DATE DUE

CONTEMPORARY SYRIA

CONTEMPORARY SYRIA
Liberalization between Cold War and Cold Peace

Edited by
EBERHARD KIENLE

Preface by
PATRICK SEALE

British Academic Press
in association with the
Centre of Near and Middle Eastern Studies
School of Oriental and African Studies
University of London

Published in 1994 by
British Academic Press
45 Bloomsbury Square
London WC1A 2HY

In association with the
Centre of Near and Middle Eastern Studies
School of Oriental and African Studies
University of London

175 Fifth Avenue
New York
NY 10010

In the United States of America
and Canada distributed by
St Martin's Press
175 Fifth Avenue
New York
NY 10010

A full CIP record for this book is available from the British Library

Library of Congress catalog card number: 93–60182
. full CIP record for this book is available from the Library of Congress

ISBN 1-86064-1350

Typeset by Philip Armstrong
Printed and bound in Great Britain by
WBC Ltd, Bridgend, Mid Glamorgan

Contents

Acknowledgements

This collection of essays has grown out of a conference on Economic and Political Change in Syria, held in May 1993 at the School of Oriental and African Studies (SOAS) in London. Like other publications with similar origins it does not include every paper presented on that occasion; however, if the papers by Nazih Ayubi and Abdallah Dardari are absent from this volume, this is not because of any disagreement about their quality, but rather because both authors had other, more pressing commitments. While most contributors had the opportunity to attend the proceedings and enjoy two days of discussion and debate, Raymond A. Hinnebusch and Hans Günter Lobmeyer were unfortunately unable to attend and therefore deserve particular recognition for their efforts. Fida Nasrallah, for her part, must be praised for replacing another speaker literally overnight.

The conference was held and the present volume published only thanks to the generous financial support of various sponsors, in particular the British Academy, the Damascus office of the British Council, the Arab-British Chamber of Commerce, Capital Trust Ltd (London), Deminex (Essen), and SOAS itself. Special thanks go to Charles Tripp, who introduced the proceedings, and to Tony Allan, Patrick Seale and Philip Robbins, who chaired the three sessions. I am also indebted to Giacomo Luciani for his practical advice; to Lynne Townley of the Centre of Near and Middle Eastern Studies (CNMES) at SOAS for her admirable preparation and technical organization of the conference; and to Patrick Quow of the SOAS printroom for copying the conference papers at very short notice. Technical editing was provided by Diana Gur of the CNMES. Specialized editorial support by Simonetta Calderini (SOAS) and further copy-editing by Janet Law. Daphne Trotter proofread the final text.

Eberhard Kienle

Preface

Patrick Seale

One of the most intriguing subjects in Arab politics today is the future
of Syria, a country at the very heart of the Middle East power system
which has, in recent years, resolutely embarked on capitalist development, virtually switched camps from East to West following the Soviet
collapse, begun serious peace talks with Israel, and yet, despite these
dramatic changes, remained in its form of government a personal
autocracy as absolute as any the region has known in modern times.
Hafiz al-Asad, still only 63 at the time of writing, continues to rule
Syria without inhibition or serious challenge as he has for the past
quarter of a century.

This then is the central puzzle addressed by this book: will the far-
reaching changes in Syria's foreign and economic policies lead to a
liberalization of its political system? The answer would seem to be a
fairly emphatic no, or at least not so long as Asad, the monarchical
president, occupies the seat of power in Damascus. For him there seems
to be no *necessary* connection between economic freedoms and political
freedoms, between encouragement for the private sector and progress
towards democracy, between increasingly cordial relations with the
United States and power-sharing or respect for human rights at home.

Two remarks addressed to me by President Asad in recent years
have remained uppermost in my mind. When I taxed him about the
fortunes amassed by some grandees of the regime, and mentioned the
grumbling caused by their gross consumerism, he replied with a touch
of irritation that 'there is no law in this country against getting rich'.
He seemed to be reminding me that, despite his peasant background
and the populist underpinning of his rule, he is not and never has been
a doctrinaire socialist. On wresting power in 1970 from his more radical
comrade Salah Jadid, Asad immediately set about cautiously reassuring

and encouraging the business community. This process of economic liberalization (*infitah*) was relaunched more forcefully in the late 1980s after a decade-long interruption, due principally to the long struggle against the Muslim Brotherhood (1977–82), when the country was in a virtual state of siege, and to the severe foreign exchange crisis of the mid-1980s. Today, the commitment to free market economics seems irreversible, with Investment Law no. 10 of 1991 serving as a landmark on the capitalist road.

On another occasion I asked him whether, to suit the changing circumstances of the times, he was considering adjustments to the political system he had put in place at the beginning of the 1970s, over twenty years earlier. To which he replied, with evident surprise at my question, that the system was just beginning to work well and that he saw no need for change. Whereupon he launched into a lengthy disquisition about the merits and respective roles of the National Progressive Front (a grouping of minor political factions around the dominant Ba'th Party), the mass movement 'popular organizations' of workers and peasants, the People's Assembly, the regular elections for various municipal and national bodies, and indeed for the presidency itself. All this, which outsiders might dismiss as the thin disguises of absolutism, was for him evidence of pluralism and respectable constitutionality.

Asad seems not to be troubled by self-doubt. He has confidence in the system he has built, in the soundness of his principles and the correctness of his policies, reflected in his characteristically unhurried approach to problems. He likes to give the impression that his courses of action are determined by his own analysis of what is best for Syria, by his free and independent choices, and are not forced upon him by events. He would, for example, reject the notion that it was the withdrawal of Soviet support that caused him to enter the Arab–Israeli peace process or that it was external pressure, say from the IMF, which prompted the second phase of economic liberalization, or 'second *infitah*' of the late 1980s.

No doubt many Syrians would like more political freedoms and more protection under the law. Certainly they would like the president to curb the blatant corruption and arrogant excesses of a few hundred top people. But against this must be set the widespread feeling in all classes that Asad's helmsmanship has protected Syria from many dangers and humiliations, from internal strife such as has wrecked Lebanon, Algeria or Sudan, from the sort of ferocious punishment which Saddam Husayn's adventures inflicted on Iraq, from the loss of Arab nationalist credentials which Sadat's Egypt and latterly Arafat's PLO have suffered by their separate peace agreements with Israel.

In a country where national independence, self-respect and regional influence are highly prized, few Syrians would in retrospect contest the wisdom of Asad's many moves (although these were in some cases highly controversial at the time), such as his strategic alliance with Iran, his success in rescuing Lebanon from Israel's sphere of influence, his membership of the winning coalition in the Gulf War. And few would dispute his principled and unflinching stand in favour of a *comprehensive* peace with Israel based on the latter's withdrawal from Arab territories occupied in 1967, nor would fail to feel a twinge of pride at seeing him, side by side with President Clinton in Geneva, call for a 'peace of the brave'.

It would appear that Asad has come to see himself as indispensable to the security and well-being of modern Syria, and that this is a view shared by a considerable number of his fellow citizens: he alone, they seem to think, has the skill and experience to manage the delicate internal and external balancing act. The legitimacy of his rule, therefore, would seem to rest not so much on popular consent (although he would no doubt claim that as well by pointing to the 99.9 per cent of the votes cast for him at the 1991 presidential elections) but on his record of being 'right' in the many tests of will and judgement he has faced over the years. The popular outpouring of grief in January 1994 at the death of his son, Basil, could be taken as expressing a widespread concern for Asad's own health and a realization that the country's welfare in a hostile environment depends on his continued presence at the helm.

Asad was a member of the Ba'thi Military Committee that seized power on 8 March 1963, gradually imposing himself over his comrades in the next six years of often bloody struggle. He has, therefore, been close to or at the top for more than three decades and is the supreme architect of Ba'thi rule in Syria. There is nothing in his character or his record to suggest that, while there is life in him, he will willingly cede power to anyone else, whatever domestic realignments might result or new classes emerge from the current steady conversion to a market economy. In particular, the business and industrial bourgeoisie, now gaining confidence and strength, is very far from challenging his rule: on the contrary, it looks like becoming an additional prop of the regime, in alliance with, rather than in opposition to, the army and security service chiefs, the 'Alawi community, the still-powerful managers of the public sector, trade union leaders, and the mass of salaried employees heavily dependent on the state. It is only when Asad passes from the scene that this alliance is likely to fall apart in the struggle for power which must inevitably follow. For the moment he remains, in the words of one insider, 'the only pole holding up the tent'.

Three episodes in Asad's long career are, I believe, crucial to an understanding of his position. The first was the intra-party struggle of 1966–70 which saw the defeat of Michel 'Aflaq, the party founder; of the pro-Iraqi wing of the party inspired by him, resulting in a permanent estrangement between Damascus and Baghdad; and then of the rash leftist ideologues led by Salah Jadid whom Asad blamed for precipitating the catastrophic war of 1967. His 'Corrective Movement' of 1970 put the country back on course.

The second episode was the five-year trial of strength with the Islamist opposition, which ended with the Hama bloodbath of 1982. The world saw this denouement as proof of the regime's brutality and repressiveness; he saw it as the necessary punishment of terrorists who, by killing 'Alawi cadets, party functionaries, prominent government servants, and many of his own friends, sought to put the clock back and undo the achievements of the Ba'th revolution. Reconciliation between the various sects and communities which make up the Syrian population is by no means complete, but that trauma a dozen years ago is no doubt one of the reasons why Syria has since been spared the upsurge of Islamic militancy so disruptive of other states in the region.

The 'struggle for Lebanon' from 1976 onwards must be counted a third major theme of Asad's political life, its high point being his success in overturning the 17 May 1983 accord which Israel had, with American backing, imposed on its northern neighbour after its invasion of 1982. From that flowed the gradual withering of Israeli influence in Lebanon, and its replacement by Syrian influence, consecrated in 1991 by the signature of a Treaty of Brotherhood, Cooperation and Coordination. Lebanon is, for the moment at least, firmly in Syria's orbit.

The main thrust of Asad's regional policy has been to contain Israel behind its pre-1967 borders, and thereby check the expansion of its influence into the Arab Levant, a hinterland which Asad sees as vital to long-term Syrian, and indeed Arab, security. However, with the signature by the PLO of the 13 September 1993 Gaza–Jericho agreement with Israel, a new threat has emerged in the form of a potential Israeli–Palestinian–Jordanian bloc, dominated by Israel and even more dangerous to Asad's strategic vision than the Israeli–

Lebanese bloc which he managed to abort a decade earlier. If Israel were to succeed in putting together such a tripartite grouping under its aegis, bound by strong economic ties, it would have won a political prize of the first importance, to match the military hegemony it already enjoys in the region. As the peace process unfolds in the mid-1990s, Asad is certain to be increasingly concerned to thwart Israel's ambitions to restructure the region in this way to suit its own strategic goals.

Such major external worries will not encourage Asad to embark on political liberalization at home, even were he inclined to do so which, by all accounts, he is not. The release in February 1994 of long-term political prisoners, such as General Ahmad al-Suwaydani (an ally of Salah Jadid in the late 1960s), should perhaps be read as a gesture of détente directed at domestic and international critics rather than a move towards any form of power-sharing. Politically, the odds are that Asad will continue to run a tight ship, almost on a war footing.

This book is the result of a conference convened by Eberhard Kienle at the School of Oriental and African Studies in London in 1993. Its importance is twofold: it addresses some of the central questions of Syrian politics and it includes recent work by some of the best scholars in this field. The book is especially timely because it comes at a moment when every player in the region – Asad's Syria among them – is having to come to terms with great changes in the international and regional environments as the century draws to a close.

Introduction: Liberalization between Cold War and Cold Peace

Eberhard Kienle

With the promulgation of Law no. 10 of May 1991 which, after decades of restrictions, strongly encourages private Syrian, Arab and even foreign investment in areas hitherto reserved for the public sector, Syrian policy-makers clearly appeared to be joining the ever-growing league of 'liberalizing' economies. The new law appeared to mark a substantial departure from previous policies which, more in line with the Ba'thi precepts of Arab socialism, favoured a brand of economic nationalism built upon a dominant public sector within an economy that was also subject in general to a high degree of control and intervention by the state. These policies were, of course, slowly and gradually amended after 1970 when Hafiz al-Asad wrested power from his Ba'thi predecessors and initiated his 'corrective movement' (*al-haraka al-tashihiyya*) and 'open-door policy' (*infitah*) which were both legitimated as a critique of earlier development models. In the wake of the major foreign exchange crisis of the mid-1980s, the process of economic reform gained significant momentum and in the course of this second *infitah* the role of the private sector expanded impressively. However, even then transitions were managed discreetly and old principles were never abdicated as openly as in 1991.

As elsewhere in the world, new, private-sector-orientated policies in Syria can be analysed as a response to the failure, if not in principle then in their actual workings, of previous models of economic development. And as in many other cases, changing international conditions played a major part in this failure. The Syrian combination of a dominant public sector, whose social functions and lack of efficiency would be more than made up for by rent transfers from the major Arab oil producers, had run into trouble even before the latter's decreasing oil revenues led to more restrictive spending policies. Indeed, Syrian policies towards various Lebanese actors, the PLO and Iraq (the latter having just started its war against Iran) began to have an adverse effect on rent transfers in the early 1980s, at a time when oil revenues had risen steeply for the second time in less than ten years. Syria consequently not only received less, but also incurred additional expenditure due to rising prices. None the less, unlike other countries, Syria still had the support of a major non-capitalist power, the Soviet Union. More than any other factor, the rapid decline of the USSR in the late 1980s, the collapse of its markets and its insistence on the repayment of substantial military debts that previously seemed to have been forgotten, highlighted the need for economic reform in Syria. Fortuitously, the Iraqi occupation of Kuwait in 1990 afforded Damascus an opportunity to side openly with the winners of the Cold War who soon won the Kuwait war as well. New, external resources could thus be attracted into the country in order to give a new impetus to economic reform. Yet the ongoing conflict with Israel continued to exert dampening effects both on investors who feared for their assets and on a government which feared for its political independence.

The implications of the legal changes of 1991 and their relatively respectable results have not so far been given much coverage from this or any other perspective in specialist publications; nor have they captured the attention of a wider public accustomed to seeing Syria as a security problem or, alternatively, as an insignificant backwater of the region. A few academic and policy-orientated pieces apart, current economic change in Syria and its political implications have, if at all, been merely described as they unfold, with explanations never reaching beyond the most immediate relationship between causes and effects.

Syria may not have – and will possibly never acquire – the strategic importance of Egypt; but it is certainly not an irrelevant part of the region, as is demonstrated by European and US policies towards the Levant, inter-Arab rivalries and the Israeli–Arab conflict. At the time of writing, it is obviously the interplay between the chances for a permanent settlement of this particular conflict on the one hand, and changes within the country on the other, that highlight the role and importance of Syria as an actor and as an object of analysis. From the perspective an outside observer, the question is largely to what extent economic change in Syria will influence the country's policies towards Israel and Palestine, either because political power is redistributed in the process, or because Syria becomes more dependent on foreign capital and markets. Conversely, Syrians might ask how to ensure a sufficient flow of external resources without accepting unfavourable peace conditions. But whatever the merits of examining the nexus between internal change within a given country and its relations with the surrounding world, they should not detract from the need to analyse the implications of such change for the inhabitants of the country itself who are most directly concerned. At the same time, returning to wider perspectives, processes of liberalization can hardly be analysed thoroughly on an empirical basis restricted only to the study of 'major' cases such as Egypt.

Two years after the enactment of Investment Law no. 10, at a time when its first effects could be evaluated, it seems important to look at the Syrian experience more closely, not only to examine the changes that have already taken place but also to discuss their likely implications in the short and medium term. Thus, the plan for a conference was born in which Syrian and foreign experts would together take stock of recent changes and develop scenarios for the future. Reflecting the title of the conference, which took place at the School of Oriental and African Studies (SOAS) in London on 27 and 28 May 1993, the present volume comprises the papers that were presented in the three panels concerned with economic reform proper, its potential for internal political change on the one hand and for international realignments on the other.

As implied by this order, the aim was to analyse actual and potential political change on the basis and in the light of economic change, bearing in mind, of course, the specific constraints posed by the conflict with Israel. Although economic change has largely resulted from new economic policies, which in turn responded to new economic challenges, this change in policy did not reflect political change in the sense of the redistribution of power or the rewriting of the rules of political participation. Chronologically at least, the policy-induced absolute and relative growth of the private sector over the second half of the 1980s, and attendant processes of increased social differentiation and stratification, preceded the pluralistic face-lift of the legislative elections in 1990. In these elections voters had a better choice between candidates and could – and did – elect a greater number of 'independents' than at any time since the Ba'thi 'revolution' of 1963. Similarly, certain features of political change may be linked to simultaneous economic change or at least to projects for such change. While Volker Perthes correctly points out (in Chapter 3) that the formation of the National Progressive Front (NPF) in 1972 preceded the more substantial measures of economic liberalization of that decade, it is equally true that this new domestic alliance tied potentially critical forces to the regime and thus contributed to prepare the ground for the first *infitah*.

If in the past economic change could be linked to the creation of new institutions or, more generally, to the rewriting of certain rules governing political participation, the same may apply to the future. As economic liberalization in the 1990s is more thorough and far-reaching than it was in the 1970s or even in the 1980s, Syria may now be heading towards more substantial modifications of its political system. Therefore, the question arises as to whether in the future Syria will still be a country dominated by a military establishment hailing largely from a specific societal background, which may be identified with the 'Alawi section of Syrian society. This portrait of Syria, sketched in many variations, invariably refers to the relevance of vertical divisions within society for political participation; the regime's rural origins and its traditional constituency among 'farmers and workers', including the urban salariat at large; the patrimonial, praetorian and authoritarian-populist character of the regime; the importance of informal patron–client relations behind the facade of formal institutional politics; and the role of the Ba'th Party as either a chief instrument and support of the regime or even as one of its seats of power.[1] This portrait certainly contains important truths, but it is equally important not to over-emphasize its various features, thus unduly simplifying complex realities. Under no circumstances must the portrait be replaced by its more popular caricature of a government purely by and for all 'Alawis, at the expense of everybody else, guided by strict adherance to some sort of Soviet-like party doctrine and mechanisms. With further economic change, however, in theory even the more safely established features may not remain as they are, but gain or lose importance, or even disappear and give way to others. In particular, private capital may move out of the shadow of the state within which it has grown and operated so far. Labour may oppose measures of liberalization or, alternatively, fragment along the divide between the public and private sectors. Finally, any such modification of the class structure may affect the vertical divisions of society, including the relations between 'Alawis and others.

On the surface this perspective could be misunderstood as an economistic one that considers political change simply as a mechanical function of economic change. Naturally, neither the convenors of the conference nor the participants intended to establish such a simplistic relationship between these spheres, which are, moreover, rather

artificially constructed areas of analysis. Instead, the link was formulated
as a hypothesis, strongly suggested by events in the 1980s and 1990s,
but one that needed to be explored, refined and possibly relativized.
The authors of this volume agree that there is generally a strong
association between economic and political developments in contemporary Syria, but show that it is a subtle and complex link adorned
with various caveats, not least the one pertaining to the conflict with
Israel.

To the limited extent to which economic reform in Syria since the
1980s has been discussed, it has been described as a process of
'liberalization' or as a second *infitah* that broadened and deepened the
transformations initiated under the first *infitah* of the 1970s. (See
chapters 1 and 3 in this volume for an overview of the first *infitah*.)
The metaphor of *infitah*, translated as 'open-door policy', captures
perhaps more accurately than the much used and abused notion of
'liberalization' the key feature of change which consisted precisely of
the opening up of exclusion zones, captive markets and other
monopolies or *domaines réservés* to new, private competitors. Private
business was ushered in to establish itself in economic sectors hitherto
partly or entirely reserved for the public sector, and granted new
opportunities there. There is no doubt that the notion of 'liberalization'
is commonly intended to designate processes of this kind, but, being
less clearly metaphorical than *infitah*, it may be taken to be more
rigorously defined and thus to include additional features which,
however, are absent in the Syrian case. Moreover, implicitly,
'liberalization' contains the positive connotation of greater liberties
which, in practice, may not be granted to all participants; public sector
workers and employees even tend to lose such liberties to the extent
that they depend on revenue. In this introduction, and in most of the
essays in this volume, 'liberalization' is used as a synonym for *infitah*;
in Ilya Harik's terms, it includes the 'relaxation of economic controls
and the encouragement of the private sector' and thus reflects the partial
withdrawal of the state from its hegemonic role as an entrepreneur and
as a provider of welfare and other services.[2] It need not – and in the
Syrian case so far does not – involve privatization in the sense of
transferring the ownership of state assets to private individuals or
companies, even though the growing size and role of the private sector
inevitably leads to a more general 'privatization' of the economy.

Processes of political change which accompany those of economic
liberalization are often labelled as processes of political liberalization.

However, the liberating features commonly associated with liberalization are even more doubtful in the political domain than in the economic domain, where arguably not everybody needs to be among the winners. In the public debate about economic liberalization an implicit and tacit consensus seems to have emerged in recent years that it should or even inevitably would lead to political liberalization, if not to fully-fledged democracy. Based on analogy rather than empirical evidence or even theory, this alleged linkage tends to be emphasized by the advocates of contemporary policies of structural adjustment in almost complete ignorance of a large body of literature that argues to the contrary. In the eyes of the advocates of the new credo, authors such as Guillermo O'Donnell and Albert Hirschman are deemed wholly unworthy of discussion, as they link authoritarianism and repression to certain economic strategies such as the deepening of import substitution industrialization (ISI) or more generally to the accumulation of capital, both of which are undoubtedly pursued through economic liberalization.[3] In line with the liberal assumption that economic markets favour the emergence of political markets, some contemporary writers endorse this argument with surprising ease, even in situations where the growth of the economic market remains after all modest. In addition, the argument is often flawed by the failure to distinguish between democracy and various forms and degrees of pluralism such as coalition-building and selective participation or enfranchisement. Even Ilya Harik, towards the end of an otherwise sophisticated argument, states that '[al]though it is not possible to find a direct causal linkage between privatization and democracy in either direction, it seems nevertheless clear that the two reinforce one another'.[4]

Critical of such sweeping generalizations, the contributors to this volume have sought to determine the nature of political change more precisely in the light of the actual form and extent of economic change. The various chapters demonstrate convincingly, we hope, that the nexus between economic liberalization and political change in Syria is more complex and less straightforward than can be captured by a simple judgement based on analogy.

The assessment of recent and foreseeable internal realignments in Syria by and large confirms more cautious and less extreme expectations about the political impact of economic liberalization. This is partly because, in the words of David Pool, 'economic liberalization sets constraints on political liberalization' and the process consequently is 'one of controlled authoritarian liberalization'.[5] As Sadiq Mahmud's critique of 'Asadism' shows, the Syrian regime does indeed take precautions, not least in its rhetoric where freedoms are reduced to the collective freedoms of the people. 'Liberalization' thus is eclipsed by 'liberation' from the adverse effects of the forces of imperialism and Zionism.[6] It is possible that the regime will, at some point, lose control over the process of controlled liberalization and consequently that more substantial changes will occur at the helm of the state; however, in this case a relatively solid new *bloc au pouvoir* may emerge which has little interest in general political liberalization, even though there would be a real opportunity to move towards it. (See Chapter 7 in this volume.)

As Nazih Ayubi states, programmes of privatization and liberalization may

> ... involve important changes in the ruling coalitions, [but] they do not necessarily lead to political liberalization. Rather, they tend to shift the emphasis from simple populist formulae to more intricate corporatist formulae ... [T]he transition toward an economic market does not automatically translate itself into the creation of a political market, but into a more complex picture of a multiplicity of interests and organizations in a state of competition, bargaining and intermediation.[7]

From this perspective, the central feature of political change under conditions of economic liberalization is the selective inclusion and exclusion of political actors and forces which may take on a variety of shapes. The inclusion of new forces may, but need not, lead to the exclusion of formerly established ones, and the winners and victims of these processes may find themselves either fully or only partly enfranchised or disenfranchised.

While Ayubi in principle allows for 'important changes' at the level of those who control the state, other authors favour more conservative scenarios. Jean Leca, for instance, denies that the emergence of classes or their creation by the state 'leads to class action, [i.e.] action by groups identifying themselves politically *vis-à-vis* the state'. The structural conditions for class mobilization, he argues, do not exist where political relationships determine economic ones and where informal patron–client relations and 'palace politics' are as efficient as collective action.[8]

In the same vein, a recent case-study of the effects of economic reform in Syria argues that actual political change was minimal. Focusing on the 1980s and 1990s, Steven Heydemann denies the 'notion of a structural conflict between political survival and the implementation of economic stabilization policies', even though he explicitly acknowledges the growing economic importance of private capital.[9] Heydemann holds that the 'selective stabilization program' which the Syrian regime introduced to overcome the acute resource crisis of the 1980s, and which resembled policies recommended by the International Monetary Fund (IMF), did not 'seriously disrupt the patronage-based political arrangements the regime depends on for its survival'.[10] He then concludes that:

> [t]he political constraints associated with Syria's patronage-based system of rule have not made economic reform impossible, but they do seem sufficiently powerful to prevent selective stabilization in Syria from crossing the threshold between its continuation as a piecemeal process of crisis management and its transformation into a more durable process of reform, and potentially economic adjustment and liberalization.[11]

Roughly, the spectrum of scenarios considered as most likely by the authors of the present volume stretches from Ayubi to Heydemann, even though more far-reaching change is not excluded. The boundaries of political participation are subject to more or less significant modification, but, except under the very fortunate conditions alluded to above, the larger part of society does not stand a good chance of playing much of a role in the political process. Factors other than purely economic ones need of course to be taken into account here, not least relations with Israel which may affect political openness directly by justifying, or not, a national security state as well as indirectly by influencing the degree of economic reform.

It remains doubtful, however, whether the past and alleged future resilience of the Syrian regime actually underscores Heydemann's more general claim that authoritarian regimes may survive the challenges of stabilization and adjustment, even if economic rationality runs counter to the interests of its vital and therefore 'favoured' constituencies. His critique (implicit in the above extract) of Thomas Callaghy and Stephen Haggard,[12] who emphasize the importance for authoritarian regimes, as much as for more accountable governments, of cultivating such constituencies, would apply only if the new economic policies in Syria had actually reduced the privileges of the privileged. The military establishment and its most immediate and important clients may be losing out in relative terms to private capital or, more precisely, to non-military capitalists, but so far they have certainly not incurred any serious loss in absolute terms. The losers have been others, more easy to police and less able to mount a challenge.

Whether or not the present regime in Syria is or would be as resilient as suggested by Heydemann, it is unlikely to be replaced by a democratic successor, if we apply the limits to political change sketched by Ayubi and largely subscribed to by the authors of this volume. If new forces and actors join or (partly) replace those who at present control the state apparatus, power may be less centralized, more diffusely organized and decision-making may be associated with some informal checks and balances. These developments may go beyond the present official definition of 'pluralism' (*ta'addudiyya*) and even lead to the 'return of politics', but this does not mean that *ipso facto* actual democracy is on the cards.

A major cause for scepticism is the argument developed by Leca and referred to above which, rephrased, denies that classes in themselves, be they owners of capital or labour, inevitably need to turn into classes *for* themselves and act as such. Thus the bourgeoisie remains a fiction and the perhaps equally fictitious assumption that bourgeoisies are the natural carriers of liberal and democratic political values has no chance of materializing in reality. Instead, the members of such classes might prefer alternative and largely individual strategies to further their interests. But even if they act collectively as a group or class and succeed in rewriting the rules of political participation in their own favour, they could only lose under present conditions if suffrage was generalized and society enfranchised as a whole. Thus, there is no contradiction between their constituting themselves as a class in themselves and yet welcoming the state's attempt to establish a privileged partnership against challengers from elsewhere in society.[13]

This is not to say that Syria lacks truly convinced democrats, but they are too weak to push for substantial democratization. Unlike the chambers of commerce and industry, the professional organizations of the lawyers, doctors, chemists and engineers in the past repeatedly proved their democratic credentials, most notably in the strikes and unrest of spring 1980. However, if the business community is ever pushed to speak out in favour of democratic values and procedures, it is most likely to do so in response to pressures from a resurgent Islamist opposition. Before the Islamist movements and groups who operated in the 1970s and early 1980s were crushed in and after the destruction of Hama, some, though certainly not all of them, claimed to aim at the democratization of politics. Like their counterparts in other countries, they did not always convince. Similar questions would arise if new Islamist parties and movements could mobilize the losers of contemporary economic adjustment, political realignments and their attendant features of social disruption and cultural disorientation. Even though one may imagine the emergence of an Islamic democratic party in the image of a Christian democratic party, other movements would pay only lip-service to these ideals. In a hypocritical game of overbidding, insincere grassroots democrats would then push unconvinced economic and political elites to extol the virtues of democracy. Under these conditions Syria could well turn into one of those 'democracies without democrats' discussed in a volume edited by Ghassan Salamé;[14] seen from a more optimistic perspective, the continuous bargaining and negotiating between declared but unconvinced democrats might ultimately lead to the acceptance of democratic procedures, as John Waterbury points out in the same collection.[15]

Finally, the chances for a greater degree of democracy, participation and respect for human rights may be enhanced by external pressures to which the Syrian government will be less immune in the future than it has been in the past. While the regime's former main strategic and economic backers in Moscow attached little importance to these issues, at least as they were defined and understood in the 'West', all potential supporters in the new world order have a record of emphasizing political conditionality and may therefore link material advantages to political reforms. The European Parliament repeatedly blocked financial aid destined for Syria because of human rights violations while the USA, which establishes such linkages in its policies towards other countries, might well do the same even if it removes Syria from its blacklist of alleged sponsors of international terrorism.

As already indicated, the contributors to this volume tend to agree that economic liberalization in Syria will most likely result in limited political change; in the absence of additional pressures, it will fall short of fully-fledged political liberalization or even democracy, even though there may be a 'return of politics'. However, such convergence in terms of general thrust none the less coincides with important nuances as to the precise extent and shape of change. Together with differences in focus, these nuances provide for a great degree of variety between the various essays. At the same time, overall agreement as to the limits of political change has been reached on the basis of different approaches and by each author independently, without prior consultation (and at the conference sometimes to each other's surprise). Such a spontaneous convergence in spite of different starting points reinforces the overall argument and makes the inevitable repetition of a certain amount of facts a price worth paying.

Introducing the first section of this volume, which analyses the causes and context of the reformulation of economic policies as well as their effects on macro-economic developments, Sylvia Pölling presents a detailed study of the conditions and policies which led the Syrian government to rely increasingly on the private sector and which culminated in Law no. 10 of 1991. Her contribution, moreover, highlights similarities and qualitative differences between the beginnings of economic liberalization or *infitah* in the 1970s, the early phase of the 'second *infitah*' starting in the mid-1980s, and its deepening after 1991. Although Pölling focuses on economic policies and change as such, she clearly, though sometimes implicitly, comes out in support of a cautious assessment of past and future political change.

Nabil Sukkar largely shares Pölling's economic analysis, but argues from the perspective of an insider who made his own contribution to the rethinking and redrafting of economic policies in Syria which culminated in Investment Law no. 10. Discussing the key elements of his own proposals at the time, he also compares them to those of alternative plans for reform.

The second section of the book examines the nexus between economic liberalization and domestic political change. It starts with an essay by Volker Perthes in which he discusses possible linkages between these two levels of interaction during the first *infitah* in the 1970s and the second one in the 1980s. Without denying the various political effects of economic developments, Perthes argues to the effect that change on each of these two levels largely followed a logic of its own. He concludes that in the future as well political change is likely to be contained and lag far behind economic change.

Joseph Bahout presents the results of his inquiry into the self-image and class-consciousness of the Syrian business community. In the short term, he argues, the interests of the private sector remain too much intertwined with those of the state and the officers who run the state to present a serious political challenge; however, in the long term, though depending on various developments, a greater degree of private sector emancipation and possibly of friction with the military establishment should not be entirely ruled out.

Economic reform appears to have moderate effects not only as far as demands for political participation and policy inflections on the part of its chief beneficiaries are concerned, but also with regard to the aims and programmes defined of the largely clandestine opposition groups and thus on their efficacy and importance. This is the argument developed by Hans Günter Lobmeyer who notes the general absence of these issues from the agendas of opposition movements even though Syrians can hardly be expected unanimously to welcome current policies of economic reform.

Discussing developments in Syria as a test case for Marxist and neo-patrimonial approaches, Raymond A. Hinnebusch, after a brief look back at the unfolding of *infitah*, introduces the notion of 'political decompression' to define the sort of political change now under way. If decompression may ultimately result in substantial rewriting of the rules of political enfranchisement, this sort of outcome is by no means inevitable as today's rulers have a fair chance of containing such change or at least of emerging as the future balancers of contradictory interests.

Finally, the editor of the present volume explores the possibilities for a return of politics in the sense of debate, bargain and compromise. Developing various scenarios in addition to those presented by other contributors, he concludes similarly to Bahout and Hinnebusch, but on the basis of different considerations, that the distribution of power and the criteria governing political participation are far more likely than not to change in the course of further economic liberalization. While actual democratization is the most unlikely of scenarios, various forces and actors will have greater opportunities for political participation; power will be less centralized and therefore at least politics will make a comeback of sorts.

The third and last section discusses some of the consequences which economic liberalization in Syria may have on the relationship between the regime and external forces. In a provocative essay Fida Nasrallah examines the future of Syro–Lebanese relations and the extent to which economic liberalization in Syria increases the profits and political influence of Lebanese actors in a country that militarily still seems to dominate them.

Fred H. Lawson, for his part, is more sceptical about economic liberalization increasing the external vulnerability and dependence of the Syrian regime. In the 'peace process', at least, he argues, the regime's stance was not influenced by potentially more accommodating attitudes towards Israel among the business community. The agenda of high politics therefore still remains in the hands of those who have dominated it since the early days of the Asad regime.

These last two chapters need not contradict each other as they are concerned with different periods of time. The negotiations with Israel are an issue of the present while the potential colonization of Syria by Lebanese business interests is an issue of the future. In that sense, the arguments advanced by Nasrallah and Lawson may even confirm what has emerged as the common denominator in most of these essays: the emphasis on factors which, at least in the short term, tend to limit political change in spite of more thorough economic change, but which none the less at some later stage may well lose part of their salience.

1· Investment Law No. 10: Which Future for the Private Sector?

Sylvia Pölling

Despite President Asad's 'corrective movement' (*al-haraka al-tashihiyya*) which was launched in the early 1970s and started to rehabilitate the private sector, it was not until after the mid-1980s that the latter was effectively awarded a more substantial role in the Syrian economy. (For a general overview of developments in the 1970s and 1980s, see chapter 3 of this volume.) In particular Law no. 10 of May 1991 for the encouragement of productive investment,[1] accelerated private sector growth in relative and absolute terms and had a significant impact on Syria's economic performance. In the period 1991–92 the private sector overtook the public sector in its share of imports, its share of non-oil exports and its share of fixed investment – at least on paper. The government had allocated a total of S£ 60 billion to the investment budget in these two years – figures for 1992 amount to S£ 36 billion – but, as in the past, allocated sums will probably be underspent. This compares with the private sector's total investments under the new law of S£ 93.4 billion, by the end of 1992, with a foreign exchange element of S£ 72 billion equalling US $1.7 billion. Thus, private sector input in fixed investment was about a third higher than that of the public sector. In addition, private sector job creation was put at around 56,400 for both years. In comparison, the 1993 state budget envisages the creation of some 68,000 jobs.

As it will be shown, Law no. 10, though in a sense the culmination of the process initiated in 1970, goes far beyond these earlier measures and introduces qualitatively new features. After the limited initial measures of the early 1970s, joint ventures between public and private sector enterprises dominated the liberalization agenda in the second half of the decade and in the 1980s. The most consequential pieces of legislation were: Law no. 56 of 1977 which led to the establishment of

ASCTE (Arab Syrian Company for Touristic Establishments) by the entrepreneur 'Uthman 'A'idi; Law no. 41 of 1978, which led to the establishment of TRANSTOUR (Syrian Transport and Tourism Marketing Company) by Sa'ib Nahhas; Law no. 10 of 1986 relating to mixed sector companies in agriculture; and Decree no. 186 of 1986 on the Higher Council for Tourism.

Thus one of the principal features of legislation passed in the late 1970s and the 1980s was the establishment of mixed sector companies with the government as a silent partner holding a minimum 25 per cent share.[2] The management of these companies was in private hands and was supposed to provide the expertise and most of the capital; individual private shareholders were not allowed to hold more than 5 per cent of equity capital – a provision which, however, could easily be circumvented through the involvement of additional family members. The government largely contributed in kind, providing land and real estate. Also the joint ventures were exempt from the foreign exchange regulations already in place, and permission was granted for the opening of foreign exchange accounts with the Commercial Bank of Syria. Moreover, the laws provided a wide range of fiscal and regulatory privileges, such as exemptions on income tax and import duties for periods of five to seven years or more. Thus, the Treasury lost out on tax and other fiscal revenues in return for economic growth, job creation and the transfer of technology.

It is interesting to note that tourism and tourist transport were the first areas of economic activity to be opened up to the private sector. Thus, the process of liberalization started with the service industry, continued with agriculture and only then affected manufacturing industries.

The Political Rationale of Early Investment Legislation
The tourism industry posed no real challenge to government authority and the political establishment had no vested interest in it, for various reasons. First, the industry is not by nature highly profitable and does not yield immediate benefits or quick returns but needs large initial investment capital and incurs high maintenance costs. The tourism trade is, however, highly labour intensive and is a big job creator; ideal for a country with high unemployment and rapid population growth reaching 3.6 per cent per annum. In addition, this particular type of industry provides a valuable source of foreign exchange and stimulates activity in a wide area of related industries and services. On the other hand,

tourism does remain highly susceptible to political instability and uncertainty.

Previously, the tourism industry had hardly existed, as the regime was preoccupied with its own consolidation and with the defence of the country against external threats. It therefore concentrated on heavy industries and infrastructural investment.

Moreover, internal unrest due to the rise of Islamist opposition movements and the general instability of the region at large were hardly conducive to the promotion of tourism. The explosion of bombs in Damascus discouraged potential tourists, as did conflict elsewhere in the region: the outbreak of war between Iran and Iraq in 1980, the assassination of President Sadat in Egypt in 1981 and the invasion of Lebanon by Israel in 1982.

In the 1970s, unlike the mid-1980s, there was no urgent economic or financial necessity for market reforms and deregulation in Syria in order to generate foreign exchange. Excepting 1977, when growth was negative, the years prior to the crisis in the mid-1980s recorded strong increases in real GDP on the back of the second oil price hike. Remittances from Syrians abroad and official transfers from major oil-producing countries rose to an all-time high. Net transfers increased from US \$455 million in 1976 to \$1.2 billion in 1977 and peaked at \$2.3 billion in 1980 and 1981.[3] The current account recorded only relatively small deficits and was in surplus in 1979 and 1980 (by \$950 million and \$250 million respectively). Meanwhile, the 20-year friendship treaty signed in 1980 with the then Soviet Union strengthened a strategic alliance and provided Syria with the military and material support it could not expect from the West. However, it also led to the build-up of a huge military debt to Moscow (now estimated at around \$10–12 billion).

Because of the unfavourable political climate, both internal and external, the mixed sector legislation of the late 1970s became fully operational only in the late 1980s.[4]

The first mixed sector company, set up in 1977, the Arab Syrian Company for Touristic Establishments (ASCTE), created another mixed sector company in 1983, the Cham Palace Hotels and Tourism chain. But it was only after 1987–88 that ASCTE became successful in its operations. The same applies to TRANSTOUR, the main business of which remains not so much tourist transport as the renting or leasing of cars for Mecca pilgrims. The few other joint ventures in tourism are Orient Tours, Sayyida Zaynab Company for Tourists and Visits –

catering mainly for Iranian Shi'i pilgrims – and the Amrit Company for Tourist Investment which, although set up in 1984, is still not yet fully operational. The two most important companies, ASCTE and TRANSTOUR, have a near monopoly in their field.[5] They are run by highly successful Syrian entrepreneurs close to the regime.

ASCTE, which includes the Cham Palace Hotels and Tourism chain, is without doubt the most successful of these these undertakings. The group owns and runs some 17 hotel and tourist establishments in the five-star and de luxe categories which cover the whole of Syria and are often located near the main archeological and historic sites. The holding company comprises ten subsidiaries covering, inter alia, management, construction, engineering, maintenance, marketing and tourist transport. The company currently has more than 19,000 shareholders, with 10 per cent of the capital held by company employees, roughly 6000, in what can be described as a unique experiment in popular capitalism.[6]

Most of the Cham Palace hotels were built and completed only in the period 1987–90. According to the founder of ASCTE, 'Uthman 'A'idi, who combines the functions of chairman and chief manager of the group, this was due to the undeclared war between the market reformers and the socialists in 1977–83 and to the fact that public construction works had been monopolized by the state since 1974. The turnaround took place in 1987–88 when the state relinquished its monopoly, a decision triggered by the government's inability to provide accommodation for the Mediterranean Games in Lattakia. 'Uthman 'A'idi's company completed a hotel complex providing 3000 beds in 12 months. Similarly, a hotel in Aleppo was taken over from Milihouse (Military Housing Establishment, which also engages in a wide range of civilian public construction activities), having been under construction for more than a decade. After the takeover, the hotel Aleppo Cham was completed within a year.

In contrast to the late 1970s when mixed sector legislation seemed to be largely prompted by political concerns, the economic crisis of the mid-1980s was the prime mover for further market reforms. In 1986 there was a contraction in the economy following low to negative growth in the preceding years. Inflation rose to 36 per cent, from 17 per cent in 1985 and only 9 per cent in 1984.[7] Economic activity suffered from bureaucratic obstacles, foreign exchange shortages, import restrictions, price regulations, inflation, food and consumer goods shortages and the absence of business confidence. This triggered a boom in black

market activities, smuggling, currency and real estate speculation. It
also prompted the government to pass Law no. 24 imposing severe
prison sentences for violations of foreign exchange regulations. A
popular joke circulating in Damascus at the time was: 'What do you
get for the dollar? Twenty years'. The 1986 oil price collapse caused a
slump in oil revenues and was accompanied by a sharp drop in both
official transfers – mainly from the Gulf states – and remittances from
Syrians working in the Gulf.

This gloomy economic scenario coincided with Syria's international
isolation. Its alliance with Tehran during the 1980–88 Iran–Iraq war
had alienated it from the political mainstream in the Arab world. Its
'strategic friendship' with the Soviet Union during the period of the
Cold War marked Syria as being anti-western. Relations with the West
were further strained by Syria's alleged association with international
terrorism, marked by the Hindawi affair in the UK in 1986 and the
bombing of a Berlin discotheque, incidents in which Syria was allegedly
implicated. At the same time Syrian involvement in Lebanon heightened
the possibility of a direct confrontation with Israel.

In a bid to accelerate private sector participation in agriculture –
the mainstay of the Syrian economy – and to achieve the aim of self-
sufficiency, Law no. 10 of 1986 was passed providing regulations for
the setting up of mixed sector companies. In the 1970s, agriculture
had been neglected in favour of heavy industrialization and infrastructural works. In the mid-1980s, due to the severe economic crisis,
the government was unable to commit the level of investment required
to revive the agricultural sector. It therefore resorted to the private
sector, but with limited success. Law no. 10 of 1986 provided, inter
alia: exemption from procurement prices; freedom to chose whether
goods were delivered to the state marketing organizations or sold
directly on the market; duty- and tax-free imports which importers
were allowed to trade within the public sector; and permission to set
up special accounts for foreign currency and to transfer profits abroad.
Exports and imports could be handled through these accounts and 75
per cent of the export proceeds could be exchanged at the rate prevailing
in neighbouring countries. From 1989 onwards these could be retained
for the payment of imports.

The mixed sector companies did not have to pay taxes or other duties
until seven years after their first profitable year. In accordance with
Syria's land reform law, which sets maximum limits for land ownership,
Law no. 10 of 1986 states that no single person may own more than 5

per cent of a company's share, but ways around it were easily found.

Since then (and until Investment Law no. 10 of 1991), only five mixed sector companies have been established in the agricultural sector, of which only two, BARAKA and GHADAQ, appear to have been fairly successful. In most cases, the government provides the land, because private individuals experience a major handicap in obtaining land following the land reform of the early 1960s. The companies which are profitable are owned and run by a few successful entrepreneurs close to the regime, as is the case in tourism and tourism transport. Baraka, Ghadaq, Nama's and Al-Qalamun and Al-Rabeih concentrate on local production: fish-farming, dairy-processing, bee-keeping, sheep-fattening and so on. Their main profits are reportedly derived from trade in the importing of machinery and production materials which were previously monopolized by the state. They mainly produce for the local market with some exports directed at neighbouring countries.[8]

A main handicap for the mixed sector companies in agriculture is the fact that the government has no intention of openly reversing the land reform laws of the 1960s. In Algeria, where land has been given back to its former owners and compensation paid, the upswing in agriculture has been remarkable.

Law no. 10 for the Encouragement of Productive Investment
The Investment Law no. 10 of May 1991 – designed to encourage private sector activity at a time when the public sector, which suffered from structural deficiencies, bureaucracy and political interference, failed to perform – has had the greatest impact on economic activity so far. This is, however, largely the result of regional and international developments which have prompted internal changes. The new legislation was passed in the wake of the Gulf war when oil prices and revenues were high but uncertainty surrounded the future of transfers and remittances (mainly from the Gulf). Also, the economy had to absorb some 100,000 or so returnees who fled Kuwait following its invasion and annexation by Iraq in August 1990.[9] The homecomers represented only a small burden on the Treasury but their precipitate departure from Kuwait caused Syria a major loss in private transfers and therefore depressed domestic demand. However, the returnees' know-how, expertise and business contacts in the Gulf and worldwide, combined with repatriated assets, provided value added. Many of the new boutiques and shops that have opened in Damascus in the past three years belong to the former expatriates. For them, the new

investment legislation provided a favourable legal framework that gave them added business opportunities.

The 1991 law sets out the conditions and objectives for private sector productive investment. Project applications have to be in line with the government's development plan and have to use a large local component. The investment schemes have to generate growth and create jobs; they have to be export-orientated or promote import substitution and they have to contribute to the transfer of technology, managerial know-how and expertise; at present they require a minimum investment of no less than S£ 10 million (calculated at the actual market rate of S£ 42 = US $1, this equals $240,000). In return, Investment Law no. 10 offers a wide range of fiscal and regulatory exemptions, incentives and privileges. It guarantees the free transfer of profits and capital employed, and offers tax- and duty-free imports and tax exemptions on profits for up to seven years. Investors under Law no. 10 are exempted from Foreign Exchange Law no. 24 (passed in 1986) which imposes severe prison sentences on violation of its regulations. They can open foreign exchange accounts and retain 75 per cent of their export earnings for their own import/reinvestment requirements. The remainder has to be surrendered to the Commercial Bank of Syria (CBS) at the actual market rate or 'rate prevailing in neighbouring countries'. They can also sell their foreign exchange receipts to other Syrian importers via the CBS at a market rate.

However, because of its fiscal and administrative exemptions, it does not translate into increased tax revenues for the Treasury which is thus bypassed in favour of a more autonomous private sector role. The tax exemptions, granted for the first five years of the company's operations, can be extended for another two years if 50 per cent of the revenues are earned from exports, that is, create foreign exchange. The draft law was originally intended to exclude Syrian residents and aimed to attract foreign capital to boost domestic growth and compensate for a non-performing public sector. However, this decision aroused major concern among the local business community and sparked a political controversy. The draft was consequently amended to include Syrian residents with no questions asked as to the source of their foreign exchange holdings.

The main rationale of the law, apart from its contribution to growth and job creation, is thus to attract direct inward investment on a large scale. Although it is directed at Syrian residents, expatriates and other Arab and foreign nationals, the major positive response to it has come largely come from Syrian and other Arab investors, especially from the

Gulf. However, this might well be the government's intention, as it is not keen to see the country inundated by foreign interests due to its political sensitivities and the vested interests of the establishment, and because it implies an erosion of state control and sovereignty. Meanwhile, Syrian expatriate assets held abroad are assumed to be running into tens of billion dollars.[10] The repatriation of part of this would largely be sufficient to sustain growth in Syria's economy over the next few years. However, many in the Syrian expatriate community remain reluctant to commit themselves to investing in their home market; they are doubtful of the regime's commitment to economic liberalization, and concerned about conflicting legislation (Law no. 10 of 1991 excepts investors from the 1986 foreign exchange regulations, which nevertheless remain in force), as well as about general political stability. Members of the old merchant class who left the country in the 1960s, because of the large-scale nationalization and expropriation following the takeover by the socialist Ba'th Party, complain about what they see as restrictive and arbitrary legislation concerning real estate.

Nevertheless, the results of Investment Law no. 10 of 1991 have been encouraging so far, despite its abuse by private sector investors who, for instance, circumvented the state monopoly on car imports by setting up car-leasing operations and importing private cars on a large scale.[11] Its partial success has been reflected in the breakdown of project applications so far (May 1991–end 1992): out of 732 projects valued at a total of S£ 93.4 billion, 397 schemes covered the transport sector, thus accounting for 46 per cent (S£ 42.6 billion) of the total investment value. However, projects covering food processing (107 projects at S£ 19.4 billion), textiles and clothing (62 projects at S£ 7.9 billion) and chemicals and pharmaceuticals (67 projects at around S£ 7.9 billion) have also made headway.

The institutional set-up for the implementation of the new law is a ministerial Higher Council of Investment to which is attached the Investment Bureau, charged with processing project applications (to be done within one month) and with monitoring performance. Statistical coverage so far does not provide a breakdown of external investment in terms of nationality. There is also a fear that projects remain mere paperwork exploiting legal loopholes in fiscal and foreign exchange regulations. The Investment Bureau is charged with monitoring implementation to provide a follow-up. If a project has not been started within one year, the licence will be withdrawn.

The main structural shortcoming of the new law remains conflicting legislation, in particular with Law no. 24 of 1986. But in order for the new legal framework to become fully operational, further market reforms are needed to underpin effective private sector involvement in the economy. This would have to include speeding up the unification of the multi-tier exchange rate (now envisaged for the end of 1994). It would also have to include an urgently needed overhaul of the financial and banking sectors. The archaic state banking sector is unable to provide the services required for a properly functioning market economy, whether in terms of credit allocation, interest rate policy or interbank funding. The state banks offer no incentive to the individual saver to deposit money with them and do not fulfil their role of mobilizing private funds in order to channel them into productive investment. Here, the government's half-hearted approach, reflected in its haphazard liberalization programme and its reluctance to open up the banking sector to private sector participation, has presented one of the main obstacles towards the creation of a properly functioning market economy.

A small step in the right direction was the establishment in 1992 of two investment banking branches attached to the Commercial Bank of Syria with offices in Damascus and Aleppo which are to facilitate operations of investors under Law no. 10 of 1991. However, the government's procrastination on requests to allow private banks or mixed sector joint ventures to open in Syria has led to similar projects being diverted to Beirut where all the attractions of a free market economy are being offered. In the longer term, this means that all the financial and banking transactions of Syrian entrepreneurs are likely to be conducted via Lebanon, circumventing to a large extent the domestic banking sector. This development will be further boosted by the strengthening of economic cooperation and coordination between the two countries following the Treaty of Fraternity, Friendship and Cooperation, which they signed in 1991. It is questionable whether the Syrian authorities are fully aware of the implications of this trend or whether conflicting interests within the regime prevent a timely adjustment to the new circumstances and changing environment. At the time of writing, it seems unlikely that the authorities will allow private banks to open offices in the country in the short term. The most obvious reasons behind this attitude are that the state would lose its foreign exchange monopoly and private sector competition would most probably put state banks out of business. Meanwhile, a controversial draft law for the opening of a Damascus stock exchange was, in 1993, ready for submission to the People's Assembly. However, the scheme does not appear to be viable, given that no privatization of state assets is envisaged for the time being and that there are only a few long-standing mixed sector companies whose shares could be floated. This would mean that activity on the exchange would be dominated by primary issues, that is, shares of the newly set-up companies under Law no. 10 of 1991 that would be offered for public subscription. This involves high-risk or speculative transactions with no track record of past performance to assess future returns and no means of protecting small investors. It would also give rise to a situation whereby a few big operators play the market at the expense of the small shareholder. Meanwhile, the issuance and trading of Treasury bonds and bills could easily be handled over the counter by the state banks and would not need an open exchange for trading.

Other issues that need to be and, in part, are being addressed by the government cover the reform of the labour law, which defines the status of trade unions, as well as the terms of employment, job security and entitlement to social services. Finally, the government has also begun to reduce subsidies and to amend its trade, monetary and fiscal policies.

Conclusion

The prerequisites for continued direct foreign investment and a higher level of private sector activity in the Syrian market are prevailing political stability, confidence in the economy and a legal framework that allows business to operate efficiently and provides legal protection and commercial arbitration free from government intervention. Still lacking are consultancy services which offer market research and feasibility studies, and provide management, accounting and audit services.

What the private sector has to offer in comparison with Syria's public sector is greater efficiency and profitability, work incentives (performance-related financial and career rewards), better training and better pay (up to ten times the equivalent salaries in the public sector). This has, in the recent past, led to the poaching of qualified officials in the administration (an internal brain-drain), a trend that will contribute to the natural shrinkage or paring down of the public sector.

As to the challenge to the private sector in Syria to generate enough foreign exchange to finance its import requirements in the long term, the prospects are good. Unlike the government, the private sector has access to international capital markets and commercial borrowing via family links and intermediaries and a wide network of contacts abroad. Private business will also be able to tap the substantial foreign assets held by Syrian expatriates. The slow pace of economic reform and the remaining restrictions on trade, pricing and private sector operations will not deter the local business community which has been accustomed to operating under a much more restrictive system and tougher conditions in the years of socialist rule and a centralized market economy. Remaining handicaps in infrastructure, such as the chronic power cuts which have caused black-outs for to up to 20 hours, especially in the northern city of Aleppo (Damascus's rival and once the commercial and industrial centre of the region), are now being addressed. The installation of power plants is the government's top priority and ample funding for this is being provided by the various Gulf states. Meanwhile, the ailing telecommunications system, another prerequisite for the proper functioning of international business, has improved dramatically since the completion in early 1993 of the first phase of a major programme of expansion and upgrading.

Prospects for improvements in Syria's economic management are also boosted by indications that the younger, western-educated generation is returning to Syria. They see opportunities for growth in a new market environment, marked by a more relaxed political climate and a new-found domestic stability. This is set against the current background of world recession and the collapse of many totalitarian states and their ideologies of socialism and communism. However, some critics, especially those among the expatriate community, are wary about this trend. They claim that it applies only to the offspring of the nomenclatura, the sons of the military and security services who are well placed to go into business and secure lucrative commissions in public sector industries. However, it can be argued that this generation's exposure to western education will change their perception of how their home country is run and how business is generated. In contrast to Eastern Europe, a merchant trading tradition prevails in Syria and the region, which has never been eradicated by the imposition of a command economy. Even public sector employees have at least one, if not more, private sector jobs in the parallel market to make ends meet, a fact that can be called entrepreneurship on a small scale (such combinations were unknown in the Eastern European countries where full-time employment and a rigid bureaucracy did not allow for the development of moonlighting and parallel market activity).

One central question will be whether the private sector, required to generate growth and employment in the economy, will be able to meet this target in the face of half-hearted government reforms. These policies camouflage a number of vested interests and ideological commitments. Therefore, they have so far excluded the privatization of public sector industries and are only beginning to touch upon its restructuring. For the same reason, the deregulation of the financial and commercial sectors, the unification of the exchange rates and the art of price controls have not yet gained momentum.

Another key problem is that of the maintenance of social peace in spite of the widening gap between rich and poor, between the major beneficiaries of *infitah* and its potential losers. Social peace is essential to contain future Islamist militancy, but largely depends on the government's ability to secure jobs for the fast growing population and to guarantee a minimum standard of living.

In view of these favourable economic prospects, the Syrian leadership should be in a position to accelerate economic liberalization. However, at a certain stage of this process, the present Syrian leadership may well have to make provision for wider political participation, which the business community, having grown confident in its successes, will claim is beyond the domain of economic management and policy formulation.

2· The Crisis of 1986 and Syria's Plan for Reform

Nabil Sukkar

The Structure of the Syrian Economy

The Syrian economy is classified as a low middle income economy with a GNP per capita of about US $1000. Agriculture accounts for some 28 per cent of GDP, industry for 22 per cent and services for the remaining 50 per cent. The economy, where the public and private sectors have an almost equal share, has been largely managed through a central planning system. The public sector is dominant in oil, banking, construction and, until recently, foreign trade, while the private sector has been dominant in agriculture, tourism and domestic trade. In manufacturing, the public sector owned the medium to large industries, but the sum total of small private industries accounted for more than 50 per cent of value added. The relative shares accounted for by the public and private sectors have changed following the introduction of the current reforms. The present public/private sector mixture is a result of a series of measures taken in the 1960s and 1970s, beginning with the ideologically motivated nationalization of banks, insurance companies and large industries in the first half of the 1960s, and the subsequent establishment of public sector monopolies to run these activities. Land ownership was left in private hands, but a ceiling on individual land holding was fixed as early as 1958.

The Corrective Movement of 1970 tempered the ideological fervour of the 1960s and introduced a sense of pragmatism. The nationalization drive stopped and the private sector was put at relative ease. The socialization process continued, however, with the further expansion of public sector monopolies (into internal trade and construction), and through the tightening of central planning and price controls.

In the second half of the 1970s, a significant opening into the private sector was made with the introduction of a mixed sector concept in tourism, which was extended nine years later to include agriculture. The mixed sector concept was a form of a business partnership between the private and the public sectors whereby the private sector dominated both ownership (owning up to 75 per cent of shares) and management. However, the mixed sector remains relatively small.

The Crisis of 1986

The Syrian economy grew rapidly at a rate of about 10 per cent per annum in real terms in the 1970s. This was a result of the relatively high investment rate (about 30 per cent) which was facilitated by considerable official capital assistance, derived mainly from the Gulf countries and the Soviet Union. Public investment concentrated on irrigation, roads, rural electrification, education, social services and heavy industries, and the capital inflow, from Gulf countries in particular, consisted mostly of soft loans to finance investments and grants to finance budgetary deficits. The official capital inflow was supplemented by private remittances, mostly from Syrians working in the Gulf. Official net transfers (loans and grants, less principal repayments) to Syria in the period 1973–76 amounted to a cumulative $2.1 billion, and rose to a cumulative $7.0 billion in the period 1977–81, representing 12.7 per cent of GNP.

At the beginning of the 1980s official capital inflow started to drop sharply, partly as a result of the fall in world oil demand and prices and the subsequent shortfall of resources in the Gulf, and partly as a result of differences with Syria over policies concerning the war between Iraq and Iran. Official net transfers dropped to a cumulative $3.3 billion in 1982–85. Private remittances also fell because of cuts in public spending and employment in the Gulf, linked to the drop in oil prices. As a result, and in addition to two years of drought, the Syrian economy grew at an average rate of less than 1 per cent per annum, between 1982 and 1985. With population rising at a rate of 3.4 per cent per annum, this amounted to a slide in per capita income.

The government reacted to the developing crisis by curtailing imports, making a series of exchange rate adjustments, and by aiming to make it easier for the private sector to finance imports from resources held abroad. However, the measures taken were always late and short of the actual dose required. The value of the Syrian pound (S£) against the US dollar in Beirut dropped from S£ 10 in July 1985 to S£ 18 by the end of 1985, and continued its slide thereafter. In frustration, the government introduced a law in September 1986 (Law no. 24) imposing severe penalties on illegal foreign exchange dealings. This law helped to slow down the slide in the value of the Syrian pound, but also reduced the (illegal) flow of goods across the border into Syria, adding to the rising commodity shortage. In the end, GDP dropped by 5 per cent in real terms in 1986, and the country's foreign exchange reserves dropped to about $357 million by the end of 1986, representing less than one month's imports. The government found itself unable to meet its foreign exchange obligations as they fell due.

Structural rigidities inherent in the nature of the economic and political system made it difficult for the economy to cope with the evolving crisis. The monopolistic public sector, closely linked to the central government machinery, could not adjust: it had limited scope for manoeuvre, if any, as its purchasing, pricing, marketing and employment policies were all centrally determined. Also, at the centre of such a centrally controlled economy, there was no room for monetary policy, while any available scope for quick fiscal and pricing actions was hindered by the excessive centralization within the government and the indistinct lines of economic policy-making authority between the government and the Ba'th Party.

By the middle of 1987, the scarcity of foreign exchange caused public sector enterprises to come to a virtual standstill, resulting in a severe product shortage in the economy. The private sector was able to exploit various opportunities granted by the system, thus contributing in its own way to the alleviation of existing shortages.

At the same time, the slide in external budgetary support increased government borrowing from the Central Bank, creating inflationary pressures. Government indebtedness to the Central Bank increased fourfold between the latter part of 1980 and 1985. The increase in budget deficit and in the share of Central Bank financing, together with the severe product shortage and the plunge in the value of the currency, caused a price explosion during 1986 and 1987. According to official figures, consumer prices rose by 36 per cent in 1986 and 60 per cent in 1987, but true inflation rates were believed to have increased by more than 100 per cent in each of these two years.

Diagnosis and Proposed Solutions

The manifestations of the crisis were clear but the diagnosis and the proposed solutions differed.

A study conducted in 1987 by this author identified the crisis in terms of imbalances in the macroeconomic framework, and attributed them to inadequate policies and development strategies as well as deficiencies in the economic management system.[1] It revealed the following imbalances and distortions in the economy:

- Indigenous foreign exchange proceeds covered only about 50 per cent of the country's import needs. A development strategy based on import substitution was generating heavy demand for capital and raw material imports instead of saving on imports.
- Domestic tax and non-tax revenues were covering only about 60 per cent of public budgetary expenditures; the deficit of 40 per cent, which represented about 20 per cent of GDP in 1985 and 1986, was being covered by external funds and borrowing from the Central Bank.
- Internal public debt and money supply were rising faster than production. In the period 1975–85, government internal debt grew at an average rate of 32 per cent per annum, and money supply increased at an average rate of 23 per cent per annum, while GDP increased at an average rate of 15 per cent per annum.
- Consumption, public and private, constituted about 87–90 per cent of GDP, and the propensity to consume and to import in both private and public sectors was facilitated by an overvalued currency and an administered pricing system that kept prices low for social considerations.
- Public sector enterprises, burdened by excessive centralization, inefficient management, low productivity and rising costs, were unable to generate the surplus necessary for reinvestment in the economy.[2] Government policies which were formulated to fulfil social objectives, such as the policy to maintain stable prices over a long period of time and the social employment policy, prevented the generation of such a surplus. Public enterprises were kept alive by budgetary and semi-budgetary injections of funds and by commercial loans. Net losses of public enterprises in the manufacturing sector, for example, amounted to about S£ 2 billion in 1983.[3]
- The existing banking and fiscal institutions were poised to support losses in public enterprises rather than to help them recover.
- The existing administrative price structure was misleading both to planners and markets, allocating resources to inefficient uses.

The study offered a two-stage reform programme. The first stage, to run over a three-year period, focused on stabilization and the introduction of a new export-orientated development strategy. The second stage focused on the reform of the economic system as such. The latter included proposals to abandon central planning (in favour of indicative planning), to expand the role of the private sector, reform the public sector, increase competitiveness in the economy, and facilitate the equal treatment of the private, mixed and (the reformed) public sectors. It also proposed the introduction of an investment law which would offer the same incentives to all three sectors and to local and foreign investors, differentiating between incentives by nature of the economic activity (that is, by economic sectors).

At about the same time, the General Federation of the Workers' Syndicates completed a report on the economic situation which highlighted the following imbalances in the economy: service sectors which were growing faster than productive sectors, public spending rising faster than public revenues, a growing gap between investment and domestic savings and also between exports and imports, and a rapid rise in money supply. It attributed these imbalances to international economic factors which were beyond Syria's control, to inefficiency and wastage in production, insufficient public sector control and to the heavy dependence of the economy on the outside world.[4]

To cope with these imbalances, the federation's report suggested intensifying central planning and giving the public sector a larger role in the economy. It proposed specifically:

- Increasing exports, rationalizing imports and tightening government control over foreign trade and foreign exchange transactions.
- More government control over wholesale trade.
- Making the public sector responsible for all capital intensive projects, while the private sector would concentrate on small-scale projects and on projects that would depend on public sector products.
- Protecting public sector projects from competition, both domestic and foreign, and by not allowing the private or the mixed sectors greater incentives than those given to the public sector.
- The establishment of more production and marketing collectives in agriculture and an increase in the government's role in both the supply and distribution of agricultural inputs and the purchase of output.

The new government formed in late 1987 also identified 'economic difficulties' in terms of imbalances in the Syrian economy and attributed these partly to international economic developments but also to mistakes in implementation such as deviations from existing plans, rules and regulations, negligence, and shortcomings in carrying out respons- ibilities.[5] It promised to cope with these imbalances and shortcomings individually, but did not offer a reform programme. More importantly, it did not adopt the specific public sector recommendations mentioned in the above study by the Federation. The absence of a programme reflected a lack of consensus on the type and extent of the corrective measures required.

The government measures which were implemented subsequently focused on coping with imbalances in the macroeconomic framework, on reducing supply bottlenecks through adjustments in trade, prices and exchange rates, and expanding the role of the private sector. Comments in the official press focused on issues of economic imbalance as well, but also on the defence of the existing economic system in the face of increasing world interest in *perestroika* in the Soviet Union and market economic reforms in developing countries. *Perestroika*, it was argued, is not needed in Syria, as Syria's brand of socialism left land in private hands and preserved a large role for the private sector. As for market reforms, these were nothing but attempts by the 'West' to penetrate developing countries with international capitalist monopolies. On a different level of argument, press articles criticized privileges for the private sector, the neglect of the public sector, and abuses by the mixed sector of the special incentives given to it in the fields of tourism and agriculture.

As events in the former Soviet Union and Eastern Europe unfolded in 1990, the tempo of reform accelerated, and press discussion changed to a warmer acceptance of the role of private sector and to criticism of the performance of the public sector. The system of economic management remained beyond the scope of authorized criticism. Criticism of the public sector gradually became more frank and direct but it was controlled criticism and was almost always preceded by a word of praise for the achievements of the public sector. Furthermore, criticism was never allowed to lead to the conclusion that privatization was a solution to the ills of the public sector.

Press articles focused on one or more of the following public aspects of enterprise: their strong links with central government, the multiplicity of supervisory organizations, centralized regulations for the purchasing of inputs and the marketing of outputs, poor management, old equipment, excessive employment and undercapitalization. In proposing solutions, comments focused on the need for decentralization and true autonomy, separation of ownership from management, application of economic criteria in assessing performance, differentiating between economic and social objectives and giving the public sector the same incentives as those given to the private and mixed sectors.[6]

The Government Reform Measures

As the government's reform measures unfolded, they focused on the expansion of the private sector, on trade reforms and exchange rate adjustments, on a move towards an export-orientated development strategy, and on liberalizing prices and reducing subsidies.

Expanding the Role of the Private Sector

A large feature of Syria's economic reform has been the expanding role of the private sector, particularly in foreign trade and industry. In foreign trade, the private sector was allowed to import and distribute a large number of goods which until then had been the import and distribution monopoly of the public sector. The list, which was expanded several times, was carefully selected to include agricultural and industrial products (including agricultural implements and equipment, tractors, pesticides, animal fodder, packing and canning materials) and basic food commodities such as tea, rice and sugar. Importers were expected to secure their own foreign exchange to finance their imports and were not to count on government allocations of foreign exchange.

The above move represented a major departure from the resolutions of the Congress of the Ba'th Party in 1985 which called for, among other things, the full public sector control on imports, and a public monopoly on the importation and distribution of all agricultural inputs.[7]

The private sector was also encouraged to increase its exports, and this was achieved by allowing it to retain 50 per cent of its foreign exchange proceeds (later raised to 75 per cent). Such proceeds were to be used for importing necessary inputs for industry and agriculture. It was first stipulated that the remaining part of the proceeds would be surrendered to the Commercial Bank at the official rate of exchange, but this was later changed to the 'rate prevailing in neighbouring countries' – as is shown in the daily list published by the Central Bank of Syria.

Another major step in the direction of expanding the role of the private sector was taken in December 1988 when the Ministry of Industry identified a list of 30 industries which were to remain the exclusive domain of the public sector, and another list of four industries which were to be left exclusively for the public and mixed sectors.[8] By implication, all other industries were open to the private sector. Previously, the government had identified the industries that the private and mixed sectors were allowed to enter, while entry to all other industries was the privilege of the public sector.[9]

The enactment in May 1991 of Law no. 10 for the encouragement of investment was the latest and most important indication of the government's new attitude towards the private sector. The law opened the door for Syrians at home and abroad, as well as Arabs and foreigners, to invest in Syria, either independently in the private sector or in association with the government through the mixed sector and offered investors various tax and other incentives. This law, which did not apply to the public sector, also allowed the formation of totally private joint stock companies in Syria for the first time since the beginning of the nationalization drive in 1961. (See chapters 3 and 7 of this volume.)

Economic Pluralism

While the role of the private sector has gradually been increased since the early 1970s, it was not until 1990 that the official ideological bias towards the public sector was replaced by a recognition of the importance of all sectors – public, private and mixed – in the economy. The term 'economic plurality' was coined to reflect the new attitude and has now all but replaced the concept of the 'leading role of the public sector'. The three sectors were originally said to complement each other, but it is now accepted that they should compete with each other.

Trade Reform and Exchange Rate Adjustments

In addition to expanding the share of the private sector in trading, trade reforms in the past few years have included streamlining import regulations and import payment schemes, and linking private sector imports to private sector exports. The government has been expanding the list of allowable private sector imports financed from retained export proceeds rather than by letters of credit (effectively from funds held abroad), thereby creating a market for these export-generated funds. The reforms did not include measures to liberalize trade through the reduction of protection rates, whether selectively or across the board, but from mid-1993 steps were taken to replace quantitative controls by tariffs on some commodities.

As far as the exchange rate is concerned, there has been a more realistic pricing of foreign exchange, but adjustments have been introduced slowly in order to minimize their inflationary impact. The government devalued the currency in January 1988, and then reduced the number of recognized exchange rates from eight to four. The lowest is the current official rate of S£ 11.25 to the US dollar, and the highest is the 'rate prevailing in neighbouring countries' which in mid-1993 stood at S£ 42 to the US dollar. The actual market rate in Beirut fluctuated between S£ 48 and S£ 50 to the dollar at the time. Other rates are raised gradually in the direction of the neighbouring market rate, and public sector transactions are shifted gradually from the official to the neighbouring market rate, each move effectively representing another devaluation of the currency. The objective is to move from a multi-tier into a two-tier exchange rate regime soon. It is not the intention to float the currency at present, but unifying exchange rates will make such a move easier. More than 75 per cent of all transactions have now shifted to the neighbouring market rate, the last of which was the development expenditure in the 1993 budget.

The shift, which is proving to be most difficult because of its high inflationary impact, is raising the exchange rate at which customs duties are valued from the official to the 'rate prevailing in neighbouring countries'. After a long delay, the government took a step in this direction in mid-1993 by calculating customs duties on imports subject to a duty rate of more than 75 per cent at a new exchange rate of S£ 23 to the dollar, another reflection of the step-by-step approach preferred by the authorities.

An Export-Orientated Development Strategy

The foreign exchange crisis of 1986 highlighted Syria's need to generate its own foreign exchange resources to meet its import needs. In response, the government has now placed the promotion of exports at the centre of its development strategy. Under the old strategy of import substitution, exports were promoted 'only after domestic needs have been fulfilled', which was in line with the socialist pattern of growth. The new strategy calls for exporting 'whatever can be exported', and the policy has been pursued even at the expense of fulfilling domestic needs. The dramatic depreciation of the currency since 1985 made the new strategy possible.

Allowing private exporters to retain 75 per cent of their exchange proceeds, and public exporters to retain 100 per cent, was one of the instruments provided to encourage exports. Another incentive was given under the new Investment Law, and offered companies exporting more than 50 per cent of their production an additional two-year income-tax exemption.

Liberalization of Prices and Reduction of Subsidies
Several steps have been taken to move away from social pricing to economic pricing. Price fixing for major commodities remains centralized, but prices are now being fixed nearer to their real cost, and are changed more frequently to reflect changes in cost. This applies to utility (electricity, water and telephone) prices as well to manu-facturing prices.

There has also been a major change in the pricing of agricultural products. Prices of major agricultural crops (wheat, barley, maize and cotton) are now being fixed nearer to their world market prices, which reflects a new recognition of the importance of the price incentive in achieving production goals.

At the same time, against this increase in agricultural prices, subsidies on fertilizers, seeds and pesticides have been reduced. Also quantities of the rationed food items, allocated under the existing consumer subsidy system, have been cut.

Other Reforms
However, little progress has been made in reforming the public sector, banking or the fiscal system.

Public sector prices have been adjusted to reflect costs more accurately, and enterprises have been allowed to retain their export proceeds to purchase needed imports. But as enterprises were subjected to more realistic exchange rates in pricing their imports, their costs continued to rise in advance of revenues, again enlarging their deficits.

On the fiscal side, there were some retrenchments in public expenditure and there was initially a drop in visible deficits, but deficits expanded again in 1991 as evaluation of public sector imports was shifted to the more realistic exchange rates. The 1992 budget deficit (visible deficit) amounted to 20 per cent of public expenditure.

Two important tax measures have been introduced in the past few years and there has been a noticeable increase in efforts to collect taxes. A 15 per cent sales tax was imposed on certain luxury items, and the maximum applicable income tax rate was reduced from 92 per cent to 60 per cent.

On the banking side, the ceilings on bank credits by the various banking institutions were raised to reflect new price levels following the depreciation of the currency, and plans have been announced for the establishment of two new public sector banks, one for financing exports and one for servicing new investments being set up under the new Investment Law.

The Effect of the Reforms
The effect of the reforms on the economy has been positive, but there were other factors arising from the crisis of 1986 which contributed towards economic recovery.

The Effect on the Economic Situation
After a drop of 5 per cent in 1986, GDP in constant prices grew at a rate of 2 per cent in 1987 reflecting the continuation of the crisis; but taking the period between 1986 and 1991 as a whole, the economy grew at an average annual rate of 4 per cent per annum in real terms, and 8 per cent per annum in 1990 and 1991. This growth, however, can be attributed to the reform measures only in part; mainly it has been due to growth in the production and export of high quality oil which was discovered in 1984 and started to come on stream in 1986. Production and export of new oil rose substantially in subsequent years, constituting almost two-thirds of Syria's total oil production of 560,000 barrels per day by the end of 1992. Ten years earlier Syria's crude oil production stood at 200,000 barrels a day of heavy crude.

Agricultural value added has also risen considerably during the past few years, rising at an average annual rate of 5 per cent in real terms between 1986 and 1991. In 1992, agricultural value added is believed to have increased at a higher rate, and 1993 is expected to be another good year. There have generally been good harvests in those years (except for 1989), but the reform measures should be given credit for the growth performance. Higher purchase prices fixed by the government for major crops and the removal of restrictions on the import of agricultural inputs and implements by the private sector paid dividends.

Revenues from new oil finds also played a major part in improving the country's trade and balance of payments position. Oil revenues reached $1 billion in 1989, and jumped to $2 billion in 1992, according to official figures. The revenues came just in time to replace official foreign capital assistance which had reached its lowest level of $127 million in 1990, compared with $600 million and $1.7 billion five and ten years earlier respectively. The new oil revenues were bolstered by official foreign capital inflow of over $2.5 billion received from Gulf countries during and after the second Gulf war.

The rise in oil exports, credited to the public sector, represented 70 per cent of the country's total export bill. Reflecting the reform measures and the new role of the private sector in foreign trade, the share of the private sector in non-oil exports rose from 33 per cent in 1987 to over 70 per cent in 1992, and the private sector share in non-oil imports rose from 25 per cent in 1987 to 64 per cent in 1992.

While the new oil revenues enabled the government to revive the public sector, the macroeconomic stabilization measures had a negative impact on it. The gradual application of realistic currency rates to public sector imports and payment of higher purchase prices for basic agricultural products exerted pressure on both budget and public enterprise finances. Net transfers to public sector enterprises increased and continued to be covered either from the budget, the Public Debt Fund, or from commercial loans, and eventually through increased government borrowing from the Central Bank.

The value of the Syrian pound in neighbouring countries continued its slide in the aftermath of the 1986 crisis, reflecting the continued foreign exchange shortage, particularly in the light of the rise in imports in response to the new measures of import liberalization. But the value of the pound in the Beirut market has stabilized in the past two years within a range of S£ 45–50 to the dollar.

The Effect on the Competitiveness of the Economy
The larger role given to the private sector, particularly in trade and industry, and the new opportunities opened up to it under the new Investment Law, contributed to the increase in competition in the economy and to the diminution of the role and power of public sector monopolies. The change in policy has also contributed to a reduction in the power of mixed sector monopolies and semi-monopolies that were created in the fields of tourism and agriculture under special laws in the late 1970s and 1980s. The extent of the risk of private sector monopolies emerging to replace public and mixed sector monopolies will depend on the way the new Investment Law is applied, and on the speed with which loopholes are closed and improvements are introduced

to the existing business regulatory framework of the economy.

Further improvements in competitiveness will be made when the public sector is reformed, making it possible to treat all three sectors equally in terms of incentives, exemptions, interest rates, taxes, access to credit and the like.

Distributive Effects

Despite social employment and price stabilization under central planning, the declared aim to distribute benefits equitably has not been served by the emergence of large fortunes derived from privileged parallel market and speculative activities in currency and real estate transactions.

The new reduction in state controls and the large opportunities opened to the private sector in productive activities should reduce the scope for high earning, parasitic activities and open the door for the emergence of new small and medium-sized businesses. It should also offer employment opportunities to a large number of wage-earners.

The maldistribution of income will increase, however, if groups that benefited from the large public sector and from economic shortages under central planning succeed in gaining privileged positions within the new system, and if tax exemptions offered under the new Investment Law prove to be too generous, given the highly profitable investment opportunities which now exist. There are plans to establish a stock exchange to mobilize savings and to widen the ownership base of the economy, but setting up a stock exchange should, in our opinion, be preceded by the establishment of disclosure rules in companies and by a wider regulation reform as referred to earlier. Otherwise, the stock market could become a playground for professional speculators, contributing to further inequality in income distribution.

What adds to the fears is that the sharp increase in prices following the depreciation of the currency and the gradual reduction in consumer subsidies are creating hardships for fixed income groups, civil servants and other public sector employees who have been compensated only in part for the depreciation of the currency. There has been only one increase in public sector wages and salaries since 1987. Keeping the lid on wages and salaries following depreciation is desirable from an economic point of view, but entails an undesirable social cost in the short run, especially when there are very few social safety-nets in the economy.

The Challenges Ahead

Syria's economic reform emanated from within the country. It was spurred by a domestic foreign exchange crisis which led to the recognition of shortcomings in economic policies and development strategies. But external factors, such as the collapse of the former Eastern European systems in early 1990, gave reform a momentum and a new sense of irreversibility. Furthermore, Syria's foreign exchange crisis was not embedded in a debt crisis. Official capital inflow to Syria in the 1970s was mostly in the form of grants, soft loans and credits. Syria's total external long-term debt (excluding Soviet debt) amounted to $3.1 billion at the end of 1986, representing 1.7 per cent of GDP, and its debt service ratio (debt service as a percentage of export of goods and services) amounted to an acceptable 15.6 per cent in the same year.[10]

Syria's reform programme was not formulated or imposed by the IMF, the World Bank or any other donor. The IMF and the World Bank have no current operations in Syria. World Bank group lending to Syria ceased in 1986 when Syria stopped making payments on its loans and credits to the group because of its foreign exchange shortage. It resumed current payments in the spring of 1992, with an understanding that the bank will help it find a source and arrange a plan to facilitate payment of the accumulated arrears of some $400 million. Despite its need for foreign exchange, Syria is not warming up to the two international institutions for the fear of loan conditionality. It does not want to be pushed on reform; it wants to carry out its reforms in its own way and at its own pace.

Reform in Syria has been gradual. The combination of trade, price and exchange rate adjustments, and the new role given to the private sector have helped the country to cope with its supply bottlenecks and improve the macroeconomic framework. These measures were necessary prerequisites for any subsequent institutional reform. Likewise, activating the private sector before commencing reform of the public sector, which is likely to lead to the loss of output, is a prudent sequence of reform. Also, the new export-oriented strategy and the open invitation to private capital inflow from abroad, with emphasis on Syrian expatriate capital, has prepared the ground for reduced dependency on official capital inflow which was dominant and proved to be unreliable in the past.

In this context, the next stage in Syria's reform requires:
1. Continuing the stabilization efforts in the areas of trade, price,

exchange rate and fiscal domains.

2. Creating the necessary conditions for the continued success of the first stage of the reforms (which increased the market element in the economy and the participation of the private sector both local and foreign).

3. Reforming the public sector and the system of overall economic management beginning with the official abandonment of central planning.

4. Reforming the regulatory framework for business and setting up the necessary machinery for its administration.

In moving to the next stage of the reforms Syria appears hesitant and cautious. First, because the next stage requires the explicit or at least *de facto* abandonment of certain ideological precepts, and, second, because there is no consensus within the Syrian establishment on the extent and the format of the next stage; third, there is substantial concern about the political and social consequences for further and more far-reaching reform. Public sector reform, in particular, is known to lead to unemployment, price increases, the reduction of rent-seeking activities and the reallocation of power, while Syria has been noted over the years for the priority it places on maintaining stability and on preserving political solidarity within its establishment. To gain time and to help the emergence of a consensus, an Inter-Ministerial and Inter-Party Committee was formed in 1992 to examine ways to improve the management of the economy and to reform the public sector.

The next stage of reform is moreover complicated by the inter-dependence of the various measures required. Public sector reform, leading to privatization or not, requires substantial funds which neither the banking system nor the budget, in their present conditions, is able to provide. At the same time, policy and institutional reforms in both the fiscal and financial sectors cannot be sustained until new rules have been set for public enterprise borrowing from the banking system, and until the relationship between public enterprise and the Treasury (and other budgetary institutions such as the Public Debt Fund) have been clarified. Likewise, a reform of the banking system cannot be successful until fiscal reforms, both institutional and policy, have been put in place, and until budgetary deficits, visible or hidden, have been checked. Therefore, the next stage of reform cannot be pursued piecemeal. It has to be pursued in a comprehensive way if it is to be effective, and progress has to be made simultaneously in all its parts.

Within the establishment two opposing views have emerged as far as the reform of the public sector is concerned. The first deals with the transformation of public enterprises into joint stock companies, grouping them according to their functions under a number of holding companies as, for instance, in Egypt and Algeria, as a prelude to reforming and rehabilitating individual enterprises on a case-by-case basis. This approach leaves the door open for the introduction of necessary new laws and regulations that could convert these enterprises into market-orientated profit-making entities. The other view involves amending existing laws, rules and regulations governing public enterprise operations to make enterprises more autonomous. It suggests that enterprises should be given more say in purchasing inputs, marketing outputs and price fixing, and should retain all the surpluses they generate, only handing over taxes to the central government. This view still holds, however, that price fixing should remain centrally determined, and should be guided by economic and social considerations.

In all cases, reform of public enterprises is likely to be gradual, even though in a sense the process has effectively begun by omission rather than commission. Expansion of the private sector is already attracting employees from the public sector, the number of industries that are exclusive to the public sector is being reduced, and public enterprises are increasingly exposed to unfair competition from the private and mixed sectors. In effect, the public enterprise sector is shrinking by attrition. By the time the government is ready to approach the reform of public enterprises head on, it will have a truncated public enterprise sector on its hands.

Although the government insists that it only intends only to reform and not to privatize public enterprises, privatization, at least in part, will prove to be unavoidable. A serious examination of public sector ills will reveal that the cost of restructuring and rehabilitation in terms of clearing bad debts, replenishing equities, rehabilitating old equipment, and setting up deployment and training programmes and social safety-nets is going to be enormous. This would require massive funds, and borrowing on a scale which Syria would not accept politically and cannot afford economically. The only alternative would be to privatize enterprises – at least in part. And a politically acceptable formula would be to transfer public enterprises into the mixed sector.

The government's recent invitation to Syrian citizens, those in residence and those living abroad, to participate in an active way in the development process of the country, fosters a new sense of national unity. It marks the end of the socialist revolution and populist politics in Syria, when the coalition of workers, peasants and petty bourgeoisie was considered as the vanguard of economic and political transformation. In practice, evolution has replaced revolution in Syria since 1970, but recent developments have prepared the ground for the emergence of a broader definition of socialism that embraces new groups and coalitions in addition to old ones.

Syria's new foreign alliances will no doubt play a role in enhancing the market element in the economy, but Syria is not likely to adopt doctrinaire market formulas. It will probably attempt to strike a balance between the roles of the markets and the state. Government responsibilities in carrying out the required development and technological transformation of the economy are enormous, and no amount of marketization or privatization will be sufficient to undertake this responsibility alone. But the government needs to define its role and responsibilities anew, and to identify the policy instruments it will use in managing the new market-biased economy. It also needs to define the role it wants to attribute to public enterprises in its new development orientation.

Syria's anticipated high population growth of 3.7 per cent per annum for the next decade requires the pursuit of a high growth strategy, which in turn requires an unusually high investment rate, and a more efficient allocation of resources. The opening to the private sector will enable the country to mobilize new investible resources, and the increased reliance on markets and realistic prices will allow for a more efficient allocation of resources. Furthermore, the new export-orientated strategy and the invitation to direct private investments from abroad will supplement official external assistance in providing the foreign exchange necessary to finance the large investments required. But the impact of the first stage of reforms will be retarded if it is not followed up by the introduction of complementary reforms required for the new private institutions and market policies, and if public sector reform does not sufficiently mobilize its large potential, which is currently either underutilized or inefficiently utilized. It is this second stage of reform which will enable the first stage to bear fruit and make economic growth internally sustainable and less vulnerable to the political vagaries of foreign aid. Syrian cautiousness may be understandable from a political and social point of view, but the increasing prospects for peace in the region may finally compel Syria to move faster in making its choices and in starting its next stage of reform if it wants to maintain and consolidate its present regional position in the changing political and economic environment and the shifting alliances in the Middle East.

3· Stages of Economic and Political Liberalization

Volker Perthes

Since the takeover of the Ba'th Party in 1963, Syria has experienced two moves towards economic liberalization or opening (*infitah*). The first, rather limited in scope, took place in the early 1970s; the second, penetrating more deeply and eventually entailing a redefinition of Syria's overall development strategy, began to emerge clearly from 1985–86. Each time, economic liberalization has been accompanied by some changes in formal regime structures, but there was a considerable time-lag in the second case. The purpose of this chapter is to examine the relationship between economic and political restructuring in each period and to ask whether the Syrian example supports the thesis that processes of economic and political liberalization in Third World countries are mutually interdependent or even 'twin processes'[1] which accompany each other naturally, being perhaps two sides of the same coin called 'structural adjustment'.

The first of these two periods of economic liberalization in Syria was directly related to Hafiz al-Asad's assumption of power in 1970. Asad, though a leading member of the regime he eventually overthrew, had long been in favour of abandoning the latter's strategy of socialist transformation. Instead he sought to reduce Syria's reliance on the USSR and the socialist bloc, to open up the private sector and to link up with the conservative Arab states. His influence within the regime had been growing since the spring of 1969, when he staged a first, partial coup. This enabled him to place some of his supporters in important positions relating both to security and to economic policy. Notably, 'Abd al-Halim Khaddam, who became Minister for Economy and Foreign Trade, was one of Asad's partisans and was known to be an economic liberal. Some cautious moves towards economic liberalization were undertaken in 1969 and 1970. A substantial departure towards a new development strategy, however, did not take place before Asad's complete takeover.

The *Infitah* of the 1970s

In his declaration of 16 November 1970, the day he completed his takeover, Asad broadly promised a new relationship between the regime and its citizens, namely the preservation of citizens' freedom and dignity. He declared that new political institutions, particularly a parliament, would be established. Significantly, he did not speak of democracy in this context. His declaration contained no reference to economic liberalization, but referred instead to the 'development of socialism'.[2] Regarded as being sympathetic in principle to business interests and to a realignment with Syria's conservative fellow Arab states, his takeover was generally welcomed, not only by the remnants of Syria's bourgeoisie and the upper middle class.

Those who expected economic change were not disappointed. As mentioned above, even before 1970 some initial measures towards liberalization had been introduced. They showed hardly any effect, however, since they did not seem to express the regime's general policy direction. Economic liberalization or *infitah* policies which created a greater impact began in 1971, grew in 1974–75 and began to peter out in 1977.

The term *infitah* has become common currency in the Arab world. It refers, generally, to policies that increase the weight of the private sector, open economies up internationally, involve a greater reliance on market forces and may include public sector reforms.[3] In Syria, the term was widely used in 1974–75.[4] Later it became somewhat discredited in official discourse since people connected it with the specific course of events in Sadat's Egypt. In hindsight, Syria's first *infitah* may be divided into three partly overlapping stages, each containing a bundle of measures bringing about, or aiming to bring about, specific social, economic or political changes.[5]

A series of initial measures which had been implemented even before Asad's takeover were mainly directed towards non-Syrian Arabs and Syrian expatriates, allowing them to open foreign currency accounts in Syrian banks,[6] to acquire real estate,[7] to obtain certain guarantees for their investments in Syria; under certain conditions, they allowed the repatriation of invested capital and of profits originating from such investments.[8] In 1971, the government underlined these rather theoretical commitments by joining the Arab Investment Insurance

Organization and ratifying an Arab agreement on the facilitation and protection of inter-Arab capital investments.[9] Primarily, these measures were declarations of principle and good intention. As such they aimed more at pleasing wealthy conservative Arab states and at attracting public sector investments from there than at encouraging private Arab investors freely to test their entrepreneurial skills in Syria. A list of conditions which potential investors would have to meet made sure that such investments would be undertaken only if the Syrian government was interested in the particular project.

Nonetheless, the new regime initiated a series of measures aimed at gaining the trust and support of the private sector. Immediately after the coup, import restrictions on certain goods were lifted, and, early in 1971, registered importers became entitled by means of the so-called 'quota' or 'Exceptional Imports system' to import certain quantities of goods which in principle were banned from importation.[10] As of 1972, imports without foreign exchange transfers were allowed in order to enable merchants and other persons who had part of their wealth abroad to repatriate some of it back to Syria. As early as January 1971, Asad had issued an amnesty on capital flight and other offences against economic laws committed prior to his coup.[11] By showing goodwill towards private business without actually abandoning any state control over private sector activities, the government generally tried to reassure the private sector and particularly to encourage entrepreneurs who had left Syria after the nationalizations of 1964–65 to return and start up new businesses. Also in 1971, a General Authority for Free Zones was established, mainly to promote investments in Syria's already existing two free zones and to further the establishment of new ones, offering private entrepreneurs an opportunity to make use of Syria's comparative advantages – essentially cheap labour and its geographical location – and to enter the Syrian market more easily without being subject to import licensing and Syrian labour laws. All these attempts met with some success. A considerable number of new, though generally small, private manufacturing and service establishments were set up, even though this policy initially triggered a surge of imports, particularly of consumer goods.

The scope of *infitah* both towards the local private sector and towards the West and western companies was substantially widened after the October war of 1973. Syria's financial capabilities improved considerably through rising oil revenues and increased capital inflows from sources abroad: Arab aid, credit easily available on the international financial market and workers' remittances. The government embarked on a gigantic growth and investment programme, involving large imports of both capital and consumer goods, and numerous contracts with foreign, mainly western, companies for the construction of turnkey industrial plants and infrastructural projects. Public development spending, at current prices, increased six-fold between 1970 and 1975 and doubled between 1975 and 1980.

Syria's overall development strategy in these years called for rapid, mainly publicly financed growth, centring upon import-substituting industries, energy and communications. All society's energy and resources were to be made use of to win the battle for 'development and liberation' which Asad viewed as an inseparable unit. The state was to lead development and the national economy; and the government would assign a role to the private sector. As a rule, private business was to concentrate on less capital-intensive ventures that would secure comparatively quick returns,[12] such as trade and services, light manufacturing industries and construction, particularly of dwellings and private sector industrial buildings. Banking and insurance, mining and oil, manufacturing industries defined as strategic, as well as others in which existing public sector establishments were supposed to cover local demand, remained out of bounds for private capital; in other industries private sector establishments would be permitted alongside the public sector.

The private sector was encouraged to take its share from public spending, mainly by importing on behalf of public sector agencies and by playing an intermediary role between the state and foreign companies; at the same time it was supposed to expand its activities in manufacturing, construction, services and internal trade. Foreign exchange controls were virtually abandoned;[13] local businessmen were allowed to operate openly as middlemen trying by different means to get government contracts assigned to foreign companies; also new credit facilities for the private sector were introduced. Even though government policies were more favourable to private trade than they were to manufacturing, the entire private sector grew considerably throughout the 1970s. Private investments increased even faster than those of the public sector, and private industrial and commercial establishments almost doubled.[14]

Besides contracting the building of industrial and infrastructural projects to western companies and increasingly importing western goods, the government actively sought to attract direct foreign investment in order to establish joint ventures with Syrian public sector companies. Western companies were not particularly interested, however, except for the oil sector. As of 1975, foreign oil companies obtained drilling concessions and production-sharing contracts with the Syrian state, a pattern that became even more marked in the 1980s.

The last substantial measures of the first *infitah* were launched in 1977 when private entrepreneurs were entrusted with a number of important projects for the development of Syria's tourism industry. A so-called 'mixed' (private–state) sector, consisting essentially of two large joint stock companies was established. These companies were private in all but name; the state held a minority share but did not interfere with the conduct of business. Each of these companies, however, was established by law and thus legally protected against competition. Not surprisingly, they could acquire quasi-monopolistic positions in certain sectors of the tourism industry.[15] Even though their establishment therefore can hardly be referred to as a matter of liberalization, it represented an element of *infitah*, insofar as it led to new openings for the private sector and included the possibility of selectively farming out privileges to certain individuals closely connected to the regime.

As pointed out, *infitah* policies were perfectly compatible with the government's development strategy of state-led growth which assigned a certain limited role to the private sector. It was also consistent with Asad's attempts to widen the social basis of the regime. Advantageous credit facilities offered by state-owned banks and equally advantageous opportunities for private merchants to import on behalf of the public sector, or to broker deals between the state and international companies, were a means of distributing some of the oil rent Syria had gained directly from its own oil exports or indirectly through Arab aid. Consumer goods imported or produced by the private sector served mainly to satisfy the demands of Syria's salaried middle classes, which for the main part were employed by the state. The living standards of this rapidly increasing stratum – making up some 10 per cent of the population at the beginning and some 17 per cent at the end of the 1970s[16] – improved considerably, enabling them to acquire consumer goods that previously had been of upper-class standards. *Infitah* policies were therefore an important instrument in winning over and maintaining the loyalty of a large and important segment of the urban population.

As of 1977, economic constraints, particularly the deterioration in the balance of payments, made the government reconsider its liberal import policies. Gradually, Syria's first *infitah* drew to a close. The private sector was assured that no return to socialism and no expropriations would take place; however, import restrictions were imposed, first in 1977 and then, on a wider level in 1981 when, after some relief due to rising oil prices, symptoms of an economic crisis became increasingly apparent. Initially, these restrictions applied to upmarket or luxury consumer items. Instead of importing, the private sector was encouraged to produce them locally which, of course, involved the importation of machinery and intermediate goods. Also, imports without foreign exchange transfers, a system which had increasingly encouraged illegal currency exports, were banned; importers again had to obtain a letter of credit from the Commercial Bank of Syria. Aside from these purely economic measures, the Economic Penalties Law – essentially an anti-corruption law – was updated in 1977,[17] and special economic security courts were established to deal with smuggling, illegal foreign exchange trade, corruption, bribery, fraud connected to public contracts and other economic offences.

Such laws were not necessarily meant to end corruption. The regime had made it clear, however, that the *infitah* policies it had pursued in the previous years were not intended to allow the private sector to determine, by its own preferences and activities, the course of economic policies. On the contrary, the regime would still be able to define the limits for private business, and individual businessmen remained subject to the goodwill of the regime. Concessions made to the private sector were revocable and could be granted, upheld or withdrawn selectively, that is, import restrictions could be lifted or imposed on certain goods and not on others, investment might be allowed in a particular sector of a particular industry, and so on. Thus, able to satisfy selectively the demands of parts of Syria's business community, the regime was in a position to fragment the private sector politically and prevent it from becoming a collective negotiator. The *infitah* policies of the 1970s had thus enhanced the economic position of the private sector without giving it even a limited share of political power.

Political Restructuring

The economic opening of the 1970s was accompanied by substantial restructuring of the political system, beginning shortly after Asad's takeover. This process of restructuring contributed to a political opening of sorts, but it also had opposite effects. Therefore, to refer to the process as one of outright political liberalization would be misleading.

Some of the most important elements of this political restructuring included the establishment of a parliament which in 1971 was appointed and after 1973 elected; the establishment, in 1972, of the National Progressive Front (NPF) as an institutionalized coalition of the Ba'th Party and a group of tolerated, smaller parties; the promulgation, in 1973, of a new constitution; and the transformation of popular organizations such as the trade unions and the Peasants Union.

Asad's takeover was warmly welcomed by the upper strata of society and the largest part of the armed forces. There was some popular support too. Being weary of the radical leftist course followed by the Jadid regime, many Syrians wanted a change, and Asad promised a new departure. There was no resistance to his coup; nonetheless, parts of the party, the unions and those younger intellectuals who had supported his radical predecessors, had to be reckoned with as potential opponents.

By establishing a parliament and the NPF and by passing a new constitution, Asad tried both to broaden his base of support and to institutionalize and stabilize his regime. A number of independent candidates – those generally not belonging to any of the legalized parties – were appointed and later elected to the parliament. For the most part they represented the middle classes and in some cases Syria's pre-Ba'thi urban and tribal aristocracy. The parties incorporated into the NPF were the Syrian Communist Party (SCP), which had already part-icipated in Ba'thi governments before Asad, the Nasirist Arab Socialist Union (ASU), and two Ba'thi breakaway factions. There was no legal basis for parties to act outside the front. Parties joining the NPF had to pay for their privilige by their consenting to toe the Ba'th Party line which, according to the NPF covenant, was binding for the entire front, and to accept a second-class position within the system. This entailed that they were not allowed to become active among students and in the armed forces; moreover, they were only allotted a handful of deputies each, while the Ba'th retained an absolute majority in the parliament as well as in the front executive. To stabilize the regime, the establishment of the NPF was no doubt a successful move; the ASU and the SCP, both with substantial followings within the trade unions, among intellectuals and in some rural regions, were weakened through the divisions that occurred over the question as to whether to accept this unequal form of participation or to choose the uncomfortable alternative of illegal opposition. With the new constitution, Asad, who had first had himself elected president in an uncontested referendum in March 1971, institutionalized his presidential and ultimately personal regime. The constitution was tailored to suit the president already in office, laying virtually all effective powers into his hands. Parliamentary elections, first held in 1973, then in 1977, left limited choice. Voting was apparently free; candidates, however, were generally preselected. The division of seats between the parties of the NPF had been arranged prior to the elections, and independent candidates – receiving approximately one-third of the seats in the elections of 1973 and less than a fifth in those of 1977 – had little chance of being elected if they were not on good terms with the regime. The exception of four oppositional deputies out of a total of 186 who were elected in 1973 proved the rule; an 'error' like this did not repeat itself in later elections. More freedom of choice was available in local and provincial (*muhafaza*) elections. The 1972 elections for the provincial councils resulted in a defeat for the regime and served as a warning that unmanipulated national elections could become dangerous. Even in later local and provincial elections the regime did not insist on a majority for the NPF parties. Local and provincial councils have somewhat non-political functions and no power of their own; therefore the regime did not mind leaving them to local notables whose activities would anyway be checked by the provincial governor, himself appointed by the president. Parliament, on the other hand, had a political function, even though in terms of actual power it remained very much 'on the margins of political life'.[18] Not surprisingly, electoral participation in legislative elections remained low, generally well under 20 per cent.[19]

Institutionalizing the regime served the goal of legitimizing it, and was in line with the obvious need to build institutions commensurate with the increased functions of an interventionist state and the tasks of a modern government. Besides the establishment of political institutions, these needs also led to the expansion and, partly, the modernization of the administration, including the establishment of several new agencies concerned with planning, statistics, economic policies and the public sector. These reforms had already been started by Asad's predecessors. Increased financial capacities made it possible in the first decade of Asad's rule to expand the bureaucracy on an unprecedented scale.[20] This expansion also had the effect that new recruits on whom the regime could count outnumbered bureaucrats connected with any of the previous regimes.

The extent to which Asad's restructuring of the political system aimed at institutionalization and control (or regime stabilization) rather than political liberalization becomes most evident if one looks to the fate of the trade unions and the Peasants Union. Both organizations, the former having a tradition reaching back to the period of the mandate, the latter founded under the Ba'th in 1964, had been largely supportive of the radical Ba'th regimes. After Asad's takeover, their leaderships were purged once again of persons unwilling to declare their allegiance to the new regime. Even though the majority of their executive bodies chose to cooperate with Asad, the trade unions in particular, with large leftist tendencies among their membership, remained a potential threat to the regime as long as they were not completely under its control. By 1974, however, the regime had largely succeeded in transforming both the trade unions and the Peasants Union from syndicalist organizations into quasi-corporatist institutions. The Peasants Union was merged with the Cooperative Unions and redefined as a 'syndicalist [niqabi] and economic popular organization'[21] comprising landless peasants, share-croppers, smallholders, medium-sized landowners, employers and agricultural engineers. Thus it ceased to be a class-based organization of the rural poor, becoming instead a sectoral organization which was dominated by the middle-class peasantry. The trade unions had to adopt the slogan of 'political' as opposed to 'postulative' unionism. This meant explicitly that national goals were to be placed above those of the working class.[22] The organization was centralized, the position of trade union functionaries and of the executive were strengthened at the expense of the ordinary members and local branches, while democratic procedures were eroded. Both the trade unions and the Peasants Union, as well as other less important popular organizations such as women's and students' unions or the official youth organization, became quasi-official, compulsory bodies, which were entrusted with quasi-governmental functions including control and supervision of their members. Their leadership was hand-picked by the regime and became part of the regime's elite. As corporatist organizations they were supposed to enrol the largest possible number of people belonging to the part of society for which they were responsible; equally, they were to represent their membership's sectoral rather than class interests, and, most importantly, they were to further and defend the developmental and political goals defined by the regime. Trade unions, the Peasants Union and other popular organizations grew considerably in terms of numbers and organizational strength. At the same time, however, they were too internally undemocratic and powerless *vis-à-vis* the regime to become effective instruments of mass political participation.[23]

The transformation and political neutralization of the unions as that of the NPF parties may have been necessary to enact *infitah* policies speedily and without resistance. There was, however, some leftist criticism of *infitah* from within the unions and from the Syrian Communist Party which expressed reservations also harboured by parts of the Ba'thi left. Thus the SCP, for instance, protested against the granting of a concession to an oil company from the USA in 1975. The unions and the front parties were allowed to voice political criticism of sorts; however, they were not able to alter the course of events. On the contrary, the decision of the SCP to voice from within the NPF their opposition to regime policies brought the activities of the front to a virtual halt; only in the late 1970s was this stalemate finally overcome.[24]

Connecting Lines
It is noticeable that the selective political opening of the first years of Asad's rule coincided with the still limited measures of economic *infitah*. Both moves essentially aimed at gaining the support and confidence of the social groups important to Asad's political project and to his development strategy. These were, in the first place, the salaried middle classes, new entrepreneurs and parts of the old urban and rural elite. An impressing sequence of referenda and elections took place to legitimate the regime; the democratic character of these electoral operations, however, was limited from the outset.[25] The regime did not talk much about democracy; instead, 'popular democracy' was the code-word, meaning that the people had to consent to authoritarian rule which pretended to serve their best interests. Nor did the population believe that liberal democracy of the kind they had occasionally experienced in the 1940s, 1950s and early 1960s had returned. Those invited to participate as junior partners in the parliament, the NPF and the government were aware that the regime had no intention of granting them a share in effective power.

After the October war in 1973, *infitah* policies were expanded, but they were not accompanied by further measures of political liberalization. Instead the trade unions, which could have challenged the regime's policies towards the private sector and the West, were brought under control, while the regime strengthened and enlarged its *mukhabarat*, special forces and other repressive agencies. An oppositional observer went so far as to claim that with the end of the October war the government had virtually declared a civil war against the majority of the population whose living standards were about to deteriorate.[26]

Actually, even though inflationary pressures were felt by wage-earners as early as 1974, the living standards of the masses continued to rise until 1976–77; it must also be said in the years immediately following the October war, there was little demand for democracy, be this on the part of the people at large or the intellectuals in particular. Asad had won popularity through his political victory in the war, while the combination of economic liberalization and growth served to meet the aspirations of most segments of the population. Per capita income was rising, albeit unequally, throughout all classes, 'development' in the form of electricity, roads and schools was noticeable in all parts of the country, and the expansion of education and of public sector employment allowed a high degree of upward social mobility.

Disappointment with the regime started to become apparent in the period 1976–78, as wages and agricultural procurement prices were affected by inflation; corruption, nepotism and the illegal enrichment of the regime elite became more obvious. Syria's regional policies, particularly its intervention in Lebanon, became unpopular and complaints over the unlimited power of the security forces increased. Oppositional forces were not able to organize politically and were thus driven into violence; between 1979 and 1982 the situation came close to that of a civil war. During these years numerous 'Alawis and persons close to the regime were assassinated while the latter resorted to indiscriminate acts of retaliation. Simultaneously, open clashes occurred between government forces and armed supporters of the Islamist-led opposition. In February 1982, these confrontations culminated in an uprising in the city of Hama which was quelled by government troops, leading to the destruction of most of the city. The authoritarian and repressive character of the regime clearly approved, not only in its response to the violent insurrections of the radical opposition, but also in its policy to crush the remaining elements of civil society such as the lawyers' union and other professional unions. In April 1980, the executive bodies of these organizations were dissolved and their members imprisoned after calling a one-day strike in support of their demand to end the state of emergency. Also, the parliament elected in 1981 no longer comprised independent deputies; even the SCP, still part of the NPF but increasingly critical of the regime, lost its seats.

At the same time, corporatist structures were further strengthened. Most importantly, a 'Committee for the Guidance of Imports, Exports and Consumption' was set up in 1981 to discuss and determine the general thrust of economic policy. The committee was headed by the prime minister and included all government ministers concerned plus representatives of the party, the trade unions and the Chambers of Commerce and of Industry.

This period of heightened internal unrest coincided with the appearance of signs of a serious economic crisis. In an attempt to rally support, the government in 1980 ordered a massive pay-rise for workers and employees in the public sector and, responding to the wishes of the Chambers of Commerce, lifted some restrictions on imports. These measures were taken purely out of political motives, and were aimed at maintaining the support both of the bourgeoisie and the public sector salariat.[27] A year later, in view of the deteriorating budgetary and foreign exchange situation, the government imposed new limits on imports, reduced the privileges applying to economic activities in the free zone, and began to adopt an austere budgetary policy. These measures clearly demonstrated that the period of state-led growth on which the *infitah* of the 1970s was founded had come to an end.

Syria's Second *Infitah*

From 1983 onwards, new measures towards liberalization began to be introduced, and by 1986–87, representatives of Syria's commercial class had begun to speak of a new *infitah*. This second *infitah* was qualitatively different from that of the 1970s. In the first period, public resources seemed almost unlimited, and the state, leading economic development, opened or expanded existing fields of private sector activities in accordance with its own socio-political and economic priorities. Throughout most of the 1980s, however, Syria faced severe economic difficulties, as the foreign exchange crisis developed into a general slump. Per capita GDP declined by 20 per cent over the decade, and the indexes of manufacturing and main crops production remained almost stagnant. [28] Diminishing public resources and austerity budgets forced the government gradually to open up additional domains to the private sector and to abandon some of its instruments of control. This eventually contributed to a change in the government's overall development strategy and to the transfer of some of its economic levers to the private sector.

Similar to the *infitah* of the 1970s, this new *infitah* was a phased and gradual undertaking. Policies were largely home-made, that is, not forced upon Syria from abroad. They obviously did not follow a prefabricated plan or schedule, even though, eventually, the reforms and changes this process entailed turned out to be very much in line with structural adjustment programmes that other countries adopted under the tutelage of the International Monetary Fund (IMF) or the World Bank.

At the time of writing, the process is ongoing. So far, we can distinguish three overlapping stages or bundles of measures and a fourth one which is is still in the making. In the initial stage, extending until around 1987–88, the development strategy of the government still centred on import substitution which, somewhat misleadingly, it called a strategy of 'self-reliance'. From 1982 it had become increasingly difficult for Syria's state-owned Commercial Bank to provide the private sector with the foreign exchange needed for imports, and by 1984 the bank virtually declined to open any further letters of credit for private importers. Against this background, the government took a series of measures intended to enable the private sector to generate its own foreign exchange and, at the same time, to increase the foreign exchange reserves of the state. The most important step in this direction was taken in 1983, and it allowed private manufacturers to keep 50 per cent of their hard currency export earnings for their own imports; the remainder had to be sold to the Commercial Bank at the official or, depending on the type of commodity, a more favourable 'parallel' rate. In 1987, this measure was extended to include all private exporters, not only manufacturers, while the percentage of export earnings which could be retained was raised to 75 per cent for certain commodities. A list of these commodities was established and constantly updated by the Ministry of Economy and Foreign Trade.[29] In addition, Syrians and non-Syrians alike were encouraged to open foreign currency accounts at the Commercial Bank to finance their imports.[30] The foreign exchange deposited was supposed to have originated from property or economic activities abroad, but it was made clear that no questions would be asked about its source. At the same time, the Ministry of Economy and Foreign Trade again began gradually to widen the scope for private imports, lifting more import restrictions than it imposed. Imports without currency transfers were again permitted in 1985.

Whatever the piecemeal fashion in which they were introduced, these measures dented the state monopoly in matters of foreign exchange, and triggered a boom in the currency black market. A new law (law no.

24 of 1986) against currency smuggling was implemented, threatening severe penalties for illegal currency transactions.[31] Since there was a demand for foreign exchange which the official sector could not satisfy, this measure did not seriously affect the currency black market. Instead, it contributed to a process of concentration and consolidation within this sector.

Apart from foreign trade and currency regulations, this initial phase of the second *infitah* involved a substantial liberalization of Syria's agricultural economy. In 1986, following the model of mixed tourism and transport companies, the establishment of mixed agricultural joint stock companies was permitted.[32] Beneficiaries of the new regulation were mainly 'new class' businessmen or crony-capitalists whose economic success depended heavily on their relationship with members of the regime elite.[33] Although the more far-reaching demands of Syrian businessmen, who sought to scrap the 1958 land reform law, were not met, the new regulations represented a fundamental departure from the agricultural policies of the 1960s which officially had been pursued to that date. Instead of limiting private property of agricultural land, the concentration of vast landed holdings into a few hands was again permitted – and even encouraged – in order to mobilize private capital, both Syrian and Arab, particularly for export-oriented or other foreign exchange earning ventures. With the same purpose in mind, new investments in the tourism industry were encouraged by offering tax holidays and exemptions from customs duties,[34] and the restrictions on free-zone investments which had been imposed in 1981 were lifted again.[35]

The emergence of the mixed agricultural sector marked the beginning of a gradual reorientation of official development strategies and thus the transition to a more deeply penetrating stage of economic liberalization. In 1988, still under the pressure of a large foreign exchange deficit, the government decided to give absolute priority to the acquisition of foreign currency. Public sector enterprises would not receive foreign exchange for their imports beyond what they obtained for their exports or, if foreign markets were inaccessible to them, from 'exports to the local market', that is, local sales of their products against hard currency. By 1989, the shift from import substitution to export orientation had become official policy. 'Just as investive spending has been the basic and appropriate feature of the 1970s,' an official paper of the Ministry of Economy stated, 'today, exports and the concentration on exports are the central element of our strategy and the appropriate feature of the 1980s.' [36]

The main element of the second stage of the second *infitah* was the phased devaluation of the Syrian currency and a considerable liberalization of trade regimes. In 1986, a new 'encouragement' rate for the Syrian pound was introduced, initially for non-commercial transactions. This rate, which hovered around S£ 22 to the dollar, was initially close to the black- or free-market rate. With the continuing devaluation of the Syrian currency, however, it soon became just another, if more favourable, artificial exchange rate. At the end of 1987, the pound was officially devalued from S£ 3.95 to S£ 11.2 to the dollar. In 1989, the Ministry of Supply announced that it would revalue imported consumer goods distributed through its outlets at a rate of S£ 40 to the dollar – a rate close to the free-market rate of that time. In the same year, the Ministry of Economy and Foreign Trade for the first time officially acknowledged, albeit on a limited scale, the validity of the free-market rate as an indicator for the value of the Syrian currency. Exporters of certain agricultural products were granted a so-called 'rate prevailing in neighbouring countries' – essentially the black-market rate – for that part of their export-earnings which they had to sell to the Commercial Bank.[37] Shortly afterwards exporters of other products were to be paid the encouragement rate instead of the official one. Gradually, the free-market rate was accepted. In 1990, the state offered to buy private export earnings at the free-market rate if exporters did not want to use them for imports. Alternatively, owners of foreign exchange could assign it to needy importers through the Commercial Bank.[38] The latter measure represented a qualitative step insofar as it allowed for a limited degree of private foreign exchange dealings, thus stripping the state of its legal monopoly and an instrument of its control. In 1991, the free-market rate was officially applied basically for all personal and private sector transactions, including that part of foreign exchange earnings which exporters still had to sell to the bank.[39] In 1992, the requirement that a certain percentage of export earnings had to be sold to the bank was dropped; henceforth cash could be replaced with exportable products. There remained limits on the sale of foreign exchange by the bank, dictated by the scarcity of hard currency, and the official rate was maintained to measure the value of public sector exports and imports as well as for statistical purposes in general.

As mentioned above, the devaluation of the currency went hand-in-hand with the deregulation of foreign trade. Among other things, the private sector was allowed to import raw materials for public sector companies unable to earn their own foreign exchange, such as the Hama iron and steel mill and the Dayr al-Zur paper factory.[40] In 1990, expatriates were granted special, though limited, rights to import goods generally banned from importation, such as automobiles.[41] Private traders were permitted to import on behalf of public sector foreign aid agencies.[42] At the same time the monopoly of public sector agencies on imports and the distribution to retailers of such basic consumer goods as rice, sugar, tea, coffee and cooking fat was abandoned. Gradually also public sector monopolies on purchasing certain fruits and vegetables from farmers were phased out. The state maintained a monopoly over the trade with agricultural products such as cotton, wheat and sugar-beet which were regarded as strategic. Procurement prices, however, gradually had to be raised.

At the end of this phase, the government had largely surrendered its control over foreign exchange to the market. The state-owned banking sector, instead of being an instrument of control over private exports and imports, was gradually reduced to the role of an intermediary. While other instruments of control over foreign trade were maintained, their use was limited so that market forces were more free to operate, thus signalling the abandonment of the idea that the state could, by means of its foreign trade policies, effectively steer the development of production and consumption.

The third stage of Syria's second *infitah* comprises a number of measures intended to liberalize investment policies and generally to encourage private investment, particularly in manufacturing industries. Overlapping somewhat with stage two, the main thrust of stage three did not appear clearly until 1991. In 1986 the government had considerably extended the list of industries open to private activities, something which had been done several times before, for example in 1981 when private businessmen had been encouraged to produce locally some of the goods banned from importation. By opening up new areas for private activities which generally promised good returns these measures had a positive effect. They did not, however, represent any substantial change of industrial policy. The government continued to use a constantly changing list of 'industries regarded as falling within the activities of the private sector permitted to be licensed in the Syrian Arab Region'. This allowed it to widen or narrow the scope for private industrial activities at will or, put more positively, according to the country's development needs as defined in the five-year plans. Potential investors could never be sure that the establishment of an industrial

firm to produce, for example, chewing-gum or herbicides – both added
to the list in 1981 – would still be permitted the following year, by
which time the government might have decided that enough chewing-
gum and herbicide producers were working in the country. A change
in this approach first became apparent in 1988 when, instead of updating
the list of authorized industrial activities, the list was replaced by a
negative list which defined those industries which should be reserved
solely for the public sector or for either the public or mixed sector. By
implication, all other industries were open to private business.[43]
Industries still reserved for the public sector were those regarded as
strategic, plus a few others such as, for instance, tomato-pulp
production. Here the preservation of a public sector monopoly was
obviously intended to protect existing public sector establishments
against competition.

A qualitative change was brought about three years later with the
implementation of an investment law.[44] Law no. 10 of 1991 greatly
opened the space for private investments, allowing Syrian, Arab and
foreign investors to launch private or 'mixed' projects in basically any
field of the Syrian economy. Capital investments were not to be below
S£ 10 million ($ 250,000), and all projects were subject to authorization
from the Higher Council of Investment, headed by the prime minister.
Applications by potential investors were to be decided upon within no
more than 60 days. Decisions were to take into account such factors as
the project's expected contribution to national income and export
promotion, its relevance for the labour market and the transfer of
technology. A new Investment Bureau was established to consult with
investors and to prepare decisions for the council. Approved projects
were granted tax holidays for up to seven years and they were guaranteed
the right to repatriate invested capital and profits. In addition they
were widely exempt from import restrictions and customs duties.
Parallel to the investment law, a new tax law was introduced which
substantially reduced business taxes,[45] from the previous at least
theoretical level of 90 per cent and more.

Results and Prospects of *infitah* Policies

The most notable result of Syria's second *infitah* was the remarkable
growth of the private sector. In 1990, for the first time since 1963,
private sector capital investment had outgrown that of the public sector.
The private sector's share of foreign trade, which had decreased to
some 10 per cent of the total in the early 1980s, rose to more than 20

per cent in 1986 and to 45 per cent in 1990.[46] The contribution of the private sector to the share of Syria's manufacturing industries in the net domestic product increased, according to official data, from 30–35 per cent in the mid-1980s to 43–44 per cent at the end of the decade.[47] According to the Damascus Chamber of Commerce, the private sector now contributed 55 per cent of Syria's domestic product, covering 98.6 per cent of agriculture, 72 per cent of transport, 62 per cent of trade, 59 per cent of finance and rents, 50 per cent of building and construction, 37 per cent of manufacturing industries, and 13 per cent of services.[48] Throughout the 1970s and 1980s, the position of the private sector had employed some 60 per cent or more of Syria's industrial labour force, including construction. In 1991, the private sector's share crossed the 75 per cent mark.[49]

The improvement of the position of the private sector in the national economy, as reflected in all available statistics, was initially the result of the deteriorating performance of the public sector.[50] Nevertheless, there was real overall growth in the private sector, accompanied by a partial restructuring within it. Branches that grew exceptionally were those which had always been regarded as the most profitable and which were now, as was the case during the first *infitah*, the prime beneficiaries of the reform–package: import–export trade and commissioneering, real estate, services as well as internal trade with imported or locally manufactured consumer goods for mainly upper- and upper-middle-class use. Industry was, and still is, regarded as the more difficult way to profit, and big business, in Syrian terms, was limited to commercial enterprise. It is notable that the main emphasis of *infitah* policies – in the 1980s as much as in the 1970s – was on private trade and the gradual relaxation of foreign exchange regulations. Agricultural liberalization centred upon measures to encourage large-scale investments, while peasants who were beneficiaries of the land reform remained restricted in their production and marketing choices. Measures to encourage domestic industrial activities came late. Only since 1985, therefore, have a considerable number of larger industrial establishments, employing a workforce of 50, 100 or even more, begun to emerge. Investment Law no. 10 of 1991 triggered a wave of new, larger investment projects. By mid-1992 a total of 430 new projects had been licensed – about half of them in industry, the rest mainly in transport. A trend towards concentration is clearly apparent with the emergence of a remarkable group of larger private establishments in terms of capital, turnover, profits, and – as far as industry is concerned – employment.

Accordingly, an increasing gap appeared between this upper stratum and the vast petty bourgeois majority of the private sector. In 1991, the average capital of newly established private industrial projects amounted to only US $25,000, whereas the average capital invested in new industrial and service companies established according to Investment Law no. 10 of 1991 exceeded $4 million.[51]

As noted, the growth in the private sector was accompanied by a substantial reduction of the role of the state. This was so not only with regard to the public sector's share in investments, production and exports. More importantly, the state's ability to lead the economy and to determine the course of socio-economic development diminished. Being forced to live on austerity budgets throughout most of the 1980s, development spending had to be reduced, employment in the administration and the public sector limited, and subsidies cut. These measures have little to do with liberalization but are part of a broader programme of stabilization or structural adjustment. The abandonment of public sector trade and production monopolies, and the deregulation of trade and currency regimes have, of course, limited the ability of the state to determine what was to be produced, sold and consumed in the country. Notably too, state planning was abandoned. A new five-year plan was drafted for the period 1986–90, but it was never published or enacted, and the development plan for 1991–95 was still unfinished by 1993.

Since the late 1980s, Syria's general economic situation has been improving. Most importantly, the balance of trade deficit fell; between 1989 and 1991 the balance of trade even showed a surplus. This was partly the result of economic liberalization and increased private sector exports, and partly of rising oil exports. Syria's net exports of crude oil and oil derivatives more than quadrupled between 1986 and 1991, with these oil exports representing 53 per cent of Syria's total export value in the latter year.[52] Additionally, official aid from Gulf countries increased remarkably after the second Gulf war, allowing the Syrian government to finance overdue infrastructural investments, some less important industrial projects and arms shipments.

The changes to the economic structure which Syria's second *infitah* brought about are certainly more than superficial. The state has abandoned some levers on the economy, and this, it seems, will not easily be revoked. Private economic interests are in a stronger position today than they were in the mid-1970s, the economic reforms introduced having shown positive effects, and the alliance between the regime elite and the business community has been strengthened. Notably, the process of reform and liberalization which began at a time of acute crisis was not only continued but even reinforced when Syria's general economic situation began to improve again towards the end of the 1980s. We can therefore expect the *infitah* process to continue in the future as well. Preparations to establish a Syrian stock exchange are under way. Sooner or later, the Syrian pound may become fully convertible, and law no. 24 of 1986, which still threatens everyone who illegally deals in currency, may then be shelved. There are demands for and discussions about the establishment of private banks, which may well materialize over the next few years.[53]

There is still no debate about abandoning the import licensing system as such, and it would be a mistake to assume that the business community was in favour of complete liberalization of foreign trade. Nor should one expect investment licensing to be abolished in the near future or to be replaced with a mere technical or ecological surveillance system. Even though in practice the government will not stand in the way of reasonable private investment projects, the current licensing system remains an instrument of political control which the regime is unlikely to relinquish easily. Furthermore, no large-scale privatization of public sector industries is to be expected. There may be further privatization of state land, and some government retail stores and service companies are likely to be leased or sold to the private sector or transformed into 'mixed' companies. Public manufacturing industries, however, seem to be exempt from these tendencies, even though reforms will probably confer a greater degree of flexibility to individual companies. However, these reforms will not lead to the dismantling of the public sector. There is some economic and a large measure of political rationality in maintaining the public sector as a producer of basic commodities. Even in the future it may not be the most cost-effective producer, but it has developed linkage effects with other sectors of the domestic economy. Whatever its flaws, the public sector still serves as a means of patronage and control on the one hand, and of social security on the other.

Although the state has definitely lost some of its control over the economy, certainly over production and foreign trade, the actual process of liberalization has been very much a regime affair. A remarkable feature of Syria's *infitah* policies, both in the 1970s and in the 1980s, was the gradual and highly selective manner in which they were applied.[54] The scope and timing of the liberalization measures were set by the regime, not completely at will but certainly in accordance with its schedule, not by the chambers of commerce or industry or by international actors such as the IMF. Quite successfully, the regime has attempted both to rid itself of financial burdens and to mobilize private resources. The concrete aim of skimming off some of the private sector profits to bolster the state's foreign exchange budget made it necessary to encourage private sector activities and to reassure private capital. Indemnification from economic failures by making the private sector responsible for a larger part of the economy may have been a liberalizing incentive too.[55] At the same time, selective liberalization and privatization serve the private interests of the regime elite, furthers their alliance with parts of the bourgeoisie, and adds to the fragment- ation of the business community. The reform process has no doubt been in the interest of private business, but the private sector was not in a position to dictate or to enforce its own agenda. With increasing oil revenues and Arab aid, the Syrian regime is even less likely than before to surrender any part of its political decision-making power to any part of society.

Political Adjustments

Syria's second *infitah* was only at a very late stage accompanied by some sort of political restructuring. In contrast to the changes affecting economic policies and structures, political reforms have been only of limited scope. Till the late 1980s, the political situation remained almost stagnant. Since 1982, when the Hama insurrection was crushed, indifference and cynicism had probably been the most salient features of popular attitudes towards the regime and towards politics in general. In the general elections of 1985 some 35 independents and a couple of communists were allowed to return to the parliament, but this failed to raise any special interest among the population or among foreign observers. The Parliament continued to keep a low profile, except for some weeks in 1987 when, as part of an anti-inefficiency campaign, the Assembly questioned a handful of government ministers, eventually passing no-confidence motions against them. No one, however, actually believed that the parliament had acted on its own initiative.

Political changes did not become apparent until the end of the decade. The Syrian regime could not but respond in some way to the sweeping changes in Eastern Europe which were attentively watched by the Syrian public. After the fall of Ceaucescu's regime in the last days of 1989, graffiti appeared in Damascus referring to the Syrian president as *Sham-*

cescu.[56] Asad's response to the Eastern European events was three-pronged: first, to bring home to his people that Syria could not be compared to the states of the socialist bloc; second, to make clear the limits of opposition and demands for change he would tolerate; and, third, to mollify public discontent with a token relaxation of political control. Paralleling this was a limited restructuring of the political system which was intended to incorporate Syria's business community, which had increased in importance, more formally into the regime's structure, while at the same time putting the Ba'th Party and parts of the public sector bureaucracy in their place. The social alliance on which the regime relied was thereby partly adjusted to changed socio-economic conditions.[57]

Thus, in direct response to the upheavals in Eastern Europe, Asad, in a couple of speeches early in 1990, stressed that Syria would not copy, and had never copied in the past, the examples of other countries. Changes in Eastern Europe were not going to compel Syria to alter its system, in as much as Syria had been ahead of these countries, implementing a multi-party system and a mixed economy as early as 20 years previously.[58] Freedom, Asad said, would have to be organized, but organized freedom should not be mistaken for restricted freedom. The Corrective Movement, that is, Asad's coup of 1970, had enhanced freedom and participation by, among other things, establishing the NPF. Some laws, he conceded, had become outdated and would have to be adjusted. Emergency laws should henceforth be limited to matters of state security.[59]

Actually, following this announcement, some 'economic crimes', that is, offences against price regulations and other provisions for internal trade (not illegal currency trade, however), were transferred from special security courts to the civil courts.[60] The measure can in fact be regarded as one of economic rather than political liberalization. In 1991 and 1992, thousands of political prisoners whom the regime deemed to be of little danger were set free. This was more than a purely propagandist move towards the domestic and foreign public. Primarily, the act expressed a certain relaxation in domestic political tension. It remained embedded, however, in the form of an authoritarian presidential monarchy granting private amnesties on occasions, and as such could hardly be seen as a sign of significant change. Furthermore, a wave of new arrests paralleled the amnesties, most notably those of a group of human rights activists who were arrested and sentenced to long prison terms for openly criticizing the presidential referendum of December 1991.

Nevertheless, the system has not remained entirely unchanged. In May 1990, a new parliament was elected, in which about one-third of the seats were reserved for independent candidates. There was considerable competition between independents and apparently only limited fraud; most candidates did their best to praise the president for his wisdom and for the democratic venture he had embarked upon.[61] In terms of its loyalty to the country's leader, the new parliament was indistinguishable from its predecessors. In 1991, it nominated Hafiz al-Asad unanimously for a fourth term of office as president, to which he was duly elected with a majority of 99.9 per cent.

The general elections of 1990, which resulted in the largest ever number of independent members of parliament since the early 1960s, were nonetheless a significant event among the members of the new assembly, even though there remains an absolute majority of Ba'this representing all those forces that formed the traditional basis of the regime. Most Ba'thi deputies, apart from representing the party itself and its mass organizations, at the same time represent the bureaucracy and public sector. The independents, on the other hand, are mainly professionals, other members of the educated middle class or rising businessmen; others are tribal leaders and men of religion, several of whom had served as independent deputies in previous parliaments. The increase in the number of independents illustrates the relative decline in importance of the bureaucracy and the public sector and moreover reflects the regime's attempt to extend its social base into the private sector. It also indicates that the Ba'th Party has lost its ideological leadership and its once central role in policy-making, even though it continues to play a role in the control of some sectors of the population and as a means to generate networks of patronage. The Ba'thi majority in parliament is still useful in guarding the regime against the future ambitions of the representatives of the new economic forces. The Ba'thi deputies for their part are unlikely to exploit their numerical majority or to put any obstacles in the way of the government's policy decisions. The party has quietly accepted that, as a political force, it has gradually been removed. Since 1985, no party congress has been convened. With regard to the importance of domestic and international developments which have taken place since then, party officials concede that a congress has been an urgent necessity for some time, but that, for 'reasons we do not know', none had been called. Ba'thi deputies know that they represent forces on the losing end of the economic restructuring process. For the 'liberalizing' president, it seems, his own party with its 'pre-

modern' functionaries and their socialist–radical discourse has become
somewhat annoying. The party has increasingly been forced to keep a
low profile, most conspicuously so during the presidential campaign of
1991 from which it was virtually absent.

The incorporation of new elements into the parliament and the
heightening of its profile, for instance by giving it greater media
coverage, is not tantamount to an actual democratization of political
life. The duties, or rights, of parliament remain limited. There are
certain boundaries which must not be crossed in parliamentary or public
discussion. Essentially, any criticism of the President and the policy
areas regarded as his own prerogative – security, defence, and foreign
policy[62] – remains off-limits. Parliamentary discussion and decision-
making powers are confined to rather 'non-political' issues. In an
address to parliament in December 1991, Prime Minister Zu'bi
explained that the 'democratic system in Syria' was based on the
cooperation of government and parliament through which 'the people
participate in the making of all decisions which relate to their economy
and their daily affairs' – and not to grand politics.[63] The Syrian
parliament, in this sense, functions as a consultative, quasi-corporatist
forum, resembling to some extent the *shura* councils of more traditional
regimes.[64] For the regime it is a place for consultation on request. For
more than a decade, all laws passed by parliament were introduced by
the executive, and this has not changed since the elections of 1990.
The economic performance of the government may be discussed, and
so may public services, as well as various local and group interests of
acknowledged groups. Some deputies who entered the 1990 parliament
have privately voiced disappointment over their role. They had begun
to realize that they could not influence even the budget and that the
chamber had not developed, and was obviously not supposed to develop,
into a democratic counterweight to the government.

Although the Syrian media and representatives of the regime still
occasionally refer to the country's political system as democratic, simply
dropping the prefix 'popular' a new, more cautious term is increasingly
used, namely 'pluralism' (*ta'addudiya*). In the intellectual discourse of
the Arab world, 'democracy' has increasingly become identified with
the concept of liberal democracy, including features such as human
rights, free political organization, government accountability and the
change of government through periodic elections.[65] It is plain that this
is not what the Syrian regime offers its population. In unambiguous
terms, Asad explained to parliament in 1992 that there were different

forms of democracy, that Syria was not about to import other countries' concepts, and that Syrian democracy was essentially a matter of both political and economic pluralism.[66] This recent emphasis on the pluralist character of the regime expresses, however euphemistic it is, some conceptual change. While it does not legitimate calls for a 'liberal' democracy, it nonetheless implicity acknowledges the existence of different legitimate interests in an increasingly complex society. The pluralist project of the Syrian regime demands a selective incorporation of certain economic and social interests, namely, those which are indispensable to generate necessary economic resources for the survival of the state and the satisfaction of the regime elite. In this context, the private sector is able to meet most of the economic and social demands of the regime: it generates surplus and foreign exchange; it relieves the state of responsibilities which the latter had previously assumed but was not able to fulfil, particularly employment and distribution; and it provides opportunities for parts of the regime elite to transform some of their wealth into capital. The creation of openings for other social forces, such as urban intellectuals, rural notables or men of religion, may be advisable for political reasons – as a substitute for the loss of allegiance on the part of the losers of economic adjustment. Any deeper structural changes in the system are not to be expected, as Asad himself pointed out in his 1992 speech to parliament. Pluralism, as a regime project, is certainly not intended to lead to a gradual loss of power, but rather to consolidate, reinvigorate and probably to rationalize the power and legitimacy of the regime.

If the regime's efforts at liberalization remain limited and selective, the question arises as to whether other parts of society, particularly the business community or bourgeoisie, have alternative, more far-reaching projects, and whether they are able and willing to push them forward. Since the state is in need of resources mobilized by the private sector, one might assume that the bourgeoisie has gained substantial bargaining power. A closer look at the Syrian private sector, however, suggests that as a whole and despite its enhanced economic position, Syria's business community is still politically weak.[67] It is highly fragmented, both economically because of its overwhelmingly petty bourgeois structure, and as a socio-political force. Different parts of the Syrian bourgeoisie have repeatedly demonstrated that they are likely to respond positively to the regime's policies of divide-and-rule and that they will choose individual advantages rather than gamble for collective gains. The few entrepreneurs who command the country's few big companies have certainly acquired sufficient bargaining power to enable them to gain exemptions from certain rules and preferential access to public resources. However, as they are not representative of the entire private sector, and their importance remains confined to certain sectors of the economy, such individual bargaining power is unlikely to translate into any substantial pressure on behalf of the private sector as a whole. Individually, Syrian businessmen may still be prosecuted for various economic offences and crimes, in particular tax evasion and illegal currency transactions. As most business people are involved in such illegal activities, they tend to keep a low profile and refrain from pressing political demands. As noted, business representatives have been incorporated into decision-making bodies, but this has been only on a consultative level. Since the bourgeoisie is obviously too weak to push through its economic policy objectives according to its own schedule, it is hardly imaginable that it would be able to impose on the regime a timetable for democratic change. Moreover, it does not appear that the bourgeoisie has any such timetable or list of democratic demands in the first place. Parts of the bourgeoisie are doubtless interested in at least some democratization, particularly in increased government accountability, transparency of decision-making and the rule of law. Others, notably those who have the largest influence upon regime decisions, are not really interested in such details. Thus, one part of the bourgeoisie and petty bourgeoisie is in favour of more democracy but lacks any particular bargaining power, while another part possesses more bargaining power and closer relations with the regime but is not interested in democratic change. Consequently, private sector pressure for democratization will remain very limited.

There are other societal forces whose interest in democratic change can be said to be more genuine. Their political position is, however, even weaker than that of the business community. This applies to forces within civil society such as professional unions of lawyers, medical doctors, engineers and so on – who were crushed and lost all independence in the events of 1980. The fate of Syria's budding human rights groups in 1992 was a clear warning that people should not try to establish independent, liberal associations. It is highly indicative of the weakness of civil society in Syria that the number of social, cultural, scientific, educational, religious and charity organizations permitted in Syria, which was extremely low to begin with, has actually decreased over the last decade from over 650 to only 504.[68] In general, Syria's civil society is deeply penetrated by the state. In the case of the trade

unions, for example, whose counterparts in other countries have
occasionally proven to be an effective challenge to authoritarian rule,
the leadership is incorporated into the regime elite. In addition, the
unions are very much on the defensive, trying, at best, to protect their
membership, from bearing the full brunt of the costs of economic
restructuring.

Conclusion

The Syrian case contradicts the convenient argument, still often heard
in western debates on development policy, that economic and political
liberalization are inseparable, that economic liberalization both helps
to further and eventually relies upon political liberalization and
democratization. Syria is not unique in this respect.[69] Rather, it can be
understood as 'one example of a variety of approaches adopted by
Middle Eastern (and other) states to manage economic change without
provoking disruptive political change'.[70]

The two moves towards economic *infitah* which Syria experienced
in the 1970s and 1980s were brought about against distinctively different
economic backgrounds. In the first case, abundance provided the motive
for economic opening; in the second case scarcity of resources or, put
less mildly, the threat of state bankruptcy. In the 1970s, *infitah* policies
served as a means of distributing Syria's increased political and oil rents;
in the 1980s, the objective was to mobilize domestic, private resources
to make up for the inability of the state not only to maintain previous
growth rates, but also to secure the supply of imported consumer goods
and production inputs both for the private and the public sectors. This
is not to deny that a number of crony-capitalists managed to secure
high rents (that is, non-competitive gains) through that process too.
On the whole, Syria's *infitah* of the 1980s served its purposes, even
though the remarkable improvement in Syria's overall economic
situation has to a large extent been due to increased oil exports and,
since the Kuwait crisis of 1990, to Arab aid (that is, to the acquisition
of new rent elements).

While granting a higher degree of autonomy to the private sector
and thereby surrendering some economic levers, the regime has not
relinquished any of its political powers. Limited and selective pluralism,
as granted by the regime, can be regarded as a matter of 'system
maintenance' rather than democratization or substantial political
liberalization.[71] It aims at regaining lost legitimacy and helps to secure
the incorporation of indispensable groups into regime structures.

Economic liberalization, the Syrian case tells us, is possible, and quite successfully so, without being paralleled by substantial political change. It may require a new formula of societal incorporation, including the demobilization of strata which have been or will be pushed to the losing end of the reform process. It does not, however, necessarily require a new form of government.

4· The Syrian Business Community, its Politics and Prospects

Joseph Bahout

Should *infitah* be envisaged as a zero-sum game? In political terms, who gains and who loses in the liberalization process? How could the emergence of an important entrepreneurial group alter the nature of the state–society relationship in Syria?

Indeed, the Syrian private sector is alive and well. However, the very existence of that sector, its size, importance and the scope of its activities are still very dependent upon, and have to submit to, political direction. The complex relationship between the public and private sectors in Syria has largely determined the nature and composition of the entrepreneurial group – or business community – and determines to a large extent its political consciousness and potential political role.

Syrian Entrepreneurs: Social Actors or Social Class?
The business community, although constituting an economically influential group, cannot simply be called a 'bourgeoisie', principally because it is far from being a simple sociological category. Rather, it is a hybrid and heterogeneous group, whose various components have been formed during three decades of sometimes brutal and radical changes in economic policies, and in the context of a frequently unclear relationship between the public and private sectors.

Therefore, this business community bears little similarity to its 'compradore' ancestor: the rural landed and urban 'aristocracy' that virtually ruled Syria from the mid-nineteenth century until the late 1950s. Although some individuals and families who belonged to this historical bourgeoisie are now part of the new business community, the core of this community and its recent members have different origins. In this sense, the wealthy Syrian upper stratum is an amalgam of a new and a renewed 'class'. From a methodological point of view, this aspect raises a problem of classification. Following a typology suggested by Volker Perthes,[1] we will, in this chapter, use the terms 'entrepreneurial class' and 'business community' to designate a group whose members come from four distinct backgrounds.

The first group is comprised of remnants of the old bourgeoisie, whose origins can be traced back to the Ottoman era, and whose power was strengthened under the French mandate. Historically, this land-owning class recycled its economic surplus in urban activities, such as trade and medium-scale industry. In the wake of independence, it is this same stratum which exercised political power in Syria.[2] Later on, the successive waves of nationalizations, if failing to eliminate this class completely, at least weakened it to a very large extent. Nationalizations first began in 1958, with the setting up of the United Arab Republic under the leadership of Nasir's Egypt; they were then carried on – after the *Infisal* and a brief episode of liberal parliamentary rule – by the successive Ba'th regimes, starting in 1963. The initial waves of nationalization measures, centred mostly on land reform, particularly hit the rural component of the Syrian upper class; subsequent measures later affected other components as well. Today, by claiming for themselves the denomination of 'national bourgeoisie', the survivors of these economic policies wish to remind us that, in spite of economic and political hardships, they have continued to invest in productive sectors inside Syria; they aim at the same time to differentiate themselves from the new capitalists whom they perceive as both usurpers and parasites. Ironically, the old bourgeoisie was not only hit by the nationalizations, but is now again threatened by liberalization measures which expose its weaknesses in an open competition with a new set of powerful economic players.

The second group is one of medium-size entrepreneurs, mostly active in small industry, manufacture, commerce and some types of services, more directly the by-product of the *infitah*. This group constitutes an important part of what could be a Syrian 'new middle class' and, in a sense, it contains the most enterprising of today's Syrian entrepreneurs, who are risking small or medium assets to start businesses in a still uncertain environment. However, their political culture, behaviour and attitude towards the state are more those of a 'petty bourgeoisie'. They are petty bourgeois to the extent that they are still at an intermediary stage of class formation – most of them being of modest origin – but they aim to become a part of the upper class. They have grown and acquired their managerial skills within an environment of administrative and bureaucratic constraints, and have thus familiarized themselves with the wheels of corruption set up by the state and its apparatus. As far as their interests are concerned, they seem to be asking for greater economic freedom as well as maintenance of the political status quo. One of their weaknesses is that their political consciousness is limited and not clearly defined. Their fragility bars them from clearly articulating and pursuing their political demands, even though as medium-sized entrepreneurs they actually suffer most from the arbitrary application of government regulations.

The third group is the upper stratum of nouveaux riches, or the 'new class' (*Tabaqa jadida*), this latter term being used by the Syrians themselves to designate those entrepreneurs whose origins go back to the indirect oil rent Syria has benefited from since 1973. Far more than the medium-sized entrepreneurs this group benefited from the first and second *infitah* of 1973 and the late 1980s; and it is indeed this success which differentiates it from the former. Consequently, they are much more closely connected to the circuits of the public economy and are solidly linked with the state and administrative apparatus. Mostly as intermediaries, and through their connections with the bureaucracy, the party and/or the army, they managed to control, in a quasi-monopolistic way, the realization of the major infrastructural projects launched by the government since 1973. In this respect, they constitute what Issam Khafaji, describing one of the Iraqi capitalist circles, called the 'contractors' bourgeoisie' (*burjwaziyyat al-muqawilun*).[3] After the mid-1980s, this 'new class' diversified its business activities, investing in real estate, construction, agro-business, tourism and transportation. The size and real power of this entrepreneurial category still cannot be accurately determined, although its external manifestations are sometimes spectacular. The present situation and attitudes of this 'new class' are, however, paradoxical: its members have greatly benefited from public expenditure and from the protection of major political and military officials, as well as from a set of contradictory legal regulations.[4] But now that they have strengthened their economic position, they increasingly feel the need to detach themselves from their former protectors, having become more conscious of their importance for the country and the regime. In that respect, and with time, they would probably find it useful to ally themselves with the medium-sized entrepreneurs in order to articulate demands for greater and more audacious change. Members of this 'new class' have an interest in such an alliance, especially because the smaller entrepreneurs of the medium strata are still not competitive enough to constitute a serious threat to their vested interests.

The fourth and final group is comprised of prominent members of the select club of the 'state or bureaucratic bourgeoisie'. The members of this group are at the same time members of the regime or at least occupy key positions in its military or bureaucratic apparatus. They often use their position, privileges and immunity to promote their own material interests. Interestingly, however, some members or their sons, have relinquished or refused positions in the apparatus in order to devote themselves entirely to private business activities.

The 'Military-Mercantile Complex': Organic Unity or Competitive Alliance?

Some 15 years ago when Elizabeth Picard analysed the nature of state–society relations in Syria and the ethnic, familial and clientelistic networks built up by its elite, she coined the term of a 'military-mercantile complex' and proposed to label the regime as a 'militaro-merchant dictatorship.[5] This approach has, since then, become the dominant framework to analyse the political sociology of power in contemporary Syria. Since the beginning of the 1970s, a new hybrid elite has indeed tightened its grip over the power stucture; an elite including officers from different origins, top-ranking officials, public-enterprise managers, and a group of new businessmen – mostly speculators and brokers.

However, the formation of such a dyadic elite was a function of, and the response to, a precise historical situation: at the beginning of the 1970s when the military members of this emerging new elite took over, power seemed to have moved into the hands of geographically peripheral, socially ascending and ethnically minoritarian sectors of society. Not so much inclined towards commerce and business, but having control of the coercive and propagnda apparatus, the new masters extended their protection to the merchants who, in turn, became one of the most solid of the regime's bases of support.

If today the regime is reluctant to complete the process started with the Corrective Movement in 1970 and in spite of important legal changes refuses to retreat from the economic arena, the reasons must not be sought in any sort of residual ideological commitment to the Ba'th values. Indeed, the use of the coercive apparatus could compensate for a deficit in terms of ideological resources. Rather, the real risk of economic liberalization is a likely decrease in the regime's capacity to control economic activity, the distribution of wealth and its political consequences. By controlling the greater share of material resources, the state clearly aims at depriving other social forces, particularly the private sector, of political tools which could hardly be neutralized with mere repression.

Therefore, we may perceive that the recent liberalization measures, although unavoidable from a macro-economic point of view, are nevertheless intended to remain, at least in the short-run, cosmetic. In the view of Syria's political leadership, the optimal formula in terms of political economy would be: 'a prosperous, submissive, and parasitic private sector, yes; a true national bourgeoisie, no.'[6] At the same time the upper stratum of the entrepreneurial community, that is, the 'new class', in the short-run, still seems to be in need of an omnipotent bureaucracy, if not of a strong state. This stratum developed itself within the protective environs of state capitalism, and was nurtured by the prebends the state allocated in the form of public works contracts. In the near future, the survival and paradoxically even the consolidation and growing independence of this group will depend upon an accomplice bureaucracy which keeps competitors away, controls access to public markets and continues to apply laws and regulations selectively and in a sense arbitrarily. One wonders whether the innovation brought about by the much praised 'mixed sector', with the package of economic and symbolic advantages and privileges it confers on the private sector 'protégés' of the state, is not after all the supreme form of institution-alizing a very particular kind of partnership between the state and the 'new class'.

According to the 'military-mercantile complex', a rather odd couple is governing Syria. It is a couple within which a constantly changing balance of power is at work, and whereby any exogenous change is used by either of the two parties to redefine the initial equilibrium to its own advantage. However, such changes need not be a zero-sum game and at times both parties may benefit.

Consolidation and Emancipation

Increasingly over the years, the military have emancipated themselves from liegemen in the business world to whom they extend protection in exchange for a share in their profits. Power and public life have progressively led the military establishment into business, by and for themselves. It is possible to assume that their progressive entry into this sphere will weaken their spartan character. Consequently, we may envisage that with time the strength and intensity of its original '*Asabiyya*,'[7] could be loosened and replaced by bonds of interest much more material than symbolic.

In fact, many indicators support the hypothesis of a gradual 'demilitarization' or 'de-praetorianization' of the Syrian regime. First, the importance of the armed forces as the recruiting ground for the ruling elite is declining. A growing number of political cadres are now recruited from civil and technocratic backgrounds. Second, the army is not the sole, or most accessible, instrument of upward mobility for more peripheral sectors of society. Third, the army has lost its privileged place in the processes of elite reproduction. Instead of joining the military, many sons of high-ranking officers are establishing flourishing businesses, and they undoubtedly belong more and more to the merchants' establishment than to that of the barracks.[8] Fourth, the slow and still incremental demilitarization of Syrian society is visible through a decrease of military expenditure allocated within the general budget. Of course, this last aspect is largely exogenous, and has to do with regional and international geopolitical considerations as well.[9]

On the other side, Syrian entrepreneurs increasingly tend to see their cooperation with the state as merely tactical. They are consolidating their position within the private sector, aiming first at becoming equal partners, before stepping over the limits designed for them, in order to become an autonomous economic, social and even political force. It is interesting to note that a growing number of top bureaucrats share this view and anticipate a greater role for the private sector who no longer consider a career in the public sector or civil service as a step towards initial capital-formation. A trend is therefore appearing, the result of which is a potentially stronger mercantile branch of the original alliance. At the same time the various components of the Syrian business community are merging, through business partnerships, and even through family alliances on the basis of inter-marriage. With time, one should expect that 'bureaucratic entre-preneurs', members of the 'new class', ambitious sons of the old bourgeoisie who play by the new rules and successful new *infitahi* entrepreneurs will tend to form a more homogeneous social force.

Scenarios for Liberalization: Environmental Parameters and Constraints

Syria's evolution from a state economy to a market economy and the however timid evolution of the Syrian political system towards a greater degree of 'civilianization', are not the only *aggiornamento*s of the last ten years. The transformation is also touching Syria's foreign policy and its ability to influence regional and international changes.

In a sense, Syria is moving towards what may be called political and economic 'normality', which seems to be the price to pay in order to be accepted within the still undefined 'new world order'. In that process of realignment, it appears that the Syrian regime expects its entrepreneurs to play an important instrumental role in generating a prosperity that the exhausted possibilities of the rentier-state can no longer provide.

However, contrary to the regime's expectations, the business community need not remain a functional instrument; the exogenous changes occurring in Syria's environment cannot but affect the equilibrium between it and its military 'allies'. In the medium term, the relationship between the military establishment on the one hand, and the civilian entrepreneurs on the other could follow one of several scenarios, depending on the three variables: income from oil, the Arab–Israeli conflict and developments in Lebanon.

Oil

In the coming years, the share of oil revenues in Syria's national income may rise significantly.[10] If optimistic expectations were to be met, public revenues would increase, and the state's financial autonomy *vis-à-vis* the private sector would be enhanced, thus delaying further progress towards greater and more audacious economic liberalization.

The Arab–Israeli Conflict

Developments in the Arab–Israeli conflict could play both ways. Peace would deprive the Syrian state of another rent it has been receiving in the name of the 'confrontation with the Zionist enemy'; peace would also further add to the demilitarization of the political system. Both factors would thus increase dependence on the private sector, and on the wealth its activities could generate. Ultimately, this scenario would strengthen the political bargaining power of the business community.

Inversely, however, Syria, like Egypt after Camp David, would probably benefit from the 'peace dividends' in the form of aid and investments, mostly from the Gulf states channelled through the state, these revenues would enhance the latter's financial capacity, and allow it to hold out for a while, against a rising private sector. Nevertheless, such beneficial effects for the state would be limited in time, as peace would give *infitahi* tendencies greater ideological legitimacy, thus strengthening here too the bargaining position of the business community.

Lebanon
There remains Lebanon, whose function is increasingly that of a zone of compensation for Syrian losses elsewhere. The profitability of the *espace libanais* is nevertheless dependent upon the degree of prosperity Lebanon can regain and hence upon its future political stability. Therefore, this profitability also depends upon the relations between Syria and those who could provide the resources for Lebanon's economic recovery, that is, most probably, the major Gulf states, the western powers, as well as the Lebanese business community itself. In this scenario, both the Syrian state and Syrian private entrepreneurs would benefit.

Is *infitah* a Zero-sum Game? Prospects for Political Change
Hypotheses assuming that the growth of the business community in numbers as well as in importance will increase the constraints on the rulers and widen the autonomy of civil society inevitably question the survival of the 'military-mercantile complex' or at least of its present internal *status quo*.

While conserving a degree of validity in the Syrian case, such hypotheses nonetheless need to be applied with care. As Jean Leca pointed out, the impact of economic on political change may be limited:

> Corresponding to the economic market opened by the establishment of a private sector, there should exist a political market opened by the establishment of class groups or factions. There is no empirical proof of this. The private sector growing up in the shadow of the state (and thanks to the public sector) certainly has an interest in gaining freedom of economic action, more access to credit and fiscal facilities, the freedom of cross-border traffic; but why should it have to undertake open political action when it can try to obtain all this at least cost to itself, by remaining entrenched in bureaucratic or palace politics, where informal networks of family, regional, and factional solidarity is at the heart of the game?[11]

Moreover, the existence or the emergence of a class does not automatically imply that this class will be politically active. The clear perception and the structured and organized voicing of the interests of this class presupposes the formation of class consciousness over quite a long period, which enables a 'class-in-itself' to become a 'class-for-itself'.

In Syria today, the establishment of a political market ensuring the autonomy of social groups – and ultimately their political participation as independent actors – is not only prevented by the resilience of an authoritarian-corporatist state; it is also hampered by the fact that the rising business community is not yet a bourgeois class-for-itself.

This is, first, because of its internal heterogeneity and the existence of differences in the economic bases supporting its various components and, therefore, because of the divergence of interests that it embraces. Without doubt, there are active Syrian entrepreneurs; however, there is not yet a Syrian bourgeois class.

Second, it is not a bourgeois class because of its political culture and attitude. When asked whether he thought that economic liberalization would bring about political liberalization, one prominent industrialist and trader of Damascus replied: 'Not only do I not think so, but I do not really wish it. All we want is economic freedom and political stability; for us, democracy often means a coup d'état every two years.'

Syria's business community still has to achieve its 'bourgeois revolution', and to fill the deficit of its democratic tradition; a tradition constantly and periodically aborted by the recurrence of open and, sometimes, more subtle forms of violence.

5· *Al-dimuqratiyya hiyya al-hall?* The Syrian Opposition at the End of the Asad Era

Hans Günter Lobmeyer

'I do not want anybody to keep silent on mistakes and I do not want any deficiency and any neglect of duty to be covered.' Several times a week this quotation from a speech by President Hafiz al-Asad can be found in the Syrian daily *Tishrin*. The phrase is the motto of a column which is entitled '*Tishrin* and the citizens' concerns'. Here the newspaper invites its readers to complain about everyday difficulties with the bureaucracy, about malfunctioning public services or shortages of basic commodities, and promises to intervene in favour of the citizen. This modest Syrian version of the ombudsman is only one of the features of public life which the regime regards as proof of its 'democratic' character.

But there are only a few who share this view. When, in the middle of the 1980s, the Soviet leader Mikhail Gorbachev implemented his political reforms, he became extremely popular (at least in Europe and the USA) and was awarded the Nobel Peace Prize in 1990. Very soon the Russian term for reform, *perestroika*, was understood all over the world and there was no more need to translate it. But Gorbachev seems to have been a mere plagiarist and world public opinion obviously applauded the wrong man. Although Hafiz al-Asad is by no means as popular as Gorbachev, and although outside Syria and the Arab world only a few specialists catch the meaning of the notion 'Corrective Movement' – to say nothing of the Arab term *al-haraka al-tashihiyya*, the official name for Asad's coup of 1970 – *Tishrin* made it quite clear that it was Asad who, as early as 1970, staged 'the world's first *perestroika*'. Moreover, what happened in Eastern Europe was nothing but 'the introduction of a corrective movement in the socialist camp'.[1]

This euphemism for Asad's putsch is certainly the linguistic highlight of the regime's attempts to counter growing concern inside and outside Syria at the dictatorial and oppressive manner with which it has ruled the country for nearly a quarter of a century. Since the overthrow of Asad's Romanian counterpart, Ceaucescu, in December 1989, Syria's rulers have taken great pains to convince the Syrians that they are living in a 'democratic' country without any need for political reforms. Yet again Syria's rulers refer to the achievements of the 'Corrective Movement' which, indeed, imparted an aspect of democracy to the political system. In the early 1970s Asad created the National Progressive Front (NPF; *al-jabha al-wataniyya al-taqaddumiyya*), a coalition of several parties under the tutelage of the Ba'th Party.[2] He granted the first permanent constitution under Ba'thi rule, convened a parliament – the People's Assembly (*majlis al-sha'b*) – whose deputies are elected every five years, and permits himself to be elected president by plebiscite. All this is presented by the regime as striking evidence of democracy based, as Asad pretends, on political pluralism and power-sharing: 'For more than twenty years we have assured political pluralism ... and the parties which belong to the NPF share responsibility in the state leadership.'[3] Referring to the last parliamentary elections in May 1990, when the number of independent deputies was considerably increased, Asad emphasized that 'the great number of candidates and the intense competition [among them] proved the climate of freedom and democracy'.[4]

But when considering Syrian political life one cannot avoid the impression that Syria's leadership is talking about any country other than Syria. For reality is quite different and has little or nothing in common with democracy. The constitution only confirms the president's (that is, Asad's) omnipotence and merely renders Syria's political system a constitutional dictatorship rather than, as Article 1 stipulates, a people's democracy: the parliament has hardly any legislative power; the Ba'th Party is, according to Article 8, the country's leading party; and the NPF as a concrete institution is not even mentioned in the constitution.[5] Still worse than constitutional theory is political practice: with the exception of the Ba'th Party, the member parties of the NPF have no influence on political decisions and are mere puppets with Asad holding the strings.[6] Political competition between these parties does not occur, while plebiscites regularly turn out to be a farce and are far from being free and secret. The same applies to elections, even though those to the People's Assembly in 1990 resulted in a planned and intended reduction of Ba'thi deputies relative to independents. Whereas the ingredients necessary for a democratic political system have at least a formal existence, another basic feature of democracy is completely lacking: there is no legal opposition, nor does the regime accept the mere idea of such an opposition, that is of a political force which does not support the government but which presents itself as an alternative, intending to replace it, though without changing the political system as such.[7] The political forces which legally exist alongside the Ba'th Party, and the independent members of parliament, are far from being oppositional: they are allowed to articulate their special interests only for as long as their demands do not contradict the regime's general policy.

According to the constitution, Syria is a republic (the Arab term for which is *jumhuriyya,* which literally translated means 'of the popular masses'), and, according to the constitution, the President of the Syrian Arab Republic is to be elected by plebiscite every seven years; thus the theory. Official Syrian propaganda is more honest and its linguistic creations fit Syrian reality much better than the constitution does. Syria is not, as the propaganda states, the 'Syria of the masses' but *suriya asad* or, in other words, Asad's personal principality. He is not the 'President of the Republic', his official title, whose term of office is limited to seven years, but '*qa'iduna ila al-abad*', 'our leader into eternity'. This title is highly significant in manifesting Asad's absolute claim to power and in illustrating why the regime cannot allow or tolerate any kind of opposition and why there is not even any need for it. First, Asad is rendered a godlike being and his grip on power is very clearly emphasized. Second, the formulation 'our' suggests that the people rally unconditionally behind their president. Logically, therefore, any opposition to Asad would seem to be directed against the people's will.

Thus the formation of an opposition is hindered from the outset.[8] Every kind of organization founded, be it political or not, comes under the regime's strict control and has to commit itself unconditionally to Asad.[9] Above all, freedom of opinion and expression, though stipulated in the constitution, do not exist. Criticism is not completely banned, but the limits to any criticism are extremely narrow and do not go far beyond the possibilities offered by the ombudsman column of *Tishrin*. Everybody can complain about overcrowded buses, incompetent low-ranking officials or corruption, even some political topics can be relatively frankly discussed, for instance policies to overcome the country's dramatic economic situation. Ever since the 1970s, for instance, it has been *en vogue* to criticize very harshly the mainly

Damascus-based 'parasitic class' (*al-tabaqa al-tifiliyya*), a relatively small stratum of businessmen who owe their occasionally extreme wealth to illegal profits gained in cooperation with high-ranking officials. Though tolerance of such connivance is part of Asad's strategy to keep the bourgeoisie on his side, anybody who dares to allot responsibility for such major corruption to the Asad regime or to hint at the involvement of high-ranking officials can expect an invitation to see the *mukhabarat*, the intelligence services. The same applies to criticism of foreign and internal policies, the security apparatus, the predominance of 'Alawis in the power centres, or permanent violation of human rights, to say nothing of Asad being in power. All the subjects are strictly banned from public debate.

Opposition in Syria therefore can exist only illegally, that is, outside the officially recognized arena of politics. Many observers tend to equate opposition in Syria more or less with the Muslim Brotherhood and its other Islamist allies, certainly the most outstanding oppositional force until their defeat in the Hama uprising in 1982. But the present and past role of the secular opposition is generally neglected, even though it contributed a great deal to the near overthrow of the Asad regime at the end of the 1970s and the beginning of the 1980s[10]. However, what the Islamists called *jihad* attracted much more attention than the generally non-violent struggle of the secular opposition and proved more effective in mobilizing the population, as even the oppositional wing of the Communist Party – commonly called CP-Politbureau (*al-hizb al-shuyu'i al-suri*; *al-maktab al-siyasi*) – recently stated: 'Why have the fundamentalists ... succeeded in rallying the street behind them? The people rallied behind their actions and not behind their programme.'[11]

The secular opposition became active much earlier than the Islamists and suffered from persecution at a time when the regime took hardly any notice of the Muslim Brotherhood. In the post-Hama era the long-time leader of the Brotherhood's armed organization, 'Adnan 'Uqla, can live in Syria without being persecuted by the regime,[12] whereas Riyad al-Turk, the leader of the CP-Politbureau, has been in prison since 1980, facing the same destiny as Asad's Ba'thi rival Salah Jadid, who died in the summer of 1993 after almost a quarter of a century of imprisonment.

The illegal status of any kind of opposition means that, as a consequence, any political force which aims to replace the regime in power has also implicitly to strive for the replacement of the formal and, above all, the informal political structure on which Asad's power is based. The constitution, the legal framework for Asad's omnipotence, does not define presidential powers in general but is tailored to reflect those of a specific president: Asad. The military, the praetorian militias and the internal security apparatus are his personal power institutions which, as far as the militias and the security services are concerned, are not collective achievements of the so-called 'Ba'th revolution' of 1963 but rather were created by Asad in the 1970s. They are institutions which exist outside the legal framework of the state and form what can be described as an over-state. Neither the constitution nor the security apparatus is, so to speak, a transferable power institution; to topple this structure is thus a prerequisite for toppling the regime. That is why opposition of whatever ideological tendency must be against the system as such, rather than against the regime only. This is not only the case with the regime's ideological antipodean, that is, the Islamist groups which already in the 1960s struggled against the Ba'thi state on grounds of ideology; a great part of the secular opposition also turned into an anti-system force in 1973 when almost all the leftists who had not joined the NPF openly rejected Asad's permanent constitution because of its deeply undemocratic character.[13] Even the followers of Asad's former comrade-in-arms, Salah Jadid, who are organized in the Democratic Socialist Arab Ba'th Party (*hizb al-ba'th al-dimuqrati al-ishtiraki al-'arabi*), formerly the Movement of 23 February (*harakat 23 shubat*), as well as the pro-Iraqi branch of the Syrian Ba'th Party, are no exception to this and can be considered anti-system although they commit themselves to the same ideology as the regime in power.

In 1980 Asad succeeded in crushing the secular opposition, including the professional associations. At the time of the Hama revolt in February 1982 he was anxious to defeat also the Islamist opposition, and this once and for all.[14] The violence used by the regime at Hama went far beyond what was needed to quell the revolt. From this point of view Hama was, indeed, a victory for Asad and he was eventually able to get rid of his most uncompromising and relentless enemy from within. In the aftermath of Hama, the hitherto well-developed Islamist infrastructure was almost completely destroyed, and most Islamist activists who survived and were not imprisoned fled abroad. Whereas the secular opposition was badly shaken but not completely neutralized, the Islamist camp has not recovered from its defeat at Hama. The Islamic Front in Syria (*al-jabha al-islamiyya fi suriya*), a coalition of 'ulama and Islamist groupings has ceased to exist, and in the early 1990s there is no organized Islamist movement inside the country.[15] However, despite its domestic organizational weakness, the Muslim Brotherhood cannot be considered negligible in terms of the future. Outside Syria it maintains a relatively strong organization and it has a lot of powerful friends in the Arab world. As in the past, Asad's numerous regional rivals are always ready to support the Brotherhood, hoping to push the Syrian regime into domestic trouble. Above all, the Muslim Brotherhood has a dangerous political weapon at its disposal: Islam remains a highly efficient instrument of mobilization, and the traditional religious milieu, particularly the small urban traders and artisans, continues to be receptive to religious-political propaganda. Moreover, following Hama, a considerable part of the population at large held the Brotherhood in a certain esteem because of its struggle against Asad and the enormous number of victims from its ranks.

There is no doubt that in the early 1980s the Syrian opposition lost the war, not just a battle. Since 1982 opposition activities of whatever source have become rare in Syria and the opposition has fallen into a state of paralysis. There were some violent attacks, particularly in the mid-1980s, but these were isolated operations whose authorship is not entirely clear.[16] One of the main reasons for the defeat in the early 1980s as well as for the opposition's actual situation is the notorious disunity present even inside the various parties. The most extreme case is that of the Muslim Brotherhood; since the late 1960s its political energy has been absorbed by endless disputes over how to fight the regime and, of course, who leads the organization. To a considerable degree these internal differences contributed to the 1982 defeat. Disunity among the opposition has become one of the most efficient political weapons at Asad's disposal; by offering negotiations to almost all opposition groups he yet again succeeded in fortifying and accelerating the existing rifts. To a considerable degree the 1986 split of the Muslim Brotherhood was generated by internal controversy over the regime's offer to enter negotiations.[17]

The inability of the opposition to join forces was already highlighted in the late 1970s and in the early 1980s when the Islamists and the secular camp failed to establish a common front. This was not only caused by ideological and political differences, particularly concerning the violent means of the Islamists and their extreme anti-'Alawi bias; the Islamists and the leftists preferred to dispute over the leadership of the opposition movement and sometimes even fought each other instead of fighting their common adversary.[18] The National Alliance for the

Liberation of Syria (*al-tahaluf al-watani li tahrir suriya*), which consisted of the Muslim Brotherhood and some secular parties, was established only after the events at Hama, when any effort to join forces was, indeed, too late. Behind the Alliance was Asad's chief Arab rival, the Iraqi Ba'th regime, that had already supported the Islamists and some other opposition groups during the preceding years. After Syria's pro-Iranian stance in the first Gulf war, the Iraqi regime tried to sustain the Syrian opposition to Asad. Being an Iraqi puppet right from the outset, none of the more secular parties agreed to join it. Neither the Alliance nor its sucessor – the National Front for the Salvation of Syria (*al-jabha al-wataniyya li inqadh suriya*), founded in 1990 – have ever been represented inside Syria and therefore remained powerless.

In the post-Hama era some secular parties, though considerably weakened, constitute the only political opposition of importance inside the country. One of the most active among them is the Party (formerly Association) of Communist Action (PCA: *hizb [rabita] al-'amal al-shuyu'i*) which, like many other leftist opposition parties, recruits many of its activists from among the 'Alawis and other minorities.[19] The PCA, however, did not join the National Democratic Gathering (*al-tajammu' al-watani al-dimuqrati*), a leftist alliance whose establishment in 1980 had contributed greatly to Asad's decision to strike a blow against his leftist adversaries. The Gathering's leading parties are the CP-Politbureau and the oppositional wing of the Arab Socialist Union (ASU) led by Jamal al-Atasi, who at the same time figures as the chairman of the Gathering at large. Apart from these two parties the Gathering also comprises the Revolutionary Workers' Party (*hizb al-'ummal al-thawri*),[20] the pro-Jadid Ba'th-Party and the oppositional wing of the Movement of Arab Socialists (MAS; *harakat al-ishtirakiyin al-'arab*);[21] in contrast, the official wing of the MAS, like that of the ASU, participates in the PNF alongside the official Ba'th Party. Paralysed by the shock of Hama, widely regarded as a catastrophe by the whole opposition, the Gathering and its parties have since been fully occupied with sustaining their fragile clandestine infrastructure. After having erased the Islamist opposition, the regime's oppressive apparatus turned its attention to the secular opposition and still continues to persecute activists and sympathizers. Under these circumstances the opposition's freedom of action is extremely limited, and its activities remain largely restricted to the distribution of leaflets and the publication of numerous manifestos.

The breakdown of the Eastern European single-party systems and the increasing role of democracy and human rights in western political discourse have, however, stirred up the political opposition in Syria. Though it has not yet overcome its crisis and is still far from being able to challenge the regime, it is about to wake up from its slumber. The different parties are clearly making an effort to overcome their traditional disunity; the Marxist-oriented and dogmatic PCA, hitherto isolated from the opposition movement, has for some years now been closely cooperating with the Gathering which is dominated by its rival, the more reformist CP-Politbureau. The Gathering, too, has tried to form itself into a more effective alliance. These efforts are most perceptible on the level of political propaganda. Thus in 1991 the CP-Politbureau ceased publication of its underground paper *nidal al-sha'b* (People's Struggle) in favour of a common publication of the Gathering, *al-mawqif al-dimuqrati* (Democratic Point of View), which has since been regularly distributed inside Syria, an operation which continues to be dangerous. A similar development within the Muslim Brotherhood suggests that the organization is about to be reunited too. The Iraqi-backed wing has also ceased publication of its underground paper *al-nadhir* (the *Warner*). And the former organ of the rival Saudi-backed wing, *al-bayan* (the *Communiqué*), now represents both wings.[22]

The political opposition of the 1990s not only seeks to reverse the splits of the preceding decades; in spite of the different ideological orientation of its various Islamist, Ba'thi, Nasirist, nationalist and communist components, it is, at least verbally, united in its call for 'democracy'. This is, of course, not merely a recent concern; the great revolt of the late 1970s and the early 1980s implied democratic rather than Islamist aspects, and for years 'democratic freedoms' have been among the demands of most opposition parties, above all the CP-Politbureau. In the post-*perestroika* period, however, the claim for 'democratic freedoms' has been increasingly replaced by the claim for 'democracy' as a political system. Thus democracy is categorically demanded by the Gathering: 'Now as never before democracy has become a national necessity, a political demand that does not permit any delay, and an urgent popular requirement.'[23] Democracy is not necessarily considered the perfect solution for all problems, but it is understood to be the best available solution. Representing the political point of view not only of his own party but of all opposition forces, a member of the CP-Politbureau states: 'it is difficult to say that democracy implies magic solutions for our Arab countries' problems; it is easy to say that ... [democracy] is the right way to face the challenges which are imposed on our nation.'[24] This statement is an admission that the CP's own (Marxist) concept has failed.

'Democratic', there is no doubt, has become something like the opposition's trademark. Its generalized claim to represent a democratic opposition rather than anything else cannot pass unnoticed. The secular groups are busy creating new periodicals or renaming their old ones, most of which now carry the words 'democracy' or 'democratic' in their titles.[25] The opposition's political slogans also reveal this new political approach. The Revolutionary Workers' Party (hizb al-'ummal al-thawri), for example, emphasizes in its motto its claim to overcome the opposition's disunity as well as its claim to democracy: 'That we fight for the sake of a broad patriotic democratic front – the national democratic revolution is our way to the [national] awakening [nahda] and to progress.'[26] However, no party has worked out an actual political programme or even defined what it means by 'democracy'. The actual political situation in Syria and its manifest connection with the collapse of dictatorial 'people's democracies' in Eastern Europe leave no doubt that in general the opposition has a liberal version of democracy in mind.[27] But in all cases the opposition parties are in sharp contrast, or even absolute contradiction, to their respective ideologies: Communism, Ba'thism, Nasirism, Islamism. None of these provides an adequate theoretical framework for a concise concept of democracy. Ideological postulates are, however, not abandoned; democracy is simply considered the most suitable vehicle for realizing them. According to Jamal al-Atasi, the national awakening (nahda) 'begins with democratic changes and the establishment of our civil society on a democratic base',[28] thus, 'the national democratic revolution is our path to accomplish the project of the Arab national awakening'.[29]

The Muslim Brotherhood is the most extreme and downright classic example for both the 'democratization' of the political discourse on the one hand and the contradiction between this new discourse and ideological commitments on the other. By 1980–81 it already had a political programme with primarily democratic rather than Islamist overtones.[30] Generally, however, at that time the discourse of the Brotherhood like that of other Islamist groups remained dominated by the anti-'Alawi elements, while democratic ones were almost completely lacking.[31] Since the late 1980s, however, these democratic references have come to dominate the discourse and have, to a considerable degree, superseded the still existing but relatively moderate anti-'Alawi tendency. In a communiqué in early 1990 the Brotherhood's Saudi-backed wing listed ten principal demands under the title: 'Which change is wanted?' Not one of them mentions what the Islamists once called 'the enemies of Islam' or 'the hate-filtered sect', that is, the 'Alawis. The 'abolition of political confessionalism' is all that is required. Most remarkable is the fact that almost all the demands have much in common with democracy, while none reflects a genuine Islamic principle. Thus the Muslim Brotherhood claims 'respect for human rights', the 'equality between all citizens' and 'political pluralism to enable the people to choose ... the governmental system'; only one point refers to religion, when the organization in rather general terms demands 'to respect ... Islam, its symbols, and the freedom of Islamic practice'.[32]

All this is not presented in a religious context, but in a communiqué dealing with the importance which processes of democratization at the global level have for Syria. In this way the demands, which could easily be deduced from Islam, implicitly but clearly suggest that the Brotherhood's political project is a democratic one, without directly saying so. Unlike its rival, the Iraqi-backed wing of the Brotherhood is ideologically less scrupulous. According to a member of its leadership, the Brotherhood envisages democracy and considers it 'the most suitable platform for political competition'. Asked if the Brotherhood was also ready to accept a freely elected 'Alawi communist as president, he answered in the affirmative.[33] When the Muslim Brotherhood espouses democracy – be it implicitly or explicitly – it has not, of course, revoked its ideology but has adopted another mobilization strategy. After the failure of its religious strategy in the 1960s and the anti-'Alawi strategy in the 1970s and 1980s, it is trying the democratic option in the 1990s. It is beyond the question that democracy is not the Brotherhood's political aim but a means to another end: the assumption of power. The late Sa'id Hawwa, the Syrian organization's chief ideologist, confirmed without much ado that the Islamists are categorically against democracy: 'The Islamists fight democracy in the Islamic world, because the western notion of democracy can prohibit and allow, whereas ... in Islam the source of law cannot be interpreted.' However, at the same time he admits that

> democracy is a suitable means to pave the way for the future victory of the Islamists. [...] Democracy means the will of the majority and freedom for all; if the Islamists are given freedom ... they undoubtedly can mobilize the majority for the benefit of Islam; in this way generations are educated which will be capable

of administrative and political work.[34]

The Muslim Brotherhood is only one illustration of the possible incompatibility of certain ideologies with declared commitments to democracy. In addition to such ideological stances, historical experience also casts doubt on the democratic values proferred by various movements; in the past indeed they happily wedded domestic discourse to undemocratic policies. The call for democracy must therefore be considered in part as a means to strengthen opposition forces *vis-à-vis* the omnipotent regime in power. Democratic claims are very likely to generate support for the group in question from among all sections of society. Moreover, each party is aware of its own organizational weakness and knows that a joint effort from all opposition groups is necessary to challenge the regime. As all ideologies exclude each other, the pluralist aspect has much to recommend democracy as a kind of surrogate ideology for tactical purposes. But it certainly would be unfair to impute to the opposition only tactical motives. The prevailing international discussion on 'democracy' on the one hand and the actual domestic situation in Syria on the other hand have rendered that notion an antonym of almost all existing evils in the country. This perception is clearly visible in an essay of Jamal al-Atasi where he states:

> The revolutionary intellectual ... is someone who stands up for freedom and who stands up against oppression, exploitation, despotism, external colonialism, and against that internal colonialism of these cliquey regimes which are the masters of politics, economy, and ideology. The banner, that [the revolutionary intellectual] holds in his hands, is the banner of democracy. He propagates and strives for a popular democracy that is directly linked to the life and the will of the popular masses.[35]

Thus, domestic events are observed and valued first and foremost in terms of democracy. The Muslim Brotherhood no longer complains about the regime's unIslamic performance, and the "Alawi dictatorship' has become a subordinate topic. The nationalist and Nasirist opposition does not care very much about Asad's 'Arab' policies. The communists seem to be the opposition force least concerned about Arab or Islamic identities, and they normally apply their classical instrument – Marxist class analysis – when examining the international and domestic situation. Needless to say, the opposition's evaluation of what is going on in Syria is far from being positive. Above all it is almost completely unimpressed by Asad's moves towards domestic détente; the regime's attempt of early 1990 to enter into negotiations with exiled opposition personalities was completely unsuccessful and, ironically, it was only the Muslim Brotherhood which spoke of 'small positive steps'[36] when the regime released political prisoners in 1990.

From the opposition's point of view there is, indeed, no inducement to be ecstatic about these most modest of measures which, as far as domestic policy is concerned, can hardly be labelled 'liberalization'. But it is the nature of these measures rather than their limited scale that makes the opposition assume an attitude of aloofness – no matter how many political prisoners are released and how many independent deputies obtain a seat in the parliament. But mercy is the obverse side of arbitrary rule and a rare event on top of it. Despite these acts of mercy, repression continues, the prisons are refilled with other political opponents and the parliament remains powerless. All political moves by the regime towards a relaxation of the domestic political situation leave the basic power structure of the political system untouched. Therefore the opposition, *qua* anti-system force, considers these measures as wholly insignificant.

Whereas the domestic policy of the regime has little or nothing in common with 'liberalization', this label has suited economic policy since the middle of the 1980s. But the opposition feels only a small concern for this topic and widely disregards the so-called 'second *infitah*'. The reason for this is, of course, not indifference or a lack of awareness with regard to the overall impact of economic liberalization, but that Syria has already experienced the political and social outcomes of an earlier phase of *infitah* since the 1970s, such as the impoverishment of the lower classes and the rise of a parasitic bourgeoisie in the shadow of the regime. In the eyes of the opposition, the immediate impact of the 'second *infitah*' is therefore unlikely to go far beyond the economic sphere and will not have any new political and social implications but rather cement and aggravate existing conditions.

Since the 1970s all opposition parties have continued to pillory the deepening of socio-economic cleavages and the inglorious role of the parasitic bourgeoisie. Today both issues remain paramount for the entire opposition's indictment of the regime, and the leftist opposition, particularly the CP-Politbureau, has analysed them in depth in the context of the regime's economic policy. The Muslim Brotherhood's attitude towards the *infitah* remains, however, ambivalent. To be sure, it has always attacked the parasitic bourgeoisie and has assailed the regime for the deteriorating social conditions of the lower classes. But with regard to its ideological commitment to free enterprise and its political following among traders and entrepreneurs, it has never openly criticized the policy of *infitah*. Its 'analysis' of the socio-political situation has always confined itself to pointing to the moral decay of the regime.

The secular opposition has maintained its critical attitude towards *infitah* not in spite of but because of the fact that democracy has become its principle yardstick to measure progress. Indeed, in Syria there is less reason than anywhere else to share the illusion that a growing role for the private sector quasi-automatically paves the way for democracy or for real political liberalization. In the 1970s, *infitah* set the stage for unprecedented repression rather than liberalization, to say nothing of democratization. Against that background it is quite understandable that *infitah* offers opposition groups no encouragement to become optimistic over future prospects for democracy under the present regime. Whereas the Muslim Brotherhood continues to keep silent on *infitah*, the leftist opposition is even more pessimistic than ever.

One of the rare opposition statements on economic issues was published after the implementation of the new Investment Law in 1991. On that occasion the leftist Gathering defined at length its attitude towards the regime's economic policy. After a general criticism of *infitah*, the Gathering detailed its view of this policy in the light of the domestic economic as well as political situation. Although the Gathering defended the leading role of the public sector, it did not oppose private enterprise or the Investment Law as such. It emphasized, however, that the deep economic and political crisis could not be solved by laws but only by political means. Moreover, it argued that it is not economic liberalization which is a precondition for political liberalization but vice versa:

> The Investment Law is worth being discussed and useful only if adjustments are realized within the framework of an overall political solution of the crisis. At the moment a new law is but another entry in the body of laws of a state that is not a state of law and justice but a state where legally the law of emergency rules and practically the law of the jungle. [...] What is the use of a dozen investment laws in a political situation [that is characterized by] the reign of the *mukhabarat* state? This does

not encourage investments. When the citizen cannot be sure of his life and his future, how can he be sure of his capital and his property?[37]

The Gathering is even more gloomy in its analysis of political prospects than in its analysis of economic prospects. The socio-political implications of the Investment Law are considered 'possibly the most dangerous', as the law is perceived as a 'manifestation of the hegemony of the parasitic bourgeoisie', which is, again according to the Gathering, 'interrelated with the diminution of the national democratic awareness, the weakening of the national democratic forces, the impoverishment of the popular masses and their political marginalization'.[38] From the Gathering's point of view the Investment Law – and thus *infitah* – aims at 'the legal settlement of the supremacy of the parasitic bourgeoisie', that is, the supremacy of 'a political tendency in society that is opposed to the national democratic project'. Thus the economic policy in general and the Investment Law in particular is regarded by the Gathering not only as a halt on the long road to democracy but even as a step backwards:

> Contrary to the widely shared illusions on political opening and democratic changes, [the supremacy of the parasitic bourgeoisie] will result in an increase of oppression and a decrease of freedom and [of the respect for] human rights. This group lacks not only democratic awareness and traditions, but it is an enemy of democracy and thus the people's enemy.[39]

Indeed, the regime seems to be immune to the most modest form of democracy and nobody in Syria expects much immediate progress in this direction. The regime may be the main hindrance, but it is surely not the only one. The opposition, at least in theory the alternative to the regime, lacks 'democratic traditions' as much as the regime does. As far as actual 'democratic awareness' in the ranks of the opposition is concerned, the question arises as to whether this awareness is real or pretended and whether it should not be understood as 'awareness of suffered oppression'. It is true that the answer to this question is potentially irrelevant in view of the opposition's actual situation. In the 1990s there has not been the slightest sign of that *intifada* which, according to the leaders of the most important opposition parties, is the only way to topple the Asad regime.[40] The extremely unsuitable and, one must not forget, dangerous conditions under which any clandestine group has to work inside the country immensely hinder all efforts at mobilization. These difficulties are compounded by the fact that the Gathering and some small leftist groups which are organized inside Syria are over-intellectualized. In their pamphlets, highly abstract and sometimes even purely theoretical topics prevail, which have little or nothing to do with what is going on in Syria. The majority of these articles deal with problems that may stimulate the interest of academics, and the slogans may sound revolutionary, but none of this affects the ordinary Syrian who tries hard to surmount the difficulties of everyday life and who is tired of political slogans. Unlike the secular opposition, the Muslim Brotherhood undoubtedly makes use of a more popular discourse but is not represented inside Syria.

Today, the opposition parties are not the only forces to challenge the regime which in all appearance is questioned even from within its own constituency. This is certainly the case within the Ba'th Party, which, despite its declining importance, continues to be an essential instrument in mobilizing large parts of society. In early 1993, for instance, 30 party members were arrested in Raqqa, among them a candidate for the post of local party secretary who was eventually tortured to death.[41] More significant is the re-emergence of what may be called 'societal opposition'.[42] In 1989 a number of lawyers founded a human rights organization called the Committees for the Defence of Democratic Freedoms and Human Rights in Syria (CDF: *lijan al-difa' 'an al-hurriyyat al-dimuqratiyya wa huquq al-insan fi suriya*). About a year later, during the Gulf crisis, two groups of intellectuals each published a communiqué sharply criticizing the allied attack on Iraq and thus indirectly accusing the Syrian regime of participating in what one communiqué considered a 'criminal war'.[43] The regime's reaction was as usual: the leading members of the CDF as well as some of the signatories of the two communiqués were arrested and, as far as the CDF members are concerned, have not yet been released.

Occasional manifestos on the part of a societal group have a moral rather than a political impact. This, however, should not be under-estimated in view of the *étatisation* of Syrian society whose members generally have few chances to articulate their concerns in an autonomous way. The importance of the CDF goes far beyond that; though it sets great value on not being a political party, it has developed into a semi-political opposition whose activities attract much attention inside and outside Syria. But neither the intellectuals nor the CDF seek to replace the political system. The opposition parties which have declared this their political aim will in the near future not be able to reach their objective. The Syrian propaganda thus was not completely incorrect when it invented Asad's title, although he might not be 'our leader into eternity', he surely will be 'our leader for lifetime'.

6· Liberalization in Syria: the Struggle of Economic and Political Rationality

Raymond A. Hinnebusch

Syria, as one of the Arab states which has experimented with economic liberalization yet has appeared most resistant to it, gives an insight into how the contrary forces for and against economic liberalization work themselves out in Arab politics. The case also permits some examination of how such forces, once unleashed, potentially could transform the political system.

Two opposed approaches explain liberalization *or* resistance to it in authoritarian-statist regimes such as Syria. For Marxists, a crisis of state capital accumulation generates irresistible pressures which a bourgeoisie can exploit to force economic liberalization; it results from loss of the state's autonomy either through its capture by privileged social forces or in its bowing before international economic constraints. In the end, the requisites of capital accumulation dictate policy and since the state fails at it the capitalist class takes over. Because capital accumulation in post-populist states requires the 'disciplining' of the subordinate classes, authoritarian rule is required politically to demobilize or exclude them.

An opposing view, which might be called the neo-patrimonial model, sees the Middle Eastern state as an intractable obstacle to authentic economic liberalization. Patrimonial/rentier states harness the economy to their power requisites, using it as a source of patronage and control at the expense of economic rationality. The problem is precisely the state's autonomy from society, and this is typically attributed to political culture – one of authoritarianism and clientalism which is short on rationality. In this view, the state is under little pressure to liberalize politically from a weak, state-dependent bourgeoisie coopted through patronage or from masses encapsulated in clientage networks.[1]

The two approaches seem to capture opposing sides of a political-economy dynamic typical of developing states, namely, a struggle between economic and political rationality, wealth creation and power creation. However, both approaches come close to seeing public policy as either economically or culturally determined. In the Marxist model, the economic infrastructure gives policy-makers little freedom and the state chiefly serves the logic of capital accumulation; in the neo-patrimonial model, by contrast, economics serves politics, policy-makers are culturally impervious to economic rationality and patrimonial rule is quite compatible with inherited political culture.

In reality, usually neither logic can wholly prevail. Each is a legitimate task: economies must be developed but, equally, the state must be built where typically there has been a power vacuum. Modernization theory has traditionally argued that the natural compatibility of capitalism and democracy bridges the gap between the two logics: capital accumulation can take place in an economic sphere differentiated from politics where competitive elections can produce legitimate power. The negative experience of developing states with democratization brought modernization theories to acknowledge that this might be so only once certain thresholds in state formation and economic development had been passed. In developing states not yet past the threshold, there may be trade-offs between political and economic logic, and the challenge is to balance them. And the particular tilt between the two taken in any given country will be shaped, not just by economic constraints and cultural habits, but by politics – the calculations of ruling elites and the political struggle between them and their rivals.

The State as Obstacle to Economic Liberalization

Resistance to economic liberalization seems to be naturally embedded in the logic of an authoritarian-populist state dominated by a communal minority elite, as in Syria. The fact that the state emerged out of a revolution led by a plebeian/minoritarian elite in which the formerly dominant classes were levelled and new rising elements fostered and mobilized has enabled the regime to balance and play off, in Bonapartist fashion, conflicting social forces. The regime has been autonomous of a dominant class for a long time and largely remains so.[2]

This Bonapartist state possesses a formidable machinery of power. Policy-making power is highly concentrated in a virtual presidential monarchy, resting on huge civil and military bureaucracies, whose chains of command are reinforced by patronage and kinship. A Leninist-like party and a series of corporatist-like 'popular organizations' penetrate and incorporate popular sectors of society, notably the village, cutting off potential liberalizing opposition forces from this major segment of the mass public.

The regime's control of a large public sector and its access to rent (such as petroleum revenues and Arab aid) give it autonomy, especially of the bourgeoisie. Rent has not only eased pressures on the regime to foster conditions of bourgeois capital accumulation but also gave the regime the patronage resources to keep a segment of the bourgeoisie state-dependent.

The regime's autonomy has enabled it to shape its policies according to *raison d'état*, that is, its own interests, not those of a dominant class. Preservation of internal security and the extraction of resources for the external power struggle have therefore taken precedence over the capital accumulation requisites of the bourgeoisie and these power requisites have obstructed economic liberalization.

A first priority of the state is to defend its resource base. In this regard, the public sector was and remains a crucial source of revenue. It cannot currently be replaced by taxation of the private sector which, not seeing the regime as its own, is quite ready and able to evade taxes. Foreign currency is another key resource which, when it is scarce, the regime has consistently sought to control, even at the expense of discouraging business.

Second, the regime must satisfy the interests of its core elites. The fact that this elite is dominated by formerly propertyless minorities, especially 'Alawis, who use the state as a ladder of advancement, while the private economy is dominated by the majority Sunni community, gives the regime an exceptional stake in maintaining a large state role in the economy. The party apparatchiki and bureaucrats who staff the very structures of the state have ideological and material stakes in the state's economic role. The priority claim of the huge army on economic resources enjoys legitimacy as long as the conflict with Israel persists.

Third, the regime must protect its wider social base. As the product of a populist movement against the bourgeoisie, its constituents are the forces most likely to be threatened by economic liberalization: unionized workers, public employees and small peasants. The regime's precarious legitimacy rests on providing welfare and economic opportunity to these groups.

Political logic requires it to protect its peasant base from the encroachment of a revived landed bourgeoisie. The potentially dangerous urban mass, susceptible to Islamic fundamentalism, must be placated with state-provided cheap food and jobs. The regime's constituents have had some ability, through the privileged access accorded them in the Ba'th's populist form of corporatism, to defend their interests in regime councils.

While its original constituents are threatened, it is the regime's historic rival, the bourgeoisie, which is most likely to benefit from and be strengthened by liberalization. Indicative of the close link between the regime's economic policy and its relations with the bourgeoisie was the experience of the Islamic uprising: when the regime perceived a hostile Sunni bourgeoisie to be backing it, statist-minded elite factions gained the upper hand inside the regime, earlier liberalization measures which had benefited the bourgeoisie were curbed, and state economic intervention was widened. Economic liberalization therefore requires a *modus vivendi* between state and bourgeoisie. To liberalize means that the authoritarian-populist state has significantly to shift its social base toward the bourgeoisie, a task made all the harder in Syria because of a certain overlap between the state/private and 'Alawi/Sunni cleavages. This contrasts with conservative authoritarian regimes whose social base is firmly rooted in the bourgeoisie, sectors of which typically welcome liberalization.[3]

The Forces of Economic Liberalization
Economic Crisis
The forces of liberalization are indeed located, as the Marxists would have it, in the socio-economic infrastructure. Although the immediate motive for economic liberalization is usually political, the ultimate pressure for such change is normally rooted in an economic crisis.

In Syria, this crisis is rooted in the very nature of the regime's statist/populist strategy of state formation. This strategy peripheralized the private sector (pushing it largely into tertiary activities or into capital export), while failing to make the public sector a dynamic engine of capital accumulation. Public sector failure stems from bureaucratization (which produced inefficiencies in planning and management) and from politicization (which subordinated the logic of accumulation to political objectives such as patronage, job maximization and production of low-priced consumer commodities). This reflected the regime's inclusionary strategy of power-building which aimed at bringing the lower strata into politics on its side. The problem is this strategy tends to foster mass consumption over capital accumulation (which typically requires the disciplining and demobilization of workers and peasants). Building a national power base also dictated import substitute industrialization which, in Syria as elsewhere, produced dependency on imported parts, machinery and raw materials prior to development of the export capacity and foreign exchange needed to pay for them. This inevitably produced balance of payments and foreign exchange crises.

In the short run, oil-based rent (peculiarly available to Middle East states) sustained the regime's strategy, but when rent declined its weakness was revealed. The most immediate impact of the crisis of accumulation was a fiscal crisis: the state (overdeveloped as a result of rent) could no longer support its excessive size and functions when rent declined. This forced austerity – cutbacks in public spending – and a consequent declining ability of the state to finance investment, jobs and contracts. In this situation, beginning in the mid-1980s, the state began to turn to the bourgeoisie to fill the economic gap. In return, it had to be given concessions; thus the door of economic liberalization began to open.

A key complementary development in opening this door is that the economic and fiscal crisis seems to have also reduced the resistance of regime constituencies to liberalization. For those near the power centre, the state had far less patronage to dispense, while the capital they had accumulated during the state's expansive period could be put to work earning income if the market were freed up. In a diluted form, the same phenomenon is apparent in the regime's base. The typical rank-and-file Ba'thi or army officer comes from a village family with one son working the land, another in the party, military or government and another in petty business. Austerity forced them to diversify further by developing their business interests. They may see expanded room for the private sector as an opportunity, although they would not support radical contraction of the public sector. Meanwhile, the limits of the state's ability to maintain growth and create jobs needed to coopt the growing educated middle class have made it more politically dangerous to maintain the status quo than to alter it.

In short, the crisis was a sign that political logic had gone as far as it could at the expense of economic logic. If political logic was not brought into harmony with economic logic it would itself fail.[4]

Reconstruction of a Bourgeoisie

The door of liberalization was thus opened, but liberalization cannot go very far without the reconstruction of an entrepreneurial bourgeoisie which, being willing to invest, can provide a viable alternative to the public sector. Politically it has to be prepared to reach a *modus vivendi* with the state, and has to acquire the power to push for economic liberalization against statist vested interests.

In the Syrian case, the bourgeoisie appears to be in the process of reconstruction but this is incomplete. Ironically, the state helped give birth to a new bourgeoisie. The power elite was, itself, embourgeoised through corrupt activities or business on the side: private accumulation at the expense of public accumulation. At the same time, the large state development expenditures of the expansive 1970s fostered a state-dependent private bourgeoisie of agents, importers and contractors. This new class is typified by Sa'ib Nahhas who could become Syria's 'Uthman Ahmad 'Uthman. Beginning as the prime local agent for auto companies, he used political connections to corner state-sanctioned monopolies in tourism and transport. He is a partner with Gulf capital in international banks and investment companies. He has used political access to push semi-privatization schemes in which the state turns firms in which it retains part ownership over to private management. Lately, he has moved from services into joint agricultural and industrial ventures with Arab capital. Meanwhile, a key Damascene section of the old merchant class accommodated itself to the regime and took advantage of similar opportunities, while the influence of the anti-Ba'th landed 'aristocracy' radically declined.

The emergence of a new establishment, the so-called, 'military-mercantile complex' of 'Alawi officers and Damascene businessmen, signified the alliance of the 'new' state and 'old' private bourgeoisies. Patrick Seale suggests Asad deliberately sought in this way to give his regime a class underpining needed for stability.[5] The former sharp antagonism between the state and the private bourgeoisie was being bridged as the political elite acquired a stake in the new inequalities and was thereby differentiated from its populist constituency.

But is this new bourgeoisie a force for liberalization? On the one hand, it has an interest in a continued role for the state as a source of contracts, monopolies and protection. To a great extent it is rent seeking, rather than prepared to compete on the market, although historically most bourgeoisies got their start this way and this does not preclude a later interest in greater liberalization. In fact, this bourgeoisie welcomes greater access to foreign partnerships and the opening of fields formerly reserved for the state to private investment. A more market-orientated bourgeoisie is also emerging. Some new industrialists have arisen from the ranks of the *petite bourgeoisie* and have created medium-sized factories in areas such as textiles and plastics. Expatriate capital is also showing serious interest in Syria.

What is economically problematic is how far private capital is prepared to invest in productive commodity-producing sectors, given the greater opportunities and lesser risks outside Syria – except for those able to establish concessions and monopolies. State and party officials insist capital is interested only in quick, high-profit ventures and that the economy cannot do without a public sector investing in long-term strategic projects.

Politically, the Syrian bourgeoisie is still weak. It is still partly divided between the pro-regime new bourgeoisie and the older bourgeoisie, sectors of which are not reconciled with the regime. The still limited incidence of inter-marriage between the 'Alawi political elite and the Sunni business elite suggests a persistent lack of social trust. As long as the regime cannot wholly trust the bourgeoisie, it cannot afford to loosen state controls too far. The bourgeoisie has not forged alliances with other classes beyond the urban *petite bourgeoisie,* for much of the workers and peasants remain incorporated into the regime constituency and, to a great extent, are unavailable. Therefore, the bourgeoisie currently lacks both the power and the will to push for more economic liberalization than the regime wants. But that does not prevent elements of it from exploiting intra-regime cleavages by allying with the more liberal factions in the power elite or seeking to make their case directly to the president.

Elites, Public Policy and Economic Liberalization
The forces for or against economic liberalization in Syria appear to be too evenly balanced for one to rout the other. This seems to give elites the ability to balance between state and bourgeoisie and to tailor liberalization according to their own interests.

Changing Elite Ideology
How elites define their interest is shaped or at least indicated by their ideology. This has undergone an alteration favourable to liberalization which corresponds to the change in their objective situation. Embourgeoisement and the failures of statism created a greater disposition for liberalization. One watershed was the 1985 8th Regional Congress of the Ba'th Party where Asad reputedly declared that Syria's merchants were an 'honourable class' and backed a widened role for the private sector.[6] The collapse of communism in the 1990s dissipated

much persisting ideologically-rooted hostility to liberalization. The fact that the economic crisis which precipitated liberalization has eased in the 1990s without producing a reversion to statism in elite ranks suggests that the ideological change is permanent. The regime learned during the 1980s that the state alone cannot sustain economic development and this is all the more so since the collapse of the Soviet bloc as a source of aid, technology and markets. On the other hand, the elite and especially its children have increasingly gone into business, often in partnership with the bourgeoisie or as agents of foreign firms. Even the new 'Alawi generation, having been raised privileged, feel a part of the upper class and lacks its parents fear of the Sunni bourgeoisie.

But the elite also insists that economic and political logic must be reconciled: it wants to encourage the bourgeoisie as a economic engine without ceding it political power. There is also a consensus on avoiding a Soviet-like destruction of the statist economy before the market can replace it. Since it is not obvious how to reconcile these objectives, the elite is divided and ambivalent over how much liberalization and how fast. As such, to understand liberalization one has to look at the intra-elite political process. This may seem obvious but the dominant approaches neglect or discount it: the Marxists believe economic forces dictate change, the neo-patrimonialists that certain cultural habits confine economic policy to irrational outcomes. To understand economic policy and the forces which shape it, one cannot avoid examining the political process, however opaque it may appear.

The Political Process
A few observations about how liberalization is being shaped by the political process are in order. First, in Syria's authoritarian presidential regime Asad's views are decisive. His economic decisions are governed in the first place by *raison d'état* and this has tilted him toward liberalization. With the collapse of the USSR and the triumph of global capitalism, Asad is convinced his foreign policy can no longer be pursued in opposition to the USA. Détente with the West in foreign policy requires some internal liberalization. This dovetails with the economic constraints which mounted throughout the 1980s requiring greater concessions to the bourgeoisie. The two factors seem to have come together in a strategic decision on Asad's part to broaden the base of his regime by reducing his dependence on the party, army and state and including the bourgeoisie in the regime coalition in a far more

serious way than heretofore.

Yet Asad's cautious, pragmatic nature, his disinclination to be too far in front of the elite consensus in economic (as opposed to strategic) matters, has deterred a presidential intervention on behalf of a radical lurch to the right. He is, moreover, disinclined to impose the specifics of economic policy. As such, the extent of liberalization is being affected in good part by bureaucratic politics: an intra-regime struggle between liberalizing 'technos' and statist 'politicos'.

Since, in bureaucratic politics, there is no decisive way of determining policy, such as a general election, many resources must be mobilized and combined by a winning faction. High office with its legal prerogatives, funds and clients is important. Access to the president, which it often gives, is crucial. So is the ability to offer credible alternatives to failing current polices. Coalition-building is required since no actors below the presidency have independent power bases.

Who are the actors in bureaucratic politics? Certain salient figures seem to stand for opposing tendencies. Economy minister Muhammad al-'Imadi is the classic liberalizer and the brains behind most of the liberalizing experiments. He has the trust of the president despite his lack of party credentials. He has taken advantage of statist failures to promote liberal alternatives. The hand of the liberalizers has been strengthened by a tacit alliance with the business community which the regime seeks to court. On the other side, a typical figure has been 'Izz al-Din Nasir, member of the party regional command, 'Alawi and head of the trade union confederation. He has tried to put together an alliance with public sector managers to advance public sector reform as a substitute for privatization.[7] He is seen by business as a main opponent.

A crucial development is that bureaucratic politics is being expanded somewhat to include societal actors not based in the state. Asad's decision to widen his base has meant giving business both personal and semi-institutionalized access to policy-making and to the presidency. At the same time, the party has been pushed from the centre of policy-making and, with the collapse of socialism, it is ideologically exhausted and no longer a threat to private business. Business clout has therefore increased and is using its new access to persuade the president, with some success, to foster liberalization measures against the resistance of state and party elites.

Yet politics and potential alliances are by no means exclusively defined in terms of party and state vs private sector. Some public sector managers could be enlisted in reform by offering them freedom to operate on the market. Party leaders are adapting to the new era by courting elements in the private sector. For example 'Ala al-Din Abdin, the Damascus party boss, has good connections with and services the grievances of Damascene bourgeois families who dislike the regime. He welcomes private sector growth to provide employment now that the public sector can no longer absorb new graduates.

Policy Outcomes

Given this sort of political process, it is not surprising that the outcome has been incremental liberalization carefully designed to reduce state economic burdens without damaging state interests or control. On the one hand, state economic intervention is contracting, widening room for the private sector. Austerity has cut state subsidies and public investment. The end to certain state foreign trade monopolies, the liberalization of the exchange rate, and the relaxation of price controls have produced new room for the market. The private sector is now regarded not as a mere auxiliary of a 'leading' public sector, but as an engine of economic development at least the equal of the public sector. New concessionary investment and tax laws encourage private and foreign investment in most fields.

On the other hand, privatization of the public sector is not on the agenda and part of the Gulf war windfall has been ploughed into public sector refurbishment. Rather, joint private–public ventures are a substitute for open privatization. In these, the state's contribution is likely to be land or factories while the private sector contributes capital and entrepreneurship. State officials retain some control and get a share of the economic rewards, but the firms are run by businessmen for profit. They are an intermediary stage which encourages the alliances between state and bourgeoisie on which further liberalization rests.

The outcome so far is encouraging for the regime. Private investment has responded favourably to this new climate, at least as measured by the proliferation of private sector imports and exports, of new, small and medium businesses, and of investment licences. One observer argues that private investment already exceeds the state investment budget.[8] The heritage of Ba'thism will not be overcome overnight but, to the extent the state becomes more dependent on a growing bourgeoisie for economic health, it will have to make further concessions.

The Political Consequences of Economic Liberalization

The circle of political–economic dynamics is incomplete without some assessment of whether economic liberalization is precipitating an incremental political pluralization.

Calculated Decompression

The regime is currently pursuing a strategy of calculated political decompression as a substitute for substantial political pluralization and in the short run it is working. The draconian controls of the 1980s are being relaxed as the Islamic threat recedes. There is greater press freedom; ministers may now be criticized. The security forces are being reined in, and religious schools and mosques are recovering their autonomy on condition that opposition activity is eschewed.

Full-scale liberalization, however, still holds too many perceived political dangers for the regime. Asad argues that his 1970 rise to power initiated a Syrian *perestroika* – political relaxation, opening to the private sector – long before Gorbachev and that 'the phase through which [Syria] is passing is not suitable for implementing [competitive elections]'.[9] The Ba'th's dominance would be threatened and un-controllable forces could be unleashed. Until the social cleavage between state and bourgeoisie is fully bridged, the 'Alawis would be threatened by any return of power to the Sunni-dominated business establishment. Political liberalization carries the risk that Islam would become a vehicle of anti-regime mobilization as long as the ideological gap separating it from the secular minoritarian regime is so wide. The regime is determined to prevent the Algerian and Eastern European scenarios and the security forces have the firepower and personal stake in the regime's survival to defend it.

As yet, the state cannot be forced into more than limited political liberalization. There is so far little overt societal pressure for democratization. Although events in Eastern Europe, Algeria and Jordan at first stimulated some yearning for democracy among the educated classes, the accompanying disorder and Islamic fundamentalism have made its natural constituents – businessmen and intellectuals – wary of democracy. Patrimonial strategies such as clientalism remain viable since the large public sector and oil rent give the state the ability to stand above, play off and coopt the rival sectors of a fragmented society. Corporatist forms of state–society linkage may be enough to accommodate increased societal complexity for some time. Hama reminds all parties of how far the regime will go to preserve itself should these control mechanisms fail. But the seeds of potential pluralization can certainly be detected.

Political Liberalization and the Bourgeoisie

The bourgeoisie as yet has neither the desire or the power to demand political liberalization as the price of capital investment. To be sure, expatriates may have some leverage to press for liberalization; 'Umran Adham, a Paris-based expatriate published an open letter to Asad insisting that political pluralism was essential to investment: 'Economic and political freedom go together.'[10] But more valued than democracy by the bourgeoisie is stability combined with increased personal and economic freedoms to buy, sell, travel, talk and re-create a private civil society. Vice-President Musharka asserts that business and politics can be separated: traders are kept happy if they prosper. In fact, in return for business freedom and security, the bourgeoisie seems prepared to defer demands for political power. A *modus vivendi* may be shaping up between a state which needs a wealth-generating, conservative social force, and a bourgeoisie which needs the economic opportunities and political protection provided by the state. Rather than leading a democracy movement, the bourgeoisie looks to Asad to distance himself from the Ba'th, coopt more of its own into government, and accord it greater political access.

The bourgeoisie is now in fact accorded growing access to decision-makers. The formerly populist-dominated corporatist system, whereby the trade unions and popular organizations had privileged access to power, has been opened to the bourgeoisie: the prime minister's Committee for the Guidance of Imports, Exports and Consumption in which the heads of the Chambers of Commerce and of Industry are included, gives it crucial access to economic decision-making.[11] Parliamentary elections, though controlled, give some outlet to the politically ambitious. Some ten millionaires in the parliament are quite outspoken and a block of independent merchants and industrialists sometimes coordinate for common interests. This new more inclusive corporatism may foster habits of accommodation between state and bourgeoisie.

As the bourgeoisie's economic power grows, can the regime long sustain a Chinese-like strategy of denying it institutionalized power-sharing? Syria's bourgeoisie was never destroyed in a way comparable to China's and liberalization is according it greater autonomy to reconstruct a business-centred civil society. Having opted to depend on private capitalist investment, the regime will have to be responsive to bourgeois demands for greater rule of law and a general roll-back of the boundaries of state power. Yet, since the inegalitarian consequences of capitalism are likely to heighten popular discontent, neither bourgeoisie nor regime will want full democratization. As such, an Egyptian-like strategy in which the authoritarian presidency persists, but the bourgeoisie is incorporated through the ruling party and given a share of power in the parliament, might accommodate Syria's bourgeoisie. However, the Ba'th Party cannot readily be transformed into a party of business such as Egypt's National Democratic Party (NDP); it is overwhelmingly a party of those dependent on the state or threatened by liberalization, notably teachers, public employees, public sector workers and peasants, and only 2 per cent of its membership could be considered upper or upper-middle class.[12] Though a revision of Ba'thi ideology now stresses its long-neglected liberal side, accepting of freedoms and a private sector, Ba'thism, being fundamentally egalitarian, serves poorly as an ideological legitimation of the inequalities of capitalist development. An alternative is to permit the bourgeoisie to form its own party and compete with the Ba'th in relatively free elections while obstructing its access to the masses by a continuing strategy of populist patronage, a game long played by Mexico's Institutional Revolutionary Party (IRP).

Liberalization and the Islamic Opposition
There is little prospect that political liberalization can advance very far until a historic compromise between the Ba'th state and the main opposition, political Islam, can be reached. The Islamic movement lost the battle with the regime in the 1980s, but it remains deeply rooted in the *suq* where a merchant ethos mixes with a pervasive religious sensibility nurtured by the *'ulama*. With a partially autonomous economic base and a counter-ideology, the traditional city remains the milieu most resistant to state penetration.

Can the *suq* be integrated into the political system in a way that would advance pluralization as long as political Islam remains its dominant political expression? Political Islam is an obstacle in so far as it fosters communal conflict in a mosaic society and a counter-culture not readily incorporated into the secular state. On the other hand, the Islamic movement is not necessarily anti-democratic: in the pre-Ba'th era, the Syrian Ikhwan participated in electoral politics rather than creating secret organizations as in Egypt. In an attempt to broaden its appeal in the 1980s, the movement advocated a semi-liberal state. The notion of violent revolution has now been discredited in most Islamic circles.

To the very considerable extent that the Islamic movement expressed the reaction of the *suq* and sections of the bourgeoisie to economically damaging Ba'thi socialism, economic liberalization could advance a détente between it and the regime. The Aleppo bourgeoisie, which supported the Islamic rebellion out of resentment at its victimization and marginalization under Damascus-centred etatism, has been increasingly appeased by new business opportunities, such as the chance to cash in on export deals to pay off the Soviet debt. Syria's *suq petite bourgeoisie* survived and even prospered in spite of Ba'th rule; in the 1970s and 1980s merchants actually increased their proportion of the labour force from 9 to 12 per cent.[13] They may be well positioned, with accumulated capital and traditional know-how, to move into the economic space being vacated by the state. Thus, the economic roots of cleavage between the regime and Islamic opposition are melting away. Ideologically, Syria's Islamic movement has always advocated a liberal economic model; Islamic manifestos demanded state withdrawal from commerce, free enterprise and the 'natural incentives' of a fair profit. As the regime liberalizes, the ideological gap is narrowing.

Politically, there are signs of a détente between the Islamists and the regime which is trying to coopt and appease the Islamic mainstream, while marginalizing more radical elements. Moderate Islamic leaders who have cooperated with the government, such as Muhammad Sa'id Rahman al-Buti and the Mufti, Ahmad al-Kaftaru, do have some followings in Sufi brotherhoods and old quarters such as al-Maydan. Islamists have vocal spokesmen in parliament; Ghassan Abazad, a doctor and Ikhwan leader from Dera who brokered the return of Ikhwan exiles from Jordan, won a seat in the parliament as an independent. A large release of Islamists from prison in 1992 to appease western human rights critics also aimed to mollify Islamic opinion. Islamists are allowed to publish a magazine and people are no longer afraid to go to mosques as they were at the height of the anti-Islamic repression. A peaceful Islamic movement focused on pious personal behaviour is spreading and so long as it does not challenge the regime, it will be permitted as a safety-valve.

The most favourable scenario for the incorporation of political Islam into the system would be parliamentary elections which resulted in power-sharing between the regime and moderate Islamists. Asad has toyed with encouraging a moderate Islamic party; at the time of Ceaucescu's fall, a nervous regime wanted al-Buti to form such a party. The Jordanian precedent, which suggests that Islamic movements can be tamed through participation, may encourage the regime to proceed with such an experiment. Nor is it a foregone conclusion that the Ba'th could not hold its own in elections. In fact, in the only free elections of the Ba'th era, those of 1972 to provincial councils, traditional and Islamic forces won in the cities and the Ba'th in rural areas. In the recent parliamentary elections, the blocs of votes the regime can mobilize through the popular organizations and the National Progressive Front were decisive against a fragmented opposition. The Ba'th could count on the support of many westernized Sunni families and working women fearful of fundamentalism or an Algerian scenario. It is hard to imagine political liberalization advancing very far until the détente between Islam and the regime deepens enough that it can risk such experiments.

The Mass Public and Liberalization

So far, the masses have not been significant actors in the politics of economic liberalization, leaving the regime carefully to calibrate its policies and shift its social base. But if strata in the regime's constituency become the victims of economic liberalization, can they be prevented from challenging it? The trade unions have bitterly complained about it, but when a faction proposed pulling out of the Ba'th-dominated corporatist system, Asad's instinctive response was to warn that freedom had to be understood 'within the framework of responsibility', not 'contradiction and fragmentation'.[14] As the regime is increasingly committed to capitalist development, business associations will acquire a growing capacity to argue that this requires new pro-business concessions, and popular syndicates may be fighting a losing battle in regime councils. If more power-sharing for the bourgeoisie is not to mean the transformation of corporatism into an instrument for disciplining the popular classes on behalf of capitalist development, the unions and syndicates must attain the autonomy to defend their interests in a post-populist era. Otherwise, popular leaders are likely to emerge outside of or covertly within the corporatist system, as has happened in Egypt. Yet the mobilization of mass opposition to pro-capitalist policies requires a populist ideology which is currently lacking: Marxism has lost credibility while the Islamic movement, which has elsewhere mobilized the victims of economic liberalization, has in Syria espoused an ideology of the free market and, in any case, has not yet recovered from the repression of the 1980s.

An alternative outcome is that those elements of the regime constituency who are better able to take advantage of economic liberalization may gradually split off from the Ba'th. The skilled workers deserting the public sector for new, higher paying private firms, as well as rich peasants able to raise their income on the market, could realign with the bourgeoisie in a liberal coalition. Graduates, no longer guaranteed a state job, may look to private investment as their only opportunity. Even public employees who have businesses on the side may turn into liberalizers. The less ambitious or less skilled popular strata might then be left all the more dependent on state protection and unlikely to challenge it.

In the short term, the emergence of competing social groups could put the regime in a position to play off a divided society. In the longer run, it could set the stage for true pluralization. The conclusion of a peace with Israel may accelerate the disintegration of the regime coalition to the extent that the nationalist struggle has provided its legitimating cement. The regime, in need of an alternative legitimation to defend itself against the Islamic alternative, may calculate that further political liberalization is the lesser risk. Until Asad departs, there is little prospect of more than incremental liberalization, but rivals for the succession will need to bid for the support of newly revived societal sectors, and the winner may, like Egypt's Sadat, have an interest in building a base beyond the core 'Alawi/army/party complex, and in stimulating the economic growth needed to consolidate it: this will require concessions of further autonomy to the bourgeoisie and perhaps to the syndicates and unions.

Conclusion

The Syrian experience suggests that both the dominant schools are one-sided. The Marxist view that the crisis of the statist system is ultimately the root of change seems borne out. While, in the short run, economics can be put in the service of political logic, in the long run, the requisites of capital accumulation must be attended to and that seems to mean reconstructing a capitalist class. This probably does require some power-sharing and limited political liberalization, perhaps similar to post-populist Egypt. But it seems unlikely it need end in the abdication of political rationality by state elites, that is, the total abandonment of their initial statist/populist base and a bourgeois capture of state power. Nor is it certain that the incremental political liberalization which accompanies economic liberalization cannot provide political space in which the victims of capitalist development can defend their interests.

The neo-patrimonial school correctly points out the short-term contradiction between political and economic logic but it fails to see the forces working to overcome it, perhaps because it does not adequately identify the root cause of it. If it is some cultural propensity, it is relatively immutable. If it is a strategy of state formation, rooted in the regime's initially populist anti-bourgeois class base, as was argued here, then, as the class base is altered and the political strategy exhausted, economic liberalization can advance. Moreover, if the incorporation of the masses into the state was due not to a political culture of submission and clientalism but to a populist political strategy, when the populist coalition breaks down, the masses may mobilize on behalf of political pluralization.

To the extent economic and political rationality conflict, perhaps they are best pursued in separate stages. Once state formation is consolidated, the state can afford to give priority to the requisites of capital accumulation. Syria's current economic liberalization suggests that is happening there. The Syrian case does not yet offer evidence for the liberal argument that economic and political liberalization go together, bridging the gap between economic and political rationality. But in the transition to a post-populist stage in which the requisites of capital must be accommodated at the expense of populist rights, limited political liberalization may be a good strategy for state elites. It appeases the inevitable bourgeois demands for power while encouraging the regime's previous popular constituency to mobilize countervailing power. The state protects its autonomy by balancing between the two, capital accumulation advances and limited democratization helps legitimatize the roll-back of populism.

7· The Return of Politics? Scenarios for Syria's Second *Infitah*

Eberhard Kienle

Not long before he was kidnapped in Beirut in the spring of 1985, the Arabist and social scientist Michel Seurat, a close observer of political developments in Syria, vigorously attacked the country's regime for its tyrannical, even totalitarian, nature. Indeed, according to Seurat, it was only a regime in the sense of an informally constituted ruling group and not an actual government, which implies the existence of a state in the sense of more than just an extractive and repressive Leviathan. This regime succeeded in establishing its tyranny over Syria and was noticeable for its 'brutality' and 'indiscriminate violence'. It aspired to be totalitarian, in the definition given by Hannah Arendt 'with terror as its essence'.[1] Terror, he quoted Arendt, 'by pressing men against each other ... destroys the space between them; compared to the condition within its iron band, even the desert of tyranny, in so far as it is still some kind of space, appears like a guarantee of freedom.'[2] Though less cruel than the terror of totalitarianism, the isolation and the fearful dangers typical of this Syrian desert had suffocated politics in terms of debate, negotiation and compromise; only if defined as the mere exercise of power had politics survived.

Published in 1984, this indictment reflects the experience of Syria's *Grande Terreur,* which culminated in the Hama uprising of 1982 and its repression by the regime forces, leaving thousands of victims and casualties. Violence and force had replaced arguments and bargains. Dissent had become treachery, and while only a lack of means and capacities seemed to keep totalitarian projects in check, individual strategies of survival had to be based on retreat and isolation and hence led to the desertification of the remaining space between their protagonists.

It was customary for people to turn on their televisions before discussing politics so that their neighbours would not hear. Road blocks and 'security' checks dissuaded them from venturing out too late at night and from meeting friends and relatives. If informers were not actually everywhere, they were suspected to be everywhere, and rumour had it that every news and sweet stall in Damascus was run by one of them. Instead of meeting for a chat in a café, people now assembled at the departure points for the frequent and interminable *masiras* – officially organized demonstrations, preferably under huge bills and posters with the slogan of the day while large-scale portraits of the president adorned major buildings. Suspects disappeared, the prisons were full, and torture and ill-treatment, even summary executions, were the unavoidable fate of those arrested.[3]

About ten years on, a measure of internal détente is perceptible. In the 1990 elections to the People's Assembly Parliament, independent candidates were granted a larger share of the total (and increased) number of seats, which were attributed by means of a more competitive procedure than had been used since the 1963 coup or 'revolution'.[4] Road blocks have largely disappeared. People who previously did not want to be seen together in public now meet in cafés and even make the occasional political comment in the presence of a waiter whose accent denotes his origin from the 'Alawi mountains. No longer do they automatically consider him to be an informer of one of the several secret police forces. Though formally outlawed, satellite disks are a common feature in the more wealthy quarters of Damascus. Foreign newspapers are more easily available and spend less time on the desks of their censors. More importantly, numerous political prisoners have been released even though many others remain in gaol and yet others were newly arrested.

This is not to say that changes have been fundamental or even irreversible. The present and recent trials of those political prisoners who are still in gaol are legal face-lifts at best. It is curious, to say the least, to try people years after their arrest in courts that are hardly independent of the executive branch of government. In spite of various hints and minor amendments, the state of emergency has not been lifted. Under the state of emergency the regime and its enforcement agencies have more than sweeping powers to impose their will if they so wish. While releasing political prisoners and allowing for the return of some other opponents from exile, their parties are far from being legalized. More generally, state structures and institutions continue to be dominated from above, even though the wheel of fortune recently turned against some of the main characters in the apparatus.[5] Under these conditions, the ordinary Syrian is a subject rather than a citizen to whom government would be accountable.

Economic Liberalization and Political Change

This chapter seeks to examine the modest measures of political liberalization which have recently been introduced and their future against the background of recent and more substantial economic liberalization (as described in chapters 1 and 2 of this volume). Liberalization in this context means only that those who monopolize the physical means of coercion become less interventionist, be this economically or politically; that they leave more (but not all) decisions to others; and that finally they relinquish some of their means and instruments of intervention.

Though establishing a causal link between economic liberalization and political change, this chapter, like the Introduction, discards the premise that the latter necessarily amounts to liberalization in any meaningful sense of the term. More precisely, it argues that contemporary economic liberalization in Syria is likely to lead to the participation in politics of new forces, possibly even to the increasing marginalization of presently dominant actors, but not to fully-fledged democracy. As with economic liberalization in Egypt under Sadat or the situation in Syria in the 1970s, present developments in the country may at the same time disenfranchise certain forces and actors.[6]

The centrepiece of present policies of economic liberalization is the Investment Law no. 10 of 1991. Conditional on the approval of individual projects by a Higher Council of Investment, this law authorizes investors to import equipment and materials tax- and duty-free; to open foreign currency accounts in Syrian banks with exemptions from currency regulations; to repatriate imported capital five years after the launch of the project concerned; and to transfer profits abroad immediately. Moreover, the companies established under Law no.10, their shares and profits, enjoy tax holidays for periods of up to seven years.[7] For Syria today these measures are as novel and potentially revolutionary as was Egypt's famous Law no. 43 in 1974 which marked the beginning of large-scale possibilities for private investment and in many ways the beginning of Sadat's *infitah*.[8] Far less biased in favour of foreign capital than was Law no. 43, and certainly not explicitly so, Law no. 10 offers unprecedented opportunities not only to foreign (including Arab) but also to Syrian and Syrian expatriate investors. As the law has not failed to produce at least some of the expected results, the future of political change will depend largely on the extent to which investors are able to translate their economic leverage into political leverage. This leverage constitutes a potential for political change far beyond the developments of the 1970s. Although in essence the above caveats continue to apply, the chances for the return of politics in the sense of a return to politics have greatly improved.

Political change in the period of Syria's first *infitah* after 1970 obviously correlated with economic change but, as already argued by Perthes (chapter 3 of this volume), it hardly amounted to actual liberalization. As paradoxical as it seemed, the measures taken as early as 1971 to strengthen the private sector[9] were not coupled with the legalization of either the old 'bourgeois' parties dissolved in the 1960s[10] or of similar new outfits. Instead, the creation of the National Progressive Front (NPF) in 1972 gave some additional, though limited recognition to parties from the left, including the Communist Party, the Arab Socialist Union, the Arab Socialist Movement and the Organization of Socialist Unionists. After internal splits which inevitably followed when some of their members chose to cooperate with the regime, they remained the junior partners of the Ba'th Party which itself had become an instrument more than a seat of power.[11] More importantly, the NPF remained a participatory fiction whose members prior to 1992 were not even consulted before the formation of new governments. The PNF served as a façade and at the same time as an instrument to achieve the opposite of what it seemed to have been set up for. In addition to increasing political participation it served to bind political movements to the regime, which could, in a period of socio-economic change, potentially voice discontent. At the same time a controlled left could be used as a stick with which to beat the chief beneficiaries of the new economic policy, should the need arise. Though deprived of formal political structures, the latter could at least increasingly use informal channels to pursue and represent their interests;[12] however, throughout the 1970s and even the 1980s, these channels hardly granted them any more real possibilities of participation than were given to the movements incorporated into the NPF.

In the 1970s, the regime's capacity to combine economic opening with political control followed from its ability to supply the private sector with the resources necessary for its renaissance; developments are likely to work out differently in the 1990s when private resources are needed to keep country and government afloat. As illustrated by

Law no. 10, the situation of the 1990s contrasts sharply with that of the 1970s when resources controlled by the regime contributed to the relaunch of the private sector, be this directly through credit facilities or indirectly through the trickle-down from a public sector that, thanks to external financial support, was itself expanding.[13] Increasingly, over time, the new or renewed class of capital owners fulfilled economic functions that were relevant to the public sector or to the country as a whole; however, they were not yet strong enough actually to emancipate themselves from the regime that had created them.[14] Such emancipation has come a step closer in the 1990s with the former recipients now often acting as suppliers of resources. But while these suppliers may buy their right to participate in politics, others will continue to be excluded from such participation and in addition will lose some of the social advantages they owned under a regime which at least considered them as one of its constituencies.

Developments since the mid-1980s (more fully described by Pölling and Perthes in chapters 1 and 3) already give an albeit limited inkling of how things may develop.[15] Running up a growing foreign debt since the early 1980s, Syria in 1986 also suffered an acute foreign currency crisis as it continued a policy of import promotion in spite of continuous balance of payments deficits. The latter resulted from stagnant or insufficient agricultural, industrial and oil production combined with decreasing transfers from the major Arab oil-producing countries. Though not without hesitations, insufficiencies inherent to the public-sector-focused strategies were identified as important causes of these economic difficulties. (See chapter 2 of this volume.) Consequently, the private sector was encouraged to play a greater role in export-oriented activities, particularly in industrial agriculture through new joint ventures with the public sector,[16] but also in manufacturing. These policies implied the further relaxation of restrictions on private investment and foreign trade, so that in the late 1980s private investment amounted to about 50 per cent of total investment, while private sector activities accounted for more than half of the national product and almost half of registered foreign trade. Foreign exchange was thus increasingly earned through private sector activities; although convertible currency was in various ways channelled back into government accounts,[17] even the public sector had repeatedly to resort to the black market, thus highlighting even more clearly the capacities of private dealers to generate foreign exchange.

The presence in the Assembly elected in 1990 of a relatively large number of business people[18] may be read as a reward for the constructive role played by members of that profession in overcoming the crisis. Thus the suppliers of essential resources gained recognition as participants in the formal, admittedly largely symbolic, political process. To what extent they gained access to the far more important informal political processes can only be guessed. At any rate, developments after 1986 as much as after 1970 illustrate how economic change affected arrangements at the level of politics.

Considering the time lag between the partial redefinition of economic policies after the 1986 crisis and the modest political change shown in the parliamentary elections in 1990, any conjectures about the more substantial political effects of Law no. 10 seem all the more haphazard and premature as for the time being not much has happened beyond the measures mentioned above. Indeed, the plebiscite of December 1991 which returned President Asad for another seven-year term rather seems rather to indicate continuity and inertia.

None the less, it seems unlikely that the present monopolization of state power by a group of officers and their associates can be maintained under conditions in which the private sector plays an even more dominant role than in the late 1980s. The problem is not least that of actors who, though controlling the means of physical coercion, have succeeded only insufficiently, if at all, in playing the capitalist economic game without the crutches of the state. Representatives of the regime and officers in general have without any doubt greatly benefited from economic liberalization, have built up fortunes and invested in businesses, be it only indirectly through family members or other middlemen. Yet theirs do not seem to be the large Syrian fortunes owned by those who are closely linked with representatives of the regime but who are not themselves members of the regimes. Though once an obvious exception to this rule, one of the president's own brothers apparently incurred major losses. Even when officers become partners of ordinary business people and contribute capital to what may be called military–civilian joint ventures, these arrangements may depend more on their connection with the regime than on their economic skills and expertise.

Individuals and groups who provide the financial resources and the know-how necessary for economic recovery and expansion are likely to become more directly involved in the decision-making processes at the state level and then demand and obtain their share of 'power'. Such participation does not need to result in highly visible amendments or changes to the formal political process but may well remain relatively discreet and inconspicuous. Social and political climbers will be as inclined as are the present regime to exclude other actors from political participation. Such power-sharing arrangements will therefore stand an even better chance of remaining informal and invisible. They are likely to stop short of actual democratization which implies substantial change to the formal political process, such as free elections, and which therefore benefits other forces as well. Only the precise shape of these future power-sharing formulae remains a matter of speculation.

Resources and Participation

Like the policies of economic liberalization adopted in the immediate aftermath of the 1986 crisis, Law no. 10 may be seen as an illustration of the increasing inability of the Syrian regime to generate or mobilize in the usual ways the resources necessary for its own survival in power. These obviously include the resources necessary for maintaining the country at large as a viable territorial and economic basis for the regime. In spite of the increasing yet comparatively modest revenue from oil and in spite of financial transfers from the major oil-producing countries in the Gulf, the public-sector-focused development strategy no longer yielded the funds necessary for the basic needs of the regime: defending the country against external adversaries and itself against internal adversaries. Moreover, the latter task implied a degree of internal legitimacy that could not be secured without catering to the material interests of strategically important sectors of society.

Quite clearly from the regime's point of view, these resources could not be found through cuts in the defence budget as long as the Golan continued to be occupied and no definite settlement had been found for the conflict with Israel. Such cuts would indeed have contradicted the objective of defence against external enemies. In addition, as figures illustrate, the economic benefits from defence cuts, though important, would have amounted to less, possibly far less, than the actual benefits from the new investment policy (cf infra). This policy would probably have been even more successful had it been preceded by a peace accord, but Syrian or Arab-owned capital which forms the bulk of investment so far would not have been invested under an obvious *pax israeliana*.

The drawback of the new investment policy is that the mobilization of resources generated outside the regime or its public sector not only contributes to the propping up of the regime but also creates new dependencies on those who produce and supply these resources. In a more narrowly defined economic sense at least, the regime is strengthened only indirectly, while private sector investors are strengthened directly. For decades the Syrian regime has experienced a similar sort of dependency *vis-à-vis* its donors among the oil-rich countries in the Gulf to which now the dependency on direct investors will be added. In other words, the regime will depend even more upon resources, the flow of which it cannot sufficiently control. In order to secure their continued flow it will have to take into account the potential demands of suppliers whose vulnerability is generally compensated by that of the regime itself, should it decide to move against them. Naturally, much here depends on the suppliers, whether they voice demands, and whether they do this in any organized and concerted fashion which might cause the regime to be placed under pressure. Though cautious in his answer, Joseph Bahout expects private capital to develop over a period of time from a class-in-itself into a class-for-itself (see Chapter 4). This assessment, together with key indicators of the role of the private compared with the public sector, underscores the expectation of some sort of political change. Even though these figures partly appear in the contributions by Pölling and Perthes (in chapters 1 and 3) it seems useful to refer to them in some detail here before discussing the possible scenarios that can be derived from this situation.

Official Syrian figures indicate that about a year after the promulgation of Law no. 10 the competent investment authority had approved projects worth S£ 69.53 billion which at the 'rate prevailing in neighbouring countries', that is the realistic exchange rate, equal about US $1.6 billion;[19] more recent figures covering the period till December 1992 put the amount at S£ 93.38 billion, corresponding to about $2.1 billion.[20] The figure given for the period of the first 12 months is more than twice the amount of S£ 32.31 billion earmarked for investment in the 1991 state budget, if the same exchange rate is applied[21] (in the 1992 budget S£ 36.35 billion were earmarked for investment);[22] if as claimed by Syrian authorities the 'commercial exchange rate'[23] must be applied, the 1991 investment budget translates into about $1.53 billion –still slightly lower than 12 months of private investment under Law no. 10. Only if the third exchange rate used for the import of 'strategically' important goods is applied, public investment exceeds private investment and then amounts to about $2.88 billion.[24] The former more so than the latter ratio is reflected in figures given for the private sector share in gross fixed capital formation which in 1991 allegedly amounted to S£ 25 billion out of a total of S£ 47 billion.[25] In terms of GDP, private sector investment figures for 1991 amount to 22.7 per cent but public sector figures to only 10.6 per cent of an estimated total of S£ 305.6 billion.[26]

Admittedly, the figure for private investment reflects approved projects, not projects already carried out, but ultimately the same applies to a budget at the moment of its enactment. It is also likely that after an initial boom investment will later slow down. Finally, loopholes in Law no. 10 were used, for instance, to declare car imports as investments. On the other hand, it is obvious that similar distortions are reflected in the state budget figures which are less than transparent, be it only for the simultaneous use of various exchange rates. In 1991 the state budget also included S£ 10,304 million in concessionary loans[27] which by definition are of foreign origin and hence part of that larger amount of budgetary (or perhaps not even budgeted) revenues which the regime was able to raise 'politically' but not 'economically'. For its part, the investment budget for 1992 includes an undisclosed part of $1093 billion in concessionary funds for six large industrial projects recently pledged by Gulf states.[28] Probably, however, these are not the only foreign loans or grants that are included in this part of the budget. Though fraught with a number of uncertainties, this comparison gives a measure of the additional resources that could be mobilized through Law no. 10.

It is likely that, in the future, the ratio between private and public investment will not significantly change in the favour of the latter. Internal resources generated by the public sector will not substantially increase as oil revenue apparently seems to stagnate (cf infra). Official transfers from the Gulf may also stagnate at their present level, even if the new Gulf Development Fund, presently capitalized at $6.5 billion becomes fully operational. The greater part of this sum will probably be given to Egypt, so that Syria's share, if projected over reasonable time, could fall short of the amount it actually received under the arrangements agreed at the Baghdad summit in 1978.[29] Whether part of the wealth that might be created in a pacified Lebanon can be syphoned off to Syria remains in doubt. Beyond these funds only large-scale disarmament in the context of a permanent settlement with Israel and general détente in the Middle East could enable the regime to mobilize additional public resources for productive investment. These, however, may well fail to meet actual needs. Provided Syria reduces its defence expenditure from the amount of S£ 27,520 million given in the 1991 budget, roughly indicative of more recent budgets and corresponding to about 9 per cent of its GDP of S£ 305,600 million in the same year,[30] to about 4 per cent which by NATO standards is a generous ceiling (in Egypt defence expenditure thanks to US grants reaches approx. 7.5 per cent of GDP),[31] the exercise would entail a good S£ 15,000 million of annual savings. If calculated at the exchange rate applied to strategic imports of the public sector, this amounts to about $1.33 billion; if calculated at the 'commercial exchange rate' reportedly used in the budget itself,[32] the amount would correspond to about $710 million; finally, if calculated at the rate prevailing in neighbouring countries the dollar amount would once again be halved. Even in the best of cases, spending cuts from the military budget would be smaller than the sums invested in the first year of Law no. 10, though possibly bigger than the average investment over the next five years or so, and *ipso facto* smaller than present annual government and public sector investment.[33]

This new reality poses an obvious challenge to a regime that so far has been used to monopolize economic control and decision-making and that will hardly regain the initiative by simply declaring 1993 as the year of public sector industries. Investors may be seen as continuously subject to the vagaries and arbitrariness of Syrian authorities, but they also enjoy significant leverage *vis-à-vis* the government. Not only may they repatriate their investments under certain conditions (cf supra), but as the country and the regime need their substantial investments, there will be little inclination to bite the hand that feeds. Least exposed to regime pressures are probably foreign investors who are backed up by their governments on the one hand and by Syrian dependency on the other. More exposed, yet differentially, are Syrian investors. In the strongest position are those who are not permanently resident in the country or who have substantial interests abroad. However, as they are aware of their relative vulnerability they may also be expected to look for additional guarantees and securities. There is no reason why these people should not include the appointment of their own candidates to sensitive administrative and military positions. At the same time their bonds with their own country tend to make them more prone to interfering in politics even beyond narrowly economic matters. Their self-perceived role together with a dose of patriotism may easily lead to Saint-Simonian concepts of rule and decision-making.

Among the major consequences of the recent increase in private investment in absolute as well as in relative terms will be the yet further growing importance of the private sector in the supply and generation of foreign currency. In the case of Syria this is needed not only for the purchase of foodstuffs, capital goods and military equipment, but also in order to repay at least part of the public foreign debt. While the need for military hardware may decline after a peace agreement with Israel (cf supra), part of this advantage may be offset by less favourable conditions of payment than in the past. Russia like the Soviet Union in its terminal years tends to insist on convertible cash instead of payment in kind, barter deals or credit-financing (cf infra).

Considering Syria's rate of population increase of about 3.3 per cent annually[34] (at present on the basis of a population of 13.18 million this equals 434,000 people) even future increases in agricultural production may necessitate high food imports, though perhaps not equalling 21.2 per cent of total imports as was the case in 1991.[35] At the same time, the import of capital goods which Syria does not produce itself, accounting for about 38.5 per cent of total imports in 1991,[36] will hardly decrease in a period of planned economic expansion. Part and parcel of the new economic policy, these imports cannot be reduced. The fact that all projects under under Law no. 10 need the explicit approval of the government's Higher Council of Investment clearly attests to the importance of these imports in the eyes of the government. Accounting in 1991 for about 60 per cent of total imports worth $2,768 million,[37] the import of these vital commodities entailed expenditure amounting to $1,660 million, provided official figures are trustworthy and are not based on the confusion of the various exchange rates.

It should be added that the development of a local capital goods industry does not seem to be likely; neither the policy of industrialization which often continues to confuse the simple creation of industries with a coherent strategy,[38] nor the size of the Syrian market and its integration into the regional and world economies seem to favour it.

Amounting altogether to $16.8 billion in 1991, Syria's foreign debt,[39] in theory, for the next five years entails a total debt service (principal and interest) of between $1 billion and 1.2 billion annually.[40] These figures include some $10 billion to 12 billion owed to the former Soviet Union[41] which many observers doubt will ever be repaid. At least for the moment the regime is clearly procrastinating, if only by hesitating to recognize Russia as the legal successor to the former USSR,[42] even though all former Soviet republics have already done so and thus relinquished all their claims. Various partial solutions have been tried so far, ranging from the famous clearing account for Syrian exports first to the USSR and then to Russia,[43] to the export of citrus fruit.[44] Even though Russia does not seem to be excessively impatient and continues to sell arms to Syria against instant payment, preferably in cash,[45] it has not forgiven this debt and in view of its own capital shortage probably never will. Hence Syria may expect to have to pay at a later stage, particularly if it should need Russian support in any other matter. President Asad who in Lebanon and in inter-Arab affairs used to keep all his options open will probably be careful not to alienate a potential international ally as powerful as Russia. Obviously, if the Syrian government decides that such a risk is worth its while, repayment requirements of interest and principal would decrease significantly, perhaps to a mere $200 million to 300 million annually.

On the basis of the above figures, vital imports and total foreign debt alone necessitate foreign currency earnings of $2.66 billion to 2.86 billion annually. If invisibles and expenditure for military equipment, difficult to estimate, are added, the figure doubtless rises to more than $3 billion. Under the most favourable assumptions these outlays might just about be covered by total export earnings which in 1991 reached $3.4 billion,[46] but certainly not by public sector earnings which accounted for less than 50 per cent of the total[47] and thus for no more than about $1.6 billion to $1.7 billion. Public sector currency earnings would not even cover the currency requirements for imports and debt service to the sole OECD countries. As grants to the regime from its counterparts in the Gulf now largely come in the shape of project-linked concessionary grants, only important cuts in the expenditure for military equipment would bring relief. However, such cuts are conditional on external factors, particularly a permanent settlement with Israel; as already indicated, it is moreover doubtful whether these cuts could cover the shortfall.

Under these conditions the regime obviously benefits, though perhaps moderately, from its own exchange regulations according to which private businesses have to change foreign currency earnings into Syrian pounds, unless they use them to import capital goods.[48] This regulation, however, does not change the fact that these earnings originate in the private sector and that they may strengthen the self-confidence and position of its representatives.

In future the share of the public sector in the country's foreign currency earnings is likely to decrease or to remain stable at best; this is because, in spite of the inflow of substantial concessionary funds, its share in export-related investments such as manufacturing and service industries is stable or declining, but also because the country's oil production is stagnating and oil prices may continue to fall.[49] With crude oil representing 44.7 per cent of Syrian export earnings in 1991[50] corresponding to slightly more than two-thirds of public sector exports,[51] the writing is on the wall. Moreover, the state-owned Syrian Petroleum Company (SPC) which markets the crude and hence earns the foreign currency in the first instance, has to pass on a share of 45 per cent of these earnings to the foreign companies which actually drill the oil.[52] Therefore, public currency earnings from crude exports in 1992 amounted to no more than roughly $990 million (with total revenues from crude exports reaching approx $1.8 billion) and in 1993 may be expected to reach about $1.21 billion (against total crude oil revenues of approximately $2.2 billion).[53]

Through its growing share in total investment the private sector also contributes to the creation of new jobs. Widespread, though often hidden, unemployment in Syria is exacerbated by the high rate of population increase of some 3.3 per cent annually. Although a certain number of the newcomers to unemployment may in various ways be absorbed into family businesses and farms, this figure is less than matched by the jobs the government promises to create. When presenting the 1993 budget to the People's Assembly, the Minister of Finance, Muhammad Khalid al-Mahani, claimed it would lead to the creation of 68,302 new jobs.[54] This figure is almost twice as high as the 35,860 jobs which private companies established during the first 12 months of Law no. 10 pledged to create over a much longer period of time.[55] While the public sector thus continues to play the leading role, be it only through overstaffing, the contribution of the private sector is not negligible; it may be all the more important as it is likely to include a relatively high proportion of better-paid managerial and technical positions for a new generation of Syrians who crave upward mobility.

The need to create jobs may become yet more pressing if the 'peace process' actually proceeds to peace. Depending on the final settlement, peace may entail significant disarmament or at least demobilization. Neither of them is a necessary consequence, as is illustrated by the example of Egypt where the armed forces after the peace treaty with Israel in 1979 effectively grew in numbers;[56] none the less, under the changed circumstances of the 1990s, they are likely consequences of a general peace treaty.

Such an agreement will increase external and internal pressures on the Syrian regime partially to disarm and demobilize. Internally, it would be even more difficult than it is now to convince young Syrians to be conscripted for up to three years in the armed forces. If there is no other enemy, demobilization becomes an issue involving the legitimacy of the regime. Curiously perhaps, maintaining the armed forces at their present high level of 408,000 troops, that is, roughly 3.1 per cent of the total population,[57] could prove to be a more economical solution than creating new jobs. Soldiers may indeed come cheap if equipment is kept to a minimum. In the Syrian armed forces simple soldiers hardly get more than pocket money, basic food, a uniform, a helmet and a Kalashnikov. At least for the first years after peace uniforms could be darned, rifles repaired and even tanks could be symbolically maintained without too much cost; new investment would be negligible, especially as peace would reduce the need to replace or increase expensive hardware.

Conversely, and provided one excludes solutions such as over-staffing or modern versions of the *corvée* such as workfare, the creation of jobs to absorb demobilized troops leads to additional short- or medium-term expenses, even though these investments could be amortized later on. If the size of the Syrian armed forces was to be reduced to 1 per cent of the total population, which by the standards of NATO as well as Egypt is already relatively high,[58] 276,200 troops would have to be sent home; if it was to be reduced to 1.5 per cent still 210,000 troops would have to be made redundant. Under both assumptions the regime would again probably get away with the creation of fewer jobs because there are certain absorptive capacities and because many officers and soldiers already have a second job anyway. Judging from the above figures the public sector would probably be overstretched, but if the private sector lives up to its promises a critical mass might be reached.

As argued above, only in conjunction with substantial disarmament could demobilization enable the Syrian regime to liberate additional resources for investment and hence for the creation of jobs for some of the demobilized. Combined with the usual amount of public sector investment and conditional on the validity of the above ratio between public sector investment and job creation, this best-case scenario could indeed contribute to give work to one out of two or even more demobilized military personnel.

The picture that emerges from these elements is that public resources are insufficient to guarantee a level of investment that in turn generates the necessary amount of foreign exchange and reduces the existing high level of unemployment. Though contributing to the alleviation of highly unsatisfactory conditions, the effects of private investment on employment figures seem to be rather modest. However, the ratio of private to public investment in itself and the private sector's contribution to production as well as to the generation of foreign currency are substantial enough to entail 'economic' leverage with considerable 'political' effect.

The most simple manifestation of such leverage is seen when potential investors choose not to invest or even to withdraw their capital because conditions do not meet their expectations. Capital return will obviously be a major consideration, but it cannot be dissociated from more 'political' issues such as the absolute guarantee of property rights or the collision with established and vested interests of people in and around the regime. Hence investment may be incompatible with existing rules or arbitrariness, arrangements for the sharing or not of power, or even the exercise of power by certain individuals. If investors fear that their investments are not safe because they are excluded from the control of the physical means of coercion, they will either not invest or will insist on enforceable guarantees. If investors feel that their investments are safe without such direct control, they will none the less weigh heavily on those who nominally continue to exert that control and seek to influence or even determine their policy choices. In both cases, the rulers are losing some of their power to those whom they called in to strengthen the economy and thus to consolidate this very power. This is no different in Syria, even though as elsewhere the ultimate outcome hinges on the extent to which the suppliers of the new resources develop a consciousness of class and act in a concerted fashion.

Power-sharing or Showdown?

The emergence of a second 'power centre' in Syria, drawing its strength from increasingly organized owners of capital, would inevitably result in various internal realignments, some of which clearly imply the revival of debate, negotiation and deals. This is not to rule out the survival of the current status quo characterized by the unequal relationship between the military and capital. This relationship may continue if private capital fails to get organized or in the increasingly unlikely case that external rent, accruing from domestic oil production, transfers from the Gulf countries or other sources, reinforces the regime and its autonomy *vis-à-vis* society. Nor does it exclude the emergence of an arrangement which in spite of its novelty would hardly entail a return to, or of, politics. The latter caveat refers to a situation in which an emancipated and strong private sector deliberately continues its alliance with the officers, but now as a relationship between equals. Possibly this rebalanced *bloc au pouvoir* could come closer to an actual amalgamation of these two societal categories, thus cementing ties of interest through new ones based on intermarriage. While increasing over the years, such family relations have none the less remained limited in Syria so far. A social merger of this kind would obviously also imply an end to what remains of the division of labour between military and business. More precisely, the existing possibilities for officers to double in business would need to be reflected in similar possibilities for representatives of civilian capital to play a role in the running of the armed forces. Also, established capitalists such as the three major tycoons might prefer military protection with all its consequences to growing competition from other rising entrepreneurs. Already the major business people insist conspicuously less on the need to guarantee the rule of law than do their smaller counterparts who are more exposed to the arbitrariness of its enforcement at present. However, the latter version of continuity and stability would be challenged continuously and forcefully and be spiced with far greater political tension and debate than the preceding ones.

None the less, private capital may as well attempt to emancipate itself more thoroughly, if not radically, from military tutelage, distance itself from the regime and, depending on its assessment of the internal balance of power, confront and challenge it. Future conditions imposed by international financial institutions such as the IMF might further weaken the regime's position. In this case financial and economic power will, to a large extent, be separated from the control of the physical means of coercion, and competition between the two powers will ensue. Pessimists will then talk of instability and internal conflict, while optimists will interpret such conflict as a sign of the return of politics. Although in an unorthodox style, the emergence of capital as a parallel power would come down to the re-emergence of checks and balances of sorts. Should the bourgeoisie continue to rise and the military continue to decline, such a situation could ultimately lead to the latter's retirement in a Chilean-inspired scenario. This need not in itself lead to the complete marginalization of the 'Alawis, even though it would lead to the marginalization of 'Alawi officers who were unable to remould themselves as fully-fledged capitalists. It has been pointed out that historically this scenario correlated with economies turning from import-substitution to export-promotion and the strengthening of capital in this context;[59] it may thus be premature in the Syrian case, as the economy in spite of more recent emphasis on export-orientation still has a along way to go in this respect.

However, more likely than such a clear-cut cleavage between capital and the military seems to be a more complex arrangement in which civilian capitalists are joined by those officers who manage successfully to combine their military roles with non-parasitic private business. Together, capitalists of civilian and military origins would then find themselves in opposition to officers who failed to 'make it' and to replace rentier attitudes with productive or at least profitable investment. Difficult to imagine in a state of war, such an intra-military split is favoured by a peace agreement with Israel and the end of the 'national security state' or, as Waterbury would put it, the end of the 'ends-oriented state'.[60] Already, the sons of various powerful officers have spurned military careers altogether and have become entrepreneurs instead. Over time such tendencies could lead not only to intra-military splits but even to the departure of economically successful officers from the ranks of the military. As in the case of a new and more balanced alliance between the military establishment as a whole and private capital, a more restricted one between capitalists of military and civilian origin could ultimately lead to a merger of the social groups involved. In the second case, however, the economically less successful officers would find themselves excluded. In both cases such a merger largely depends on the perceived prospects of capitalist development which, in the case of optimism or euphoria, would enhance the readiness among actors to replace old ascriptive bonds with new ones based on interest and hence more germane to the logic of capitalism.

In both of the latter cases, power would be split and no single force, actor or group would be able to impose its conditions. This would naturally be the beginning of politics as compromises would have to be negotiated and floating votes to be lobbied. Against capital, officers or some among them might find allies in organized labour and the Ba'thi and other left. Labour itself, however, might split, pitting privileged private sector workers and employees against their less fortunate counterparts in often less profitable public sector companies. None the less, this alliance of losers could build on nationalist and anti-imperialist feeling which, still widely spread and deeply rooted, opposes foreign investment and the return of a comprador bourgeoisie. The Ba'th Party, in spite of its marginalization in the decision-making process, remains the only large-scale political organization with a viable infrastructure and branches all over the country, therefore it could prove to be an important asset for those opposing new economic policies in Syria. In a situation of more diffusely distributed political power it might even re-emerge as an actor in its own right. Ironically then, the demise of the present centralized power structure commonly described as Ba'thi rule could signal the comeback of the Ba'th as a political force. At any rate, however, corporatism would be replaced with class conflict.

Although the scenarios of relative continuity must not be dismissed, pluralism seems to have some chances to erode centralization and by this very token lead to the revival of politics in Syria. Once power passes into several and competing hands, there is also a chance for intellectuals to reappear on the stage, exploiting fissures in the crumbling monolith and crack it further. At the same time, associations and other institutions of civil society may re-emerge and perhaps contribute to the consolidation of pluralism. Even then, however, the likely limits of the process may be gauged from the Egyptian experience. Although there the famous Laws no. 43 of 1974 and 32 of 1977 more than 15 years ago created conditions similar to those under Syria's new Law no. 10, political change remained highly controlled and failed significantly to dent the autonomy of the state.[61]

8· Syria after Ta'if: Lebanon and the Lebanese in Syrian Politics

Fida Nasrallah

The Ta'if Agreement,[1] signed in Saudi Arabia in October 1989, marked the culmination of a series of dramatic events which shook Lebanon to its core. Its original cause lay in the constitutional vacuum in Lebanon following the expiry of President Amin Jumayyil's mandate in September 1988. As the Lebanese constitution did not provide for his re-election, President Jumayyil appointed General Michel 'Awn, who was the commander of the Lebanese army and a presidential candidate, as the prime minister of an interim cabinet. This in turn led to the conflictual coexistence of two rival governments in Lebanon, one under the leadership of General 'Awn and the other under the old Prime Minister Salim al-Huss. The latter had taken over the *'gouvernement démissionnaire'* of Prime Minister Rashid Karamé, who was assassinated in 1987.

The coexistence of two rival governments in Beirut, each vying for power and legitimacy, was a matter of deep concern for the Arab League which consequently set up a conciliatory commission consisting of six member states. Arab mediation began in January 1989 when both parties were given the opportunity to express their views.

Domestically, General 'Awn confronted the militias, seeking to break their stranglehold over the country. His first clash was with the Lebanese forces in February 1989. A month later he confronted the other militias and imposed a sea blockade on the illegally operated ports. This triggered opposition from the militias concerned and from Syria. The crisis escalated, General 'Awn embarked upon his 'rock-the-boat-policy' and finally, on 14 March 1989, launched his 'war of liberation' against the Syrian troops which had entered the country in the early days of the 'civil war' in 1976. The armed resistance embarrassed Syria and although ultimately unsuccessful, it did at least have the benefit of provoking serious debate about Lebanon at the Arab Summit in Casablanca in May 1989.

The Summit decided to set up a Higher Tripartite Committee comprising the leaders of Saudi Arabia, Algeria and Morocco. Its mandate was to explore and promote possibilities for constitutional reforms in Lebanon and to facilitate the election of a new president. The committee was to be responsible for contacting all parties in order to lay the groundwork for a comprehensive and definitive solution.

On 31 July 1989 the committee suddenly suspended its work and issued a communiqué which blamed Syrian intransigence for a lack of progress on the Lebanese question. A deadlock arose as a result of this communiqué and negotiations were suspended until early September, when the Syrian President Hafiz al-Asad, in a meeting with the Algerian President Bin Jadid in Tripoli, agreed to have Syria's presence in Lebanon debated. On 30 September, members of the Lebanese parliament met in the Saudi resort of Ta'if to discuss a plan for political reform drafted by the Higher Committee. This document came to be known as the Ta'if Agreement or the Charter of National Reconciliation.

Roughly, the Ta'if Agreement can be divided into four parts. The first relates to domestic reforms, the second to the restoration of Lebanese sovereignty over the entire territory of the Lebanese state, the third to the liberation of South Lebanon from Israeli occupation, and the fourth to the creation of a privileged relationship with Syria.

Domestic reforms led to the redistribution of power between the legislative and executive branches of government and ultimately sought to abolish confessionalism as the major principle of political representation. The reforms strengthened the position of the speaker of parliament by prolonging his mandate from two to nearly four years. They also stipulated that representation in the parliament would henceforth be on the basis of parity between Christians and Muslims rather than on the 5:6 ratio which had previously favoured the Christians. The number of seats in parliament was increased from 99 to 108 (ultimately to 128) and the boundaries of parliamentary constituencies were redrawn, with a few exceptions, so that they no longer coincided with the *qada'* (district), but rather with the *muhafaza* (province). Finally, the reforms called for the election of a first non-confessional parliament, to be followed by that of a senate.[2]

The restoration of Lebanese sovereignty over the entire territory of the state meant that within one year the emerging Government of National Unity would implement a security plan which sought to strengthen the army and the Forces of Internal Security (FIS) and to dissolve the various militias. The Government of National Unity would also aim to find a solution to the problem of the internally displaced.

The section relating to the liberation of southern Lebanon from Israeli occupation relied on the application of the United Nations Security Council Resolution 425 as a means to achieve that goal. None the less, it envisaged the recourse to all possible means, thus sanctioning armed resistance. Generally, the agreement envisaged that Lebanon's relationship with Israel would be based on the Armistice Agreement of 1949.

Finally, the agreement ended with a fourth chapter on the nature of relations between Lebanon and Syria. It recognized the existence of a special relationship between Lebanon and Syria and stated that future coordination and cooperation between the two countries should be determined by bilateral agreements in 'all domains' (*fi- shatta al-majalat*). These domains of cooperation were to include foreign policy, security and military affairs, economic relations, educational affairs and information.[3]

The major achievement of the agreement was that it ended the armed conflict in Lebanon. Indeed, Syria – which, at least since 1983, had done much to perpetuate the conflict – had by now managed to impose its dominance. From a regional and international perspective the stability of Lebanon under a new *Pax Syriana* was now both possible and desirable.

The agreement could not, and indeed did not, satisfy everyone. It was rejected outright by General 'Awn and criticized by Hizbullah, Amal, the Progressive Socialist Party and the Palestinians.[4] But the strong international and regional backing which the Ta'if process enjoyed ensured its survival and ultimate implementation.

The agreement was a success for Damascus which had always refused to withdraw its forces from Lebanon without similar moves coming from the Israeli side. This refusal stemmed from long-standing strategic considerations, particularly the perceived need to control Lebanon as a means of guarding against Israeli strikes against the Biqa Valley. Syria was nevertheless careful not to engage in military actions against areas not directly under its control, as such actions could lead to heavy Israeli retaliation and might threaten its own influence in Lebanon. Moreover, Syria was careful to avoid any further deterioration in its relations with western countries and with the then Soviet Union which any such unauthorized assault might engender.

The problem for Syria, therefore, was how to impose its authority over Lebanon without using military force. It was resolved in October 1989 when the Lebanese National Assembly endorsed the Charter of National Reconciliation which envisaged a continuing role for Syrian armed forces in Lebanon. The Charter stipulated that these forces should assist in the implementation of the security plan which had been incorporated into the agreement.[5]

Domestic opposition to the agreement considerably slowed its implementation. However, regional developments, particularly the Gulf crisis, beginning on 2 August 1990 with the Iraqi invasion of Kuwait, played a crucial role in the development and subsequent implementation of the agreement. As tactical allies of Iraq, General 'Awn and the PLO hoped that the Gulf crisis, which challenged American and Saudi influence, would weaken the regional and international consensus which supported the Ta'if agreement. The pro-Ta'if parties in Lebanon were apprehensive about the fate of the agreement in the light of the crisis and succeeded in convening parliament on 21 August 1990. This resulted in an amendment of the constitution, and the incorporation of the reforms called for by the agreement. The speed with which parliament was convened reflected renewed interest in Damascus for the Ta'if Agreement after the USA had given assurances concerning Syria's continuing role in Lebanon.

By August 1990, therefore, Syria was eager to exploit the diplomatic opportunities arising from Iraq's invasion of Kuwait and to improve its relations with Egypt and the USA. Syria supported Egypt's efforts in coordinating Arab responses to Iraq's invasion of Kuwait. At an emergency meeting of the Arab League in Cairo it was agreed to send troops to Saudi Arabia as part of a pan-Arab deterrent force in support of US efforts to deter Iraq from invading that country.

As a reward for its pro-alliance stance, Syria was now able to pursue the military option in Lebanon without fear of international censure. It was also widely believed that in return for Syria's participation in the US-led multinational force, Washington had agreed to facilitate total Syrian hegemony over Lebanon by exerting pressure on Israel not to intervene. Having received this assurance, Syria on 13 October 1990 launched an armed assault on the presidential palace in Ba'abda, the seat of General 'Awn, who was heading the opposition against the Ta'if Agreement. Indeed, this attack, and particularly the intervention of the Syrian air force, was in clear breach of the 'red lines' agreement with Israel which defined the limits of Syrian military activities in

Lebanon. That Israel did not retaliate in response to this breach may well have reflected US support for the Syrian offensive. Thus, in the wake of the Gulf crisis, the Ta'if Agreement became completely Syrianized, with American and Saudi blessing.

Measures to implement the Ta'if Agreement were stepped up in the aftermath of Iraq's military defeat in February 1991. On 22 May 1991, the Treaty of Fraternity, Cooperation and Coordination was signed between Syria and Lebanon.[6] This treaty was the natural outcome of the Ta'if Agreement which stipulated the establishment of a formal structure for the development and implementation of joint policies on a wide range of security and economic affairs. All Lebanese policies, therefore, would henceforth be conducted in cooperation with Syria.

The treaty declared that Syria and Lebanon 'had distinctive brotherly relations based on their geographic proximity, similar history, shared destiny and common interests'. Moreover, it specified the mechanism by which these distinctive relations were to be managed and developed. Five joint councils were established which would meet regularly in order to develop and implement policies concerning Lebanon. The most important of these councils was the Higher Council, which was comprised of the presidents, prime ministers, deputy prime ministers, and speakers of parliament of the two countries. This Higher Council was responsible for coordination and cooperation in political, economic, social, military and other spheres. Its decisions were binding, albeit within the legal and constitutional frameworks of both countries.

The treaty particularly emphasized economic cooperation, including agriculture, industry, commerce, transport, communications and customs. It also envisaged 'joint projects' and the 'coordination of development plans'. Considering the different economic systems of Syria and Lebanon, this may be interpreted in two different ways. It could either mean that Syria saw no contradiction in coordinating its development plans with Lebanon – a country whose very *raison d'être* rested on liberal policies and a *laissez-faire* economy – and that it had therefore decided to push the liberalization of its own economy further. Or it could mean that cooperation would be in the direction of integrating the Lebanese economy into the Syrian economy to the benefit of the latter.[7]

Security coordination, which crystallized in September 1991 with the signing of a mutual Defence Pact, implied tight control over the activities of all those who resided in Lebanon.[8] This pact sanctioned the continued presence of Syrian military forces in Lebanon, forces which were not subject to the orders of the Lebanese military leaders, and over whom the ministers and deputies had no say with regards to their deployment, composition or size.

Syrian diplomacy portrayed the treaty as the first proof that Syria had recognized the independent existence of Lebanon, since signing a Treaty with another state automatically implies recognition. However, it is difficult to agree with such a claim as Damascus still refuses to formalize this recognition by establishing diplomatic relations with Lebanon.[9]

At any rate, the various treaties signed or even ratified so far, clearly illustrate the formalization of this 'privileged relationship' between the two countries; the only missing part is the economic agreement that still remains to be signed.[10] Indeed, some form of special relationship has always been the goal of both countries, even though their representatives may not have always agreed about its scope and nature. Nor would the outstanding economic agreement be the first in this domain. A Syro-Lebanese customs union was hastily created in 1943; an economic and financial treaty was signed on 28 January 1949; an economic treaty was signed in Damascus on 5 March 1953; and yet another accord was signed on 22 December 1970. Their later abrogation or suspension has not always been in Lebanon's interest.[11]

Syria's second *infitah* (see chapters 1 and 3) presents not only Syria, but also its neighbours with new realities. This more far-reaching programme of liberalization resulted from serious economic and financial difficulties; these, in turn, were caused by long-standing structural weaknesses which were exacerbated by various additional factors such as the decreasing level of rent transfers from the major oil-producing countries. After an initially cautious and hesitant response to the crisis, the Syrian government in the mid-1980s embarked on a programme of reform which at first discreetly, then with Investment Law no. 10 of 1991 openly encouraged the private sector to play a greater role in the economy. As the law of 1991 puts Syrian, Arab and foreign capital on an equal footing, Lebanese entrepreneurs, thanks to their personal and family links as well as their geographical proximity, may acquire economic assets and significant leverage in Syria. This applies even more to Syrian expatriate entrepreneurs operating from Lebanon.

Already many Syrian companies participate in projects in Lebanon. This hardly seems surprising as much of what is called Lebanese business and banking has actually been the result of Syrian expatriate investment.

Indeed, the former head of the Lebanese Bankers' Association, As'ad Sawaya, came from Homs. Some of the biggest contractors in Lebanon, such as Abdel Rahman Hourieh who has build most of its roads, are of Syrian origin. Similarly, the village of Rabiyeh, which is one of the most successful real estate projects in Lebanon, has as its main investor Shukri al-Shammas, who is also originally from Homs. *Al-Sharika al-khumasiyya*, a Syrian company, has invested heavily in real estate in Lebanon. Syrian expatriates who have acquired Lebanese citizenship as well as other Lebanese sho live at home or abroad are at the forefront of those eager to invest in Syria once such opportunities arise. Once the second Syrian *infitah* takes off, there will be no shortage of entrepreneurial skills available to revive the Syrian economy – and capital will also be available. Entrepreneurs based in Lebanon will benefit from easier access to information and contacts than others. Their close personal and family ties across the border with Syria will be as instrumental in this respect as their ability to build on a long tradition of economic cooperation,[12] the basis of which has survived, against all odds, the years of the Lebanese 'civil war'.

Finally, the new dialogue that is opening up between certain members of the Christian community in Lebanon and Syria – albeit slow and gradual – is likely to encourage Lebanese investment, both domestic and expatriate, in Syria. Indeed, given the right kind of economic treaty, Syria's second *infitah* may very well result in its colonization by Lebanon.

9· Domestic Pressures and the Peace Process: Fillip or Hindrance?

Fred H. Lawson

Most observers claim that trends within Syria's domestic arena are pushing the regime led by President Hafiz al-Asad to adopt a more accommodative posture towards Israel in the series of Middle East peace talks that was initiated in the spring of 1991. This argument runs along one of two lines. First, Damascus is posited to have been unable to find an internally-generated solution to the country's perennial economic crisis. The regime is seen as having had to rely upon assistance and technical expertise from outside in order to implement the economic and social programmes that generate the popular support it needs to survive. Following the collapse of the communist bloc, concessionary aid from the East virtually disappeared; Damascus has therefore found itself more than ever before compelled to cultivate ties with alternative patrons, most notably Riyad and Washington, who can provide it with vital assistance and expertise. The best and perhaps the only way to open the aid pipeline from the USA, in particular, was to fall in with the Bush administration's effort to restart negotiations over the Arab–Israeli conflict. And the surest means of consolidating the fragile US connection is to adopt a moderate stance regarding the various items on the agenda of these talks, as much to convince Washington to remove Syria from the list of states alleged to sponsor terrorist activities as to relieve the country of the now inordinately expensive burden of continuing military confrontation with Israel.

Second, the Asad regime's ongoing moves to deregulate the Syrian economy have been seen as a fillip to serious negotiations aimed at ending the Arab–Israeli conflict. The successive economic reform programmes described by Sylvia Pölling and Volker Perthes earlier in this volume, and particularly the controlled liberalization that began to take shape in 1987, gradually created a class of richer private

entrepreneurs with an interest in forming closer ties to the outside
world. Whether or not these manufacturers' and merchants' sentiments
lie with the Palestinian national movement, the future health of their
businesses demands further reductions in the central administration's
hold over the local economy; this trend has been hindered by the state's
ongoing efforts to mobilize, and thereby centralize, internal production
and distribution in order to carry on the struggle with Israel. As the
re-emergent private sector assumes a greater role in the local economy,
and as private firms have become more profitable, not only can *nouveaux
riches* manufacturers and merchants be expected to put increasing
pressure on the state to relax its grip, in the ways suggested by Joseph
Bahout and Eberhard Kienle, but the regime itself has opted to take
the risk of abandoning the established network of state-supported
enterprises and is looking instead to the private sector to provide
employment opportunities and tax revenues. This step is likely to prove
hazardous enough without the lingering threat of renewed hostilities
with Israel. Therefore, the regime has strong incentives to conclude an
agreement regarding the Arab–Israeli conflict that will enable the
ambitious domestic economic reforms outlined by Nabil Sukkar to bear
fruit.

These two chains of reasoning underline a crucial component of
Syria's current dealings with Israel: the Asad regime would prefer to
have peaceful relations with its neighbour rather than persisting in a
state of cold war. But it would be a great mistake to conclude either
that Damascus can be pressured into accepting a hasty or dis-
advantageous settlement or that Syria is likely to abandon its long-
standing posture of declared support for the national aspirations of the
Palestinians. In fact, domestic factors represent not so much a fillip to,
as they do a brake against the Asad regime's acquiescence in any US-
brokered peace agreement that might injure or jeopardize Syrian
interests. And it is this dynamic, more than any other factor, that
accounts for the evident hard line that Damascus has taken throughout
most of the current negotiations.

Syria's Position in the 1991–93 Talks

Damascus evidenced a marked reluctance to jump onto the bandwagon
in favour of convening an international conference to resolve the Arab–
Israeli conflict in the immediate aftermath of the second Gulf war.
Following a visit with US Secretary of State James Baker in early April

1991, Foreign Minister Faruq al-Shar'a restated his government's position that the United Nations should play 'a significant role' in such a conference, and that the results of any negotiations would have to be 'based on Resolutions 242 and 338'.[1] None of the other prospective parties to the talks raised this stipulation as adamantly as did the Syrians. Although Damascus subsequently retreated from its insistence that the UN itself sponsor the talks, it persisted in demanding that the two Security Council resolutions serve as the basis for deliberations.[2] On the eve of the initial meeting in Madrid, Syrian officials announced that they would not participate in follow-up talks with Israel concerning regional environmental and economic issues unless there were clear progress towards resolving the issue of the occupied territories. This stance was unambiguously reiterated in the wake of the Madrid session.[3]

Syria boycotted the Moscow round of talks, at the end of January 1992, on the grounds that any discussion of long-term regional security issues remained premature so long as Israeli forces retained control of the Golan, the West Bank and Gaza. Lebanese and Palestinian representatives also absented themselves, but Jordanian delegates attended the conference despite intense Syrian pressure to stay away. Bilateral negotiations in Washington two months later produced virtual deadlock between Syria and Israel. Damascus attempted to focus attention on the current and future status of the occupied territories, while the Israelis complained of past Syrian threats to Israeli security. Syria's spokesperson, Bushra Kanafani, told reporters that the talks constituted 'an exercise in futility'.[4]

When negotiations resumed in late August, Syrian delegates expressed guarded optimism that the new Labour-led government in Israel would adopt a more conciliatory posture. Damascus repeated its demand for the complete return of the Golan, rebuffing Israeli hints that unspecified territorial concessions might follow the signing of a formal peace treaty. But at the same time the Syrians held open the possibility that the Golan could be demilitarized or placed under some form of international supervision. Israeli negotiators responded to this signal by stating for the first time that they considered the Golan to be covered under the terms of UN Security Council Resolution 242. Such mutual flexibility resulted in a dramatic improvement in the atmosphere surrounding the talks.

Nevertheless, the seventh round of discussions in Washington two months later evidenced none of the optimism that had pervaded the August session. Syrian spokespeople publicly denounced the Israeli

government's explicit rejection of a complete withdrawal from the
Golan, as well as its escalating air and artillery strikes in southern
Lebanon. When Israeli representatives announced that they were going
home early, the head of the Syrian team called the talks 'frustrating'.[5]
Syria's position regarding the negotiations became even more
intransigent during the early November recess. Foreign Minister al-
Shar'a responded to the results of the US presidential election by
commenting that anyone who believed that the outgoing Bush
administration had acted in an even-handed fashion with regard to the
Arabs was badly mistaken. President Bush, he noted, had authorized
the granting of sizable new loan guarantees to Israel, as well as the
rescinding of a bellwether UN measure equating Zionism with racism.[6]
When the talks resumed in mid-November, Syria restated its demand
that a full Israeli withdrawal from the occupied territories precede
discussion of any other issues. The seventh round thus concluded with
nothing to show except a commitment by all parties to reconvene in
the first week of December.

Even as the Washington talks foundered, though, President Asad
used the occasion of an interview with reporters from *Time* magazine
to soften Syria's hard line. He told the visiting correspondents on 13
November 1992 that it was conceivable, even likely, that some aspects
of the conflict might be settled in advance of others, so long as the
ultimate objective of comprehensive peace was kept firmly in mind.[7]
When a reporter asked whether Syria would sign an agreement that
did not turn over the West Bank to the Palestinians, the president replied
that he 'did not want to go into details', but that the idea of
comprehensiveness referred to the range of political aspects under
consideration, not to the amount of real estate involved. He then
repeated that as long as all the Arab delegations retained their
confidence in one another, 'it would be possible for one side to progress
more speedily than the others'.

President Asad reiterated this comparatively softer line during the
course of a keynote address to the annual convention of the General
Federation of Trade Unions in early December. He told the assembled
trade unionists that the partial withdrawal from the Golan that had
been proposed by Israel three months earlier 'does not achieve peace,
but it is a step towards peace'.[8] Nevertheless, he continued, Security
Council Resolution 338 demands not 'a partial withdrawal that
constitutes a step towards achieving peace but a withdrawal from all
parts which constitutes all steps that achieve [a comprehensive] peace'.

The president then observed that any sustainable settlement would entail 'rights and commitments', most notably 'commitments to security and peace that should be made by all parties on the condition that the security of any party should not be at the expense of the other.' He concluded by saying that 'we shall continue the peace process as we have started it, but not without an end.' Despite its relatively tough ending, the president's speech clearly opened the door to the possibility that Syria might accept a graduated Israeli withdrawal from the Golan.

Toward the end of Ramadan, on 17 March 1993, President Asad reverted to a much less compromising position in a widely publicized address delivered to a group of religious notables assembled for the annual fast-breaking (*iftar*) banquet in Damascus. The president told the assembly in no uncertain terms that any form of separate Syrian–Israeli settlement would be rejected out of hand by Syrian negotiators. He went on to assert that Damascus would under no circumstances abandon its Arab partners in the talks, but could instead be counted upon to treat issues vital to the Palestinians, Lebanese and Jordanians as vital to itself. In his words: 'The decision of our people is that there will be no concession on one grain of our rights, however difficult the circumstances or however hard the days. We must not surrender our rights, not all of them, not part of them, not even a grain of them.'[9] Knowledgeable observers inside Syria interpreted this speech as an unmistakable retreat from the more moderate sentiments that had been expressed in the president's earlier speech to the trade union federation.

Syrian delegates reaffirmed the president's harder line just prior to the ninth round of negotiations at the end of April. The head of the Syrian negotiating team, Muwaffaq al-Allaf told the Lebanese newspaper *al-Diyar* that Damascus had no intention of making a separate deal with Israel, but instead remained 'committed to a comprehensive peace and solving the Arab–Israeli conflict on all fronts'.[10] A week later, Vice-president Abd al-Halim Khaddam said in an interview with the Kuwaiti daily *al-Watan* that 'peace requires withdrawal from all the occupied Arab territories and recognition of the national rights of the Palestinian people', both of which were presently being blocked by Israel.[11] Furthermore, he asserted that 'Syria would never take any measure which might restrict the national, Syrian, Lebanese or Palestinian struggle against Israeli aggression.' At almost the same time, al-Allaf told reporters in Washington that Israeli representatives had presented nothing new in the bilateral talks that reconvened on 27 April.[12] He accused Israel of refusing to respond positively to Syria's proposal that the two sides exchange total peace for total withdrawal from the occupied territories, and remarked that the ninth round was likely to prove 'frustrating and disappointing'.[13] When the talks adjourned on 13 May, al-Allaf once again called the proceedings 'frustrating'.[14]

Damascus can thus be seen to have adopted an unambiguously uncompromising stance *vis-à-vis* Israel at virtually every stage of the peace negotiations initiated in the spring of 1991. This finding runs diametrically counter to the logic of the situation as it has been adduced by most observers of Syria's contemporary political-economic affairs. The more acquiescent posture these observers expected on the part of the Asad regime was evident on only three occasions during the two years from April 1991 to May 1993: at the beginning of the August 1992 session, in President Asad's November 1992 *Time* magazine interview and in the address that he delivered to the trade union federation a month later. Before sketching an explanation for Damascus's overall hard line, it is important to consider in detail these anomalous episodes of apparent accommodation.

Probing Labour's Bargaining Position

There can be little doubt that the momentary relaxation in Damascus's general intransigence that was evident at the end of August 1992 partly represented an overture to Israel's newly elected Labour government, and was consequently driven by the exigencies of diplomacy as much as by those of domestic politics.

As soon as it became clear that the Rabin cabinet was going to follow a negotiating strategy virtually identical to that of its predecessor, the Syrian leadership reverted to a markedly harder line. The head of Syria's team in Washington told reporters when the talks recessed on 7 September that he saw little difference between the positions taken by the successive Israeli governments. The very next day, President Asad formally received a delegation composed of prominent residents of the Golan. In his comments to the group, the president observed that it had been several years since a delegation from the area had visited the capital. He then told his guests that Syria desired

> an honourable peace accepted by our people, a peace that does not concede a grain of sand from the homeland nor any right from the national rights nor the nation's dignity ... If others agree to this peace, then peace can be achieved. But if there are

gimmicks and ambushes, then nobody can change Syria's attitudes and national principles. Surrender is not in her vocabulary.[15]

It therefore may simply be the case that the Syrian leadership cautiously proffered an olive branch to Yizhak Rabin's new Labour government, and then resumed its hard line when the overture was rebuffed.

Nevertheless, a pair of developments in Syria's domestic political-economic arena during the spring and summer of 1992 provided the broader context in which this particular accommodative move was undertaken. First, there are indications that disaffection over the regime's economic liberalization programme intensified throughout these same months. Left-wing deputies in the People's Assembly expressed considerable displeasure over the cabinet's draft 1992–93 budget when it was submitted to the parliament for consideration at the end of April. Planned reductions in social welfare spending and the generally low tax rates levied on private enterprises elicited particularly strong criticisms from members representing the Ba'th Party-affiliated trade union federation and peasants' union.[16] Discontent within the latter organization arose once again towards the end of August, when Prime Minister Mahmud al-Zu'bi told a convention of the executive officers of the country's chambers of commerce that the government planned to increase its support for export-oriented projects in the private agricultural sector.[17]

Second, new resources had begun to flow into the central administration at an exceptionally high rate. It became clear by late summer that Syria's cotton producers were going to harvest a record crop during the 1992 season. Projections estimated an increase in total output of almost 20 per cent over the level achieved in the preceding year.[18] This increase was complemented by notable rises in phosphates exports throughout the summer months. Bumper crops of foodstuffs, on the other hand, proved somewhat less profitable. The Federation of Syrian Chambers of Agriculture set up a commission at the end of August to coordinate output and marketing of such produce as tomatoes, potatoes, apples and raisins in an effort to avoid the recurrence of sharp drops in the prices of these items in the near future.[19]

Confronted by widespread grumbling within the Ba'thi popular front organizations, the regime earmarked some of these additional resources to help revitalize Syria's public sector enterprises. The board of directors of the al-Furat tractor factory, for example, announced in mid-August that it would reopen its assembly line outside Aleppo using diesel engines imported from the United Kingdom.[20] At the same time, however, state officials took steps to consolidate their ties with *nouveaux riches* private entrepreneurs. Reports were leaked in mid-September that the Ministry of Economy and Foreign Trade was prepared to revise its regulations so as to permit companies to keep 100 per cent of their export earnings to purchase imports necessary for maintaining or expanding their operations. In addition, the ministry began granting six-month lines of credit to private import firms, while the Higher Council of Investment awarded operating licences to an additional 20 private sector projects under the terms of the May 1991 investment law.[21]

Squaring the circle of placating disaffected members of the popular front organizations while at the same time buttressing the burgeoning private sector – itself the very focus of left-wing discontent – could best be accomplished in an atmosphere of heightened national concern regarding the Middle East peace talks. And although many members of the Ba'th and its affiliated popular front organizations no doubt favoured the hard line that the leadership was already pursuing in its dealings with Israel, and thus might have been expected to object to the specific content of the diplomatic initiative undertaken at the beginning of August 1992, the unmistakable shift in strategy captured the attention of the nation and held it long enough for simmering discontent over the economic situation at home to dissipate. It is worth noting that the dynamics of this situation run almost directly counter to much writing on the general connection between domestic conflict and foreign policy, which presumes that growing internal difficulties tend to prompt regimes to undertake conflictful or aggressive foreign policies, rather than comparatively accommodative ones. In the case of contemporary Syria, the Asad regime's long-standing belligerence towards Israel made a further escalation in the level of hostility directed against the old enemy considerably less effective as a means of galvanizing popular sentiment than adopting an uncharacteristic, and thus unanticipated, softer line.

The Late Tishrin Thaw

Quiet dissatisfaction with various aspects of the Asad regime's programme of economic liberalization re-emerged at the end of November 1992. The president of the Damascus Chamber of Industry, Yahya Hindi, complained during a radio interview on 2 December that the pivotal May 1991 investment law had enriched the country's merchants at the direct expense of both state-supported and some privately owned manufacturing companies.[22] His comments reflected festering resentment among less fortunate and less well-connected business people over the evident success enjoyed by a small number of entrepreneurs, even as many established manufacturing enterprises found it hard to operate at a profit in the new market-oriented domestic economic order. Meanwhile, the directors of the Damascus Chamber of Commerce found themselves subject to growing criticism for moving too cautiously to take advantage of the opportunities created by the government's economic policies. General elections for seats on the chamber's governing council were fiercely contested throughout late November and early December.[23]

More importantly, when representatives of the General Federation of Trade Unions (GFTU) gathered in the first week of December for their annual congress, they brought with them a lengthy list of grievances concerning the adverse impact that the liberalization drive was having on its membership. Skilled industrial workers were deserting the public sector in growing numbers to take higher-paying jobs in private companies; price increases on staples continued to outpace wage rises for state employees; private schools and hospitals had become clearly better equipped and better administered than those operated by the government; and the gap between the ostentatious rich and the struggling poor appeared to be widening at an alarming rate. An influential grouping within the federation was even prepared to propose that the organization's long-standing ties to the Ba'th be relaxed, so that workers' demands could be expressed outside the party's existing channels.[24]

State officials attempted to head off disaffection on the part of those who favoured preserving the extent and role of the public sector within the Syrian economy by creating an extraordinary commission to study various means of restructuring state-run enterprises. The panel announced in mid-November that it was planning to explore such options as giving the management of public companies greater autonomy in setting day-to-day policy and permitting these enterprises to keep control of the hard currency earned as a result of their activities.[25] At the same time, however, the Ministry of Economy and Foreign Trade reaffirmed its intention to set up a new bank to provide investment monies to private and mixed sector firms licensed to operate under the terms of the May 1991 law.

As was the case three months earlier, the Syrian leadership moved to ameliorate the internal strains associated with economic liberalization by undertaking highly visible initiatives in the external arena. President Asad's interview with *Time* was accorded extensive coverage in the local media, eclipsing debate over whether or not the government should permit international firms to begin re-entering the country to assist in setting up a number of large-scale private industrial plants.[26] By the same token, whatever proposals might have been put forward by the GFTU membership for revising the trade union federation's relations with the Ba'th were not only completely overshadowed but also severely undercut by President Asad's keynote speech. In the light of the gravity of the external security issues addressed by the president, it would have been trifling, if not in fact seditious, to raise the more mundane matter of restructuring trade union–party relations.

This message was driven home in the very rhetoric that pervaded the address.[27] The president began by praising the delegates for their many accomplishments in the areas of factory construction, dam building and technical training. He then asserted: 'Great as those achievements are, the greatest is our national unity, which is our pride.' The honour of the nation, he went on to say, lay in the fact 'that the achievement was accomplished within the framework of a coherent and strong national unity that achieved security and consolidated both stability and progress.' Finally, President Asad expressed his gratitude that the trade unionists 'understood freedom within the framework of responsibility and distinguished between interacting in the context of integration to reach a goal [on one hand] and contradiction and fragmentation which lead to wasted effort and crumbling power [on the other].' The necessity of forging internal unity as a means of ensuring external security could not have been stated more clearly. The assembled trade unionists undoubtedly got the message.

Domestic Pressures and Syrian Intransigence

These three relatively accommodative episodes to the contrary notwithstanding, Damascus's overall posture during the two years of peace negotiations that began in the spring of 1991 can be seen to have been consistently firm, if not actually inflexible. This stance is best explained in terms of ongoing struggles among powerful social forces for predominance within Syria's domestic arena. In particular, the overall success of the regime's programme of economic liberalization after mid-1991 dramatically increased the stakes involved in jockeying between the alliance of military and security commanders, party–state officials and public sector managers on one hand and richer private commercial and industrial interests on the other. As a result, both sides took steps to court not only the country's resurgent large landholders, but also the members of the Ba'th Party-sponsored popular front organizations.[28]

In the contest to gain control over economic policy-making, Syria's private sector merchants and manufacturers, along with richer agriculturalists in the countryside, appear to have held the upper hand in the months immediately following the second Gulf war. These forces had profited handsomely from the government's programme of controlled liberalization during the late 1980s. Capital formation in the private sector jumped 32 per cent between 1984 and 1986, despite the general economic crisis gripping the Syrian economy. Private holdings represented some 40 per cent of total fixed capital formation by 1986.[29] Agriculture and construction accounted for the largest share of the increase in capital formation. Mixed-sector farm companies producing cash crops for export and commercial real estate projects proved particularly profitable at the end of the decade. Furthermore, increases in domestic cereals production allowed the regime sharply to reduce the amount of hard currency it had to reserve for food purchases overseas.[30]

Meanwhile, the share of Syria's total trade moving through the private sector rose from 10 per cent in the early 1980s to over 20 per cent in 1986. The proportion jumped to more than 30 per cent by 1988.[31] Greater private sector involvement in the country's internal and external commerce accompanied a marked resurgence on the part of large-scale, mixed-sector and private industry.[32] The most profitable of these enterprises were the larger clothing factories, which produced underwear, shirts and socks for both domestic and foreign markets; firms specializing in the manufacture of cosmetics, fabrics and tobacco products also earned healthy profits throughout these years.

State officials were able to maintain a degree of control over the local economy during the late 1980s by channelling the goods produced in private sector industry toward markets in the Soviet Union and Eastern Europe. The value of this trade was estimated to average some $200–300 million annually throughout the last years of the decade. Syrian firms contracted with Soviet trading companies to supply increasing quantities of moderate quality goods at premium prices, generating nominal returns greatly in excess of any that locally manufactured items could command on the open market. But as the

1980s ended, trade with the communist world evaporated. Soviet authorities drastically cut the prices they were willing to offer for Syrian manufactured goods, while at the same time insisting that a greater number of counter-trading arrangements be drawn up. According to the terms of these agreements, specified quantities of Syrian products were to be shipped to Soviet buyers as a means of retiring Damascus' sizable outstanding military debt.

In response, state officials moved to subsidize commercial exchanges with the USSR and its allies. They did so by granting greater access to the state's limited hard currency reserves to those local companies which specialized in supplying manufactured items to Eastern Bloc markets. Largely as a result of this policy shift, Syrian exports to the Soviet Union rebounded in 1989–90. At the same time, though, greater incentives to produce consumer goods for sale to the East precipitated a proliferation of smaller-scale textile and food-processing factories in the suburbs surrounding Aleppo.[33] The growth of these firms buttressed the private sector within the Syrian economy, while at the same time transforming Aleppo and its environs into a centre of commercial and industrial dynamism for the country as a whole.

By the spring of 1991, private interests found themselves in a position to chart the course for the entire Syrian economy. The promulgation of the government's revised investment law that May was immediately followed by the creation of special industrial zones in several provinces to provide suitable locations for modern private and mixed-sector plants. More than 250 companies were licensed to operate under the terms of the new law during its first 12 months in force, while another 150 were authorized in the succeeding six months.[34] Public sector managers, with the active encouragement of the government, attempted to match the expansion of private enterprise by modernizing the most productive of their deteriorating plants and replacing the others with new facilities. In January 1991, for instance, Minister of Planning Sabah Baqjaji told *Al-hayat* of London that the state's 1991 budget would include a substantially larger allocation for investment in public sector industry; the General Organization for Cement and Building Materials in early May solicited bids on a project to upgrade and expand its cement factory at Hamah, while the General Fertilizer Company (GFC) tendered a proposal to do the same for its aging ammonia/urea plant outside Homs.[35]

Government planners hoped that such projects would attract the attention of western investors, but US firms in particular proved reluctant to involve themselves outside the petroleum sector of the Syrian economy. Western European companies at least evidenced a somewhat greater willingness to do business with the country: German, French and Spanish consortia bid for the contract on the GFC's fertilizer factory; Italian and German firms made offers to build a new spinning mill at Idlib; and Austrian, Italian, Japanese and German corporations tendered bids to construct a new iron and steel complex at al-Zara outside Damascus. But western capital came nowhere near being sufficient to replace the funding and technical support that had been previously provided by the communist world. Instead, it was the Arab Gulf governments which, in the wake of the second Gulf war, moved in to finance the revitalization of Syria's public sector. The Kuwait Fund for Arab Economic Development agreed in July 1991 to provide the $60.5 million needed to build the Idlib cotton mill; Saudi Arabia took responsibility for funding the al-Zara iron and steel complex, at a cost of approximately $500 million.[36]

These monies, paradoxically enough, provided Syria's military commanders, party–state officials and public sector managers with just the resources they needed to maintain their long-standing ties with the rapidly disintegrating Eastern Bloc.[37] They also enabled this alliance to defend its deteriorating position in local society in the face of the growing wealth and influence of the country's private commercial and industrial entrepreneurs. The continuation of the Asad regime's 'eastern connection' was facilitated not only by revenues flowing directly into the state treasury as a result of increased oil and phosphates production, but also by the profits and kickbacks generated through illicit trade with Lebanon.[38] These resources made it possible for government officials in the provinces to continue to contract with Czechoslovakian, Yugoslavian and Bulgarian companies for desperately needed industrial and agricultural machinery and expertise.[39]

Nevertheless, the position of Syria's public enterprises within the local economy steadily weakened relative to that of the more dynamic private sector firms as 1992 went by. Privately-owned pharmaceuticals companies, food-processing plants, spinning and weaving mills and plastics moulding factories sprouted up in the suburbs around both Damascus and Aleppo in ever-increasing numbers during the course of the year.[40] The modernization of many of the larger state-run enterprises, by contrast, suffered significant delays in funding and construction, partly due to the state's lengthy approval process and partly as a result of developments in the external arena over which the government had little if any control.[41] Privately-owned enterprises captured shares of both the country's 1992 gross domestic product and its non-petroleum exports for the year that were unprecedented during the three decades of the Ba'thi era.[42] At the same time, managers of public sector industrial plants were forced to lay off more experienced, higher-paid employees and replace them with younger labourers in an effort to cut production costs.[43] Early 1993 even saw the state-run Military Housing Establishment delay wage payments to its workers due to severe cash-flow difficulties.[44]

Under these circumstances, state officials adopted a consistently firm stance in the peace talks with Israel as a way both of mobilizing members of the popular front organizations for the defence of the nation and of reassuring public sector workers of the continuing importance of their contribution to the nation's well-being. Refusal to compromise with the historical enemy of the Syrian and Palestinian people was explicitly associated with the diligence and self-sacrifice with which the country's factory and farm labourers were expected to carry out their respective duties. As President Asad told the trade union federation: 'You were, and you still are, dear workers, the substance of economic and social changes. In addition, each gain of the Correctionist Movement's achievements was basically aiming at achieving the people's prosperity, security and stability; and you are in the front.' Inflexible positions at the peace talks therefore complemented the unwavering discipline that the regime expected from industrial workers and peasants.

By the same token, an unwavering hard line *vis-à-vis* Israel helped to prevent Syria's private entrepreneurs from becoming overly complacent about their role in the country's future economic development. In the first place, the possibility that negotiations might break down and Syrian–Israeli relations revert to outright belligerence put a damper both on moves by local businesspeople to collaborate with foreign corporations and on unbridled investment by indigenous or expatriate capitalists. Raising the spectre of renewed external conflict thus kept the expansion of the private sector within comparatively circumscribed, even manageable, bounds. Recognizing the disruptions and dangers that accompanied wholesale liberalization in Egypt and Iraq, the leadership in Damascus appreciated the necessity of imposing strictures upon speculative or non-productive private investment. But state officials then confronted the puzzle of how to regulate the activities of private capitalists and entrepreneurs without reintroducing direct state intervention into the local economy, a step which would only have frightened potential investors away from Syria entirely.

Second, the possibility that the 45-year state of war with Israel might persist entailed the potential that the Syrian economy might on short notice be recentralized for military purposes. Such a step could be expected to work to the direct benefit of the public sector, much of whose *raison d'être* was 'for the realization of economic autonomy', and thereby of national defence.[45] In this way, the state's continued purchases of sophisticated weaponry from the former Eastern Bloc effectively propped up the position of the public sector relative to that of private enterprise.[46]

On the other hand, taking a softer line towards Israel carried with it the distinct likelihood that Syria's private entrepreneurs would escalate their activities, further undercutting the collective position of the country's military officers, party–state officials and public sector managers. It may therefore have been, as the Marxists say, no coincidence that plans for both a major joint venture pharmaceuticals project and a path-breaking private aluminium fabrication mill were finalized during the brief period of accommodation that occurred at the end of November 1992.[47] More importantly, a comparatively flexible posture in the peace talks could be expected to convince greater numbers of public sector workers to abandon the state-run enterprises and seek jobs in privately-owned companies. Such a trend would make it virtually impossible for the already weakened public sector to survive, thereby dramatically raising the level of unemployment throughout the country.

Equally dangerous, from the standpoint of those advocating a continuation of state supervision over the local economy, a general exodus of skilled employees away from the public sector might provide the basis for a political alliance between private capitalists and industrial labour that would prove potent enough seriously to challenge the pre-eminence of the military officer/party–state official/public sector manager coalition. So long as workers and peasants remained at a distance from – if not actually opposed to – private interests, these forces provided a substantial counterweight to the wholesale liberalization of the Syrian economy.[48] But to the extent that the labour movement forged a common front with private capital, the distribution of power within Syria could be expected to shift profoundly. Mobilizing workers and peasants to continue the struggle against Israel thus did more than distract these forces from their rapidly accumulating domestic grievances, it also provided them with strong incentives to remain loyal retainers to the officer/party/state coalition.

Conclusion

Against the predictions of most observers of the country's diplomatic and strategic affairs, Syria adopted a consistently hard line in its negotiations with Israel throughout the two years beginning in April 1991. This trend accompanied a persistent reliance on Eastern Europe and the republics of the Commonwealth of Independent States for economic assistance and advice, as well as upon the ex-Warsaw Pact states and the People's Republic of China for military hardware.[49] The combination of intransigence towards Israel, internal economic recovery and continued ties to the former Eastern Bloc enabled the coalition of senior military and security officers, Ba'th Party and central administrative officials and managers of public sector enterprises to retain a predominant position within the country's domestic arena.

What is more intriguing is the apparent softening of Damascus's posture towards Israel at times of rising popular disaffection at home. Faced with even muffled discontent – whether among the members of the popular front organizations or on the left wing of the political spectrum – the Asad regime three times backed away from its hard line during the months between April 1991 and May 1993. These shifts left Syria vulnerable to exploitation on the part of Israeli negotiators, as well as open to criticism from radical Palestinian groups. But despite the dangers associated with a more cooperative strategy, the leadership in Damascus attempted on these occasions to manipulate foreign policy as a way of buttressing its deteriorating domestic political position. The fact that the three initiatives involved adopting a more flexible rather than a more rigid stance concerning the peace talks suggests that the officer/party/state coalition was willing to run considerable external risks in an effort to undercut its internal challengers. It also indicates that the Asad regime enjoys a notable capacity to withstand outside pressure, so long as the home front remains quiescent.

Notes

Introduction

1. For an extensive bibliography, see the following titles which to various
degrees accept or question this view of Syria: R.A. Hinnebusch,
*Authoritarian Power and State Formation in Ba'thist Syria: Army, Party,
and Peasants* (Boulder, CO, 1990); E. Kienle, *Ethnizität und Machtkonkurrenz in inter-arabischen Beziehungen: Der syrisch-irakische Konflikt
unter den Ba'th-Regimen* (Berlin, 1985); E. Kienle, *Ba'th v. Ba'th: The
Conflict between Syria and Iraq 1968–1989* (London, 1990); V. Perthes,
Staat und Gesellschaft in Syrien 1970–1989 (Hamburg, 1990); N. van Dam,
*The Struggle for Power in Syria: Sectarianism, Regionalism, and Tribalism
in Politics 1961–1978* (London, 1979); M. Seurat (partly under his pen-
name G. Michaud) reprinted in M. Seurat, *L'Etat de barbarie* (Paris, 1989);
cf also H. Batatu, 'Some observations on the social roots of Syria's ruling
military group and the causes for its dominance', *Middle East Journal*
35/3 (1981), pp 331–44. Circumspect representatives of the dominant
paradigm are moreover, A. Drysdale, 'The Syrian political elite 1966–
1976: a spatial and social analysis', *Middle Eastern Studies* 17/1, pp 3–30;
S. Mahmud, *Hiwar hawla Suriyya* (Cairo, 1992); and E. Picard, 'Y a-t-il
un problème communautaire en Syrie?', *Maghreb-Machrek* 87 (January–
March 1980), pp 7–21. For a recent critique of the attention paid to
religious or more generally vertical or 'ethnic' criteria, cf V. Perthes,
'Einige kritische Bemerkungen zum Minderheitenparadigma in der
Syrienforschung', *Orient* 31/4 (1990), pp 571–82.
2. I. Harik, 'Privatization: the issue, the prospects, and the fears', in I. Harik
and D.J. Sullivan (eds), *Privatization and Liberalization in the Middle East*
(Bloomington, IN, 1992), p 1.
3. E.g. G. O'Donnell, *Modernization and Bureaucratic Authoritarianism:
Studies in South American Politics* (Berkeley, CA, 1973); A.O. Hirschman,
'The turn to authoritarianism in Latin America and the search for its
economic determinants', in D. Collier (ed), *The New Authoritarianism in
Latin America* (Princeton, NJ, 1979), pp 61–8; for a recent discussion of
these approaches, cf S. Haggard, *Pathways from the Periphery: The Politics*

   of Growth in Newly Industrializing Countries (Ithaca, NY, 1990), ch 10.
4. I. Harik, 'Privatization', p 21.
5. D. Pool, 'The links between economic and political liberalization', in T. Niblock and E. Murphy (eds), *Economic and Political Liberalization in the Middle East* (London, 1993), p 49 (first quote) and p 50 (second quote).
6. Mahmud, *Hiwar*.
7. N.N. Ayubi, 'Political correlates of privatization programs in the Middle East', *Arab Studies Quarterly* 14/2–3 (spring–summer 1992), p 39.
8. J. Leca, 'Social structure and political stability: comparative evidence from the Algerian, Syrian and Iraqi cases', in G. Luciani (ed), *The Arab State* (London, 1990), p 183.
9. S. Heydemann, 'The political logic of economic rationality: selective stabilization in Syria', in H.J. Barkey (ed), *The Politics of Economic Reform in the Middle East* (New York, 1992), p 14.
10. Ibid., p 30.
11. Ibid., p 32.
12. Haggard, *Pathways*, e.g. p 264; T. Callaghy, 'Lost between state and market: the politics of economic adjustment in Ghana, Zambia, and Nigeria', in J.M. Nelson (ed), *Economic Crisis and Policy Choice: The Politics of Adjustment in the Third World* (Princeton, NJ, 1990), pp 257–319.
13. For such attempts on the part of the state, cf R. Owen, 'Socio-economic change and political mobilization: the case of Egypt', in G. Salamé (ed), *Democracy without Democrats? The Renewal of Politics in the Muslim World* (London, 1994), pp 183–99; on the ambivalence of the bourgeoisie, see J. Waterbury, 'The potential for political liberalization in the Middle East', in Salamé, *Democracy*, pp 23–47.
14. Salamé, *Democracy*.
15. Waterbury, 'The potential'.

Chapter 1

1. Al-Jumhuriyya al-'arabiyya al-suriyya, Wizarat al-iqtisad wa'l-tijara al-kharijiyya, *Al-qanun raqm 10 li tashji' al-istishmar min 4/5/1991 wa'l-ta'limat al-tanfiziyya min 28/5/1991* (Damascus, 1991); Al-Jumhuriyya al-'arabiyya al-suriyya, Ri'asat majlis al-wuzara', *Al-qirar raqm 7 m.w. bi ta'limat al-tanfiziyya li'l-qanun raqm 10 'l-'am 1991* (Damascus, 1991).
2. A silent partner is a shareholder who does not have any say in management decisions.
3. International Monetary Fund (IMF), *International Financial Statistics Yearbook* (Washington, DC, 1992).
4. Interview with 'Uthman 'A'idi.
5. Economist Intelligence Unit (EIU) (ed), *Syria Country Profile, 1992–1993* (by Sylvia Pölling) (London, 1992).
6. EIU (ed), *Country Report: Syria*, No. 2, 1993, p 29.
7. IMF, *Yearbook*.

8. H. Hopfinger, 'Capitalist agro-business in a socialist country? Syria's new shareholding corporations as an example', *British Society for Middle Eastern Studies Bulletin* 17/2 (1990), pp 162–70.
9. EIU (ed), *Country Report: Syria*, No. 4, 1991, p 5.
10. Interview with the Minister of Economy and Foreign Trade, Muhammad al-'Imadi.
11. EIU (ed), *Country Report: Syria*, No. 1, 1992, p 19.

Chapter 2

1. The study was N. Sukkar et al., *Nahwa iqtisad ishtiraki mutatawwar fi'l-qutr al-'arabi al-suri: muqtarahat li-i'adat al-tawazun li'l-iqtisad wa iqamat idara iqtisadiyya la-markaziyya*. It was submitted to responsible authorities in November 1987. In the next two years it was succeeded by five other volumes which covered the various sectors of the economy. A number of international consultants assisted in the early stage of the study.
2. The economic return on public enterprise fixed assets in manufacturing was calculated by the above-mentioned study at 1 per cent in 1985.
3. Syrian Arab Republic (SAR), Ministry of Planning, *Tahlil al-wad' al-rahin fi qita' al-sina'at al-tahwiliyya li al-sanawat 1979–1983* (Damascus, December 1984).
4. The General Federation of the Workers' Syndicates (General Federation of Trade Unions; GFTU), *Al-taqrir al-'amm li-mu'tamar al-ibda' al-watani wa'l-i'timad 'ala al-that* (Damascus, November 1987).
5. Ministerial statement of the new cabinet presented to parliament.
6. E.g. *al-Ba'th*, 10 July 1991, 20 January 1992, 19 February 1992; *Al-Thawra*, 19 February 1992, 20 February 1992, 23 February 1992, 29 February 1992, 3 June 1992, 11 March 1993; *Tishrin*, 17 February 1992.
7. Arab Socialist Ba'th Party, Syrian Region, Regional Leadership, *Taqarir wa muqarrarat al-mu'tamar al-qutri al-thamin* (Damascus, 1985).
8. Ministerial decree no. 4342 of 3 December 1988.
9. Ministerial decree no. 5703 of 1979 identified 68 industries which the private and mixed sectors were allowed to enter, and resolution no. 35 in 1986 raised the number of industries to 95.
10. World Bank, *World Development Report* (Washington, DC, 1988).

Chapter 3

1. S. Haggard and R.R. Kaufman, 'Economic adjustment and the prospects for democracy', in S. Haggard and R.R. Kaufman (eds), *The Politics of Economic Adjustment. International Constraints, Distributive Conflicts, and the State* (Princeton, NJ, 1992).
2. The declaration of Asad's 'Correctionist Movement' of 16 November 1970 is documented in Arab Socialist Ba'th Party (ASBP), National Leadership, *Nidal hizb al-Ba'th al-'arabi al-ishtiraki* (The Struggle of the Arab Socialist

Ba'th Party) (Damascus, 1978), pp 115–21.

3. A. Richards and J. Waterbury, *A Political Economy of the Middle East. State, Class, and Economic Development* (Boulder, CO, 1990), p 238.

4. Cf, e.g., ASBP, Syrian Region, Regional Leadership, *Taqarir wa muqarrarat al-mu'tamar al-qutri al-sadis al-mun'aqid fi Dimashq* 5 April 1975 to 15 April 1975 (Reports and Resolutions of the Sixth Regional Conference convened in Damascus) (Damascus, 1976), p 84.

5. Cf, in general, R. Qasem, 'Syria: rapid growth in foreign trade activity', *Arab Economist* 11 (April 1979), pp 23–7; M. Chatelus, 'La croissance économique: mutation des structures et dynamisme des déséquilibres', in A. Raymond (ed), *La Syrie d'aujourd'hui* (Paris, 1980) pp 225–73; F.H. Lawson, 'Political-economic trends in Ba'thist Syria: a reinterpretation', *Orient* 29 (1988), pp 586ff; V. Perthes, *Staat und Gesellschaft in Syrien 1970–1989* (Hamburg, 1990), pp 97ff.

6. Minister for Economy and Foreign Trade (MEFT), decree no. 779 of 1970.

7. Leg. decree no. 183 of 1969.

8. Leg. decrees nos 248, 265 of 1969.

9. Leg. decrees nos 50, 59 of 1971.

10. MEFT decree no. 267 of 1971.

11. Leg. decree no. 2 of 1971.

12. ASBP, Syrian Region, Regional Leadership, *Taqarir,* p 122.

13. Leg. decrees nos 172, 173 of 1974.

14. V. Perthes, 'The Syrian private industrial and commercial sectors and the state', *International Journal of Middle East Studies* 24/2 (1992), pp 207–30.

15. Perthes, 'Syrian private', p 215.

16. Perthes, *Staat,* p 217.

17. Leg. decree no. 40.

18. E. Picard, 'Syria returns to democracy: the 1973 legislative elections', in G. Hemet et al. (eds), *Elections Without Choice* (London, 1978), p 143.

19. Picard, 'Syria returns'; E. Picard, 'L'emprise du général Assad sur l'Etat syrien se renforce', *Maghreb-Machrek* 80 (1978), pp 13–14; E. Picard, 'La Syrie de 1946 à 1979', in Raymond, *La Syrie*; M. Seurat, 'Les populations, l'Etat et la société', in Raymond, *La Syrie*, pp 87–142.

20. Between 1970 and 1980, the number of civilians employed by the state and the public sector increased from 136,000 to 457,000. The entire workforce increased only from 1.6 to 2.3 million over the same time (Perthes, *Staat,* p 167).

21. Law no. 21 of 1974.

22. General Federation of Workers' Syndicates (GFWS), *A'mal wa muqarrarat wa tawsiyyat al-mu'tamar al-thamin 'ashr li'l-ittihad al-'amm li niqabat al-'ummal fi 'l-qutr al-'arabi al-suri al-mun'aqid bi Dimashq* 21–4 September 1974 (The Proceedings, Resolutions, and Recommendations of the 18th Conference of the General Federation of Trade Unions in the Syrian Arab Region convened in Damascus) (Damascus, 1974), p 34.

23. A. Filonik, *Su'ubat al-zira'a al-suriyya al-haditha* (Problems of the Modern Syrian Agriculture) (Damascus, 1987), pp 99ff; R.A. Hinnebusch,

Authoritarian Power and State Formation in Ba'thist Syria: Army, Party, and Peasants (Boulder, CO, 1990), pp 197ff; E. Longuenesse, 'Etat et syndicalisme en Syrie: discours et pratiques', *Sou'al* 8 (February 1988), pp 102ff; Perthes, *Staat*, pp 187ff.

24. Syrian Communist Party (SCP), *Al-mu'tamar al-khamis li'l-hizb al-shuyu'i al-suri, ayyar 1980* (The 5th Conference of the Syrian Communist Party, May 1980) (Damascus, n d), p 20.

25. Picard, 'La Syrie', p 176.

26. I. Hassan, 'La Syrie de la guerre civile', *Peuples méditerranéens* 12 (July–September 1980), pp 98f.

27. According to P. Seale, *Asad of Syria. The Struggle for the Middle East* (London, 1988), p 326, Asad's successful attempt to win over the Damascus Chamber of Commerce actually turned the tide in favour of the regime. The 65 per cent wage increase for public sector and state employees was of equal importance, since disenchantment with the regime had become feasible even within the lower and medium ranks of the bureaucracy.

28. E. Kanovsky, 'What's behind Syria's current economic problems?', in *Middle East Contemporary Survey 1983–84* (Tel Aviv, 1986); P. Clawson, *Unaffordable Ambitions: Syria's Military Build-up and Economic Crisis* (Washington, DC, 1989); V. Perthes, 'The Syrian economy in the 1980s', *Middle East Journal* 46/1 (1992), pp 37–58.

29. PM decree no. 1791 of 1983; no. 375 of 1987; no. 595 of 1987; MEFT decree no. 279 of 1987.

30. MEFT decree no. 47 of 1984; no. 365 of 1985.

31. Leg. decree no. 24 of 1986.

32. Leg. decree no. 10.

33. V. Perthes, 'A look at Syria's upper class. The bourgeoisie and the Ba'th', *Middle East Report* 170/21 (May–June 1991), pp 31–7.

34. PM decree no. 186 of 1985.

35. PM decree no. 1817 of 1987.

36. *al-Iqtisad*, June 1989, p 5.

37. MEFT decree nos 1048, 1593 of 1989.

38. MEFT decree no. 2184 of 1990.

39. MEFT decree no. 70 of 1991.

40. MEFT decree nos 158, 160 of 1989; Perthes, 'Syrian private', p 222.

41. Law no. 19 of 1990.

42. MEFT decree no. 905 of 1990.

43. Ministry of Industry, decree no. 4342 of 1988.

44. Law no. 10 of 1991.

45. Law no. 20 of 1991.

46. Syrian Arab Republic (SAR), *Statistical Abstract* (Damascus, 1991).

47. SAR, *Statistical Abstract* (1988 and 1991). All statistical data from Syria should be regarded with some caution, and should be taken to express trends rather than exact totals. This is particularly so for data on the private sector. There is a large informal sector whose data are neither collected by the Central Bureau of Statistics nor any other data-collecting institution such as the Ministry of Finance or the Ministry of Industry.

But even data on the formal private sector are often underestimated, since entrepreneurs, fearing taxation and other cuts from their profits, tend to hide parts of their activities. Different data-collecting agencies end up with diverging data on the same object of analysis – for example, private sector industrial activities – as a result of different methods on the one hand, and of the greater or lesser interest of entrepreneurs in providing correct data on the other. Perthes, 'Syrian private', n 21.

48. Damascus Chamber of Commerce, *Al-taqrir al-sanawi* 1990 (Annual Report) (Damascus, 1991), p 9.
49. SAR, *Statistical Abstract* (1992), p 77.
50. Gross fixed capital formation (investments) may serve as an example: private sector investments, in constant prices of 1985, dropped from S£ 6.7 billion (35 per cent of all investments) in 1983 to 4.7 billion (52 per cent of the total) in 1990; in current prices private investments increased from S£ 5.9 billion to 21.3 billion. Public sector investments dropped from S£ 12.2 billion to 4.3 billion respectively, still increasing in current prices from S£ 11.6 to 19.5 billion (SAR, *Statistical Abstract*, 1991, pp 502f).
51. SAR, *Statistical Abstract* (1992), p 168; Damascus Chamber of Commerce, *Al-taqrir al-sanawi 1991* (Annual Report) (Damascus 1992), p 15. Dollar values are calculated on the basis of the free-market rate of the Syrian pound.
52. SAR, *Statistical Abstract* (1992).
53. H.M. Ammash, *Tajawuz al-ma'ziq. Muntaliqat al-islah al-iqtisadi fi Suriya* (Overcoming the Dilemma. Points of Departure for Economic Reform in Syria) (Damascus, 1992).
54. S. Heydemann, 'The political logic of economic rationality: selective stabilization in Syria', in H.J. Barkey (ed), *The Politics of Economic Reform in the Middle East* (New York, 1992), pp 18f.
55. J. Leca, 'Social structure and political stability: comparative evidence from the Algerian, Syrian and Iraqi cases', in G. Luciani (ed), *The Arab State* (London, 1990), p 186.
56. *Sham* means both Syria and Damascus.
57. The following sections draw largely on my article 'The private sector, economic liberalization, and the prospects of democratization: the case of Syria and some other Arab countries', in G. Salamé (ed), *Democracy without Democrats? The Renewal of Politics in the Muslim World* (London, 1994) pp 243–69.
58. *Tishrin*, 4 March 1990.
59. *Tishrin*, 9 March 1990.
60. Leg. decree no. 2 of 1990.
61. V. Perthes, 'Syria's parliamentary elections. Remodelling Asad's political base', *Middle East Report* 174/22 (January–February 1992), pp 15–18.
62. P. Seale, 'Asad: between institutions and autocracy', in R.T. Antoun and D. Quataert (eds), *Syria. Society, Culture, and Polity* (Albany, 1991), p 109.
63. *al-Thawra*, 1 January 1992.
64. L.J. Cantori, 'Political participation, consultation and state-civil society

relations in the Middle East' (unpublished paper, 1991), p 6; Perthes, 'Syria's parliamentary'.

65. Amani 'Abd al-Rahman Salih, 'Al-ta'addudiyya al-siyasiyya fi al-watan al-'arabi: dirasa li'l-namuzaj al-misri wa'l-maghribi' (Political pluralism in the Arab fatherland: a study of the Egyptian/Moroccan pattern), *al-fikr al-istratiji al-'arabi* 10 (October 1991), pp 80ff; Muhammad 'Abid al-Jabiri 'Ishkaliyat al-dimuqratiyya wa'l-mujtama' al-madani fi al-watan al-'arabi' (The problematique of democracy and civil society in the Arab fatherland), *al-Mustaqbal al-'arabi* 15/167 (January 1993), pp 4–15.
66. *al-Ba'th*, 13 March 1992.
67. Perthes, 'Syrian private'.
68. SAR, *Statistical Abstract* (1981), p 476; (1992), p 413.
69. V. Perthes, 'The private sector, economic liberalization, and the prospects of democratization'.
70. S. Heydemann, 'Taxation without representation: authoritarianism and economic liberalization in Syria', in E. Goldberg, R. Kasaba and J. Migdal (eds), *Rules and Rights in the Middle East: Society, Law and Democracy* (Washington, DC, 1993).
71. G. Krämer, 'Liberalization and democracy in the Arab world', *Middle East Report* 174/22 (January–February 1992), p 24.

Chapter 4

1. V. Perthes, *Staat und Gesellschaft in Syrien 1970–1989* (Hamburg, 1990).
2. Some Syrian economic historians describe this period as one of 'bourgeois-feudal power'. See A. Hanna, 'Fasl min tarikh al-burjwaziyya al-suriyya', in M. Jadal, *al-burjwaziyya al-'arabiyya al-mu'asira* (Damascus, 1991).
3. I. Al-Khafaji, *Al-dawla wa 'l-tatawwur al-ra'smali fi 'l-Iraq* (Cairo, 1983).
4. Alongside the Investment Law no. 10 of 4 May 1991, decree no. 24 of 31 August 1986 remains in force, which heavily punishes unauthorized possession of foreign exchange. Decree no. 24 is enforced only selectively against entrepreneurs who are not politically protected. Its outright abrogation is today one of the main demands addressed to the state by the business community.
5. E. Picard, *Espace de Référence et Espace d'Intervention du Mouvement Rectificatif au Pouvoir en Syrie 1970–1982*, Thèse de III° Cycle, (Paris, 1985); see also: 'Ouverture économique et renforcement militaire en Syrie', *Oriente Moderno* 59/7–9 (July–December 1979).
6. A. Richards and J. Waterbury, *A Political Economy of the Middle East. State, Class, and Economic Development* (Boulder, CO, 1990), p 208.
7. '*Asabiyya* as used by Ibn Khaldun in the sense of 'group feeling' or '*esprit de corps*'.
8. The most notable exceptions in this respect are the two eldest sons of President Hafiz al-Asad, Basil and Mahir, who are army officers.
9. P. Clawson, *Unaffordable Ambitions? Syria's Military Build-up and Economic Crisis* (Washington, DC, 1989).

10. Exact data concerning oil revenues in Syria are still scarce and contradictory. It also seems that some figures do not appear in the national accounts; part of the oil revenue is believed to be diverted by some top officials to finance security networks. Moreover, after the euphoria of the early 1990s, some experts have moderated their expectations and are more sceptical about the future of Syria's income from oil.

11. J. Leca, 'Social structure and political stability: comparative evidence from the Algerian, Syrian and Iraqi cases', in A. Dawisha and W. Zartman (eds), *Beyond Coercion: The Durability of the Arab State* (London, 1988).

Chapter 5

1. *Tishrin*, 4 March 1990. Vice-president Abd al-Halim Khaddam invented another euphemism; he called the coup of 1970 a 'democratic revolution' (*Tishrin*, 9 March 1991).

2. There is considerable confusion about the actual composition of the NPF. Beside the Ba'th Party only five member parties are known for sure: two wings of the Syrian Communist Party (one led by Khalid Bakdash and the other one led by Yusuf Faysal); the Arab Socialist Union (ASU: *hizb al-ittihad al-ishtiraki al-'arabi*); the Movement of Arab Socialists (*harakat al-ishtirakiyyin al-'arab*); and the Organization of Socialist Unionists (*tanzim al-wahdawiyyin al-ishtirakiyyin*). The only official information originates from Asad himself who stated, in March 1990, that the Front would consist of seven parties. However, he did not name them (*Tishrin*, 9 March 1990). Beyond that no reliable information is available; which parties really form the NPF is obviously more or less a matter of speculation, and the information varies from source to source. The seven party names given by E. Kienle (*Entre Jama'a et Classe: Le Pouvoir Politique en Syrie* [Berlin, 1992], p 24) differ from those given by V. Perthes ('Syria's parliamentary elections. Remodelling Asad's political base', *Middle East Report* 174/22 [January–February 1992], p 35) who, moreover, mentions eight parties altogether including the Ba'th. To deepen the confusion, according to other information three new parties, among them a religious one, joined the NPF in 1990, none of which is mentioned by Kienle or Perthes. See A. Ayalon (ed), *Middle East Contemporary Survey (MECS)*, 14 (covering 1990) (Boulder, CO, 1991), p 654.

3. Asad on 12 March 1992 in an address to the parliament (*Tishrin*, 13 March 1992).

4. Speech on the occasion of the inaugural session of the new parliament on 11 June 1990 (*Tishrin*, 12 March 1990).

5. Article 8 mentions only the Ba'th Party's leading role in 'a national progressive front' whose political function is not specified in the constitution.

6. Only the Ba'th Party has the right to be politically active in the military and among students; for years the NPF has been denied the right to publish a newspaper of its own.

7. Rival factions within the regime and its apparatus are not considered oppositional in that sense, as they are an integral part of the regime in power and do not operate publicly.

8. Whereas a parliament can be denied any real political influence and elections can easily be manipulated, it is difficult for a dictatorial regime to create an artificial opposition. In 1989, when *perestroika* was at its height, the Syrian regime tried to launch such an 'opposition' which was given the name 'positive intellectual opposition'. This abstruse organization pretended 'to oppose the system but not the leadership of Hafiz al-Asad'. It is very likely that this organization was set up by the regime itself. Reportedly, Wahib al-Ghanam, an 'Alawi who, as one of the co-founders of the Ba'th first introduced Asad to the party, participated at the inaugural meeting of this 'opposition'. Its leader, Ra'iq al-Naqari, is an 'Alawi ex-officer of one of the regime's notorious praetorian guards, the 'Special Units' (*al-wahdat al-khassa*), and is said to have close relations with the president's brother Rif'at al-Asad. (See *Al-sharq al-awsat*, 22 and 23 June 1989.)

9. The independent formation of a political group is not tolerated even when it commits itself unconditionally to Asad. During the campaign for the parliamentary elections in May 1990 three hitherto unknown parties – the Party of Patriotic Solidarity (*hizb al-tadamun al-watani*), the People's Democratic Party (*al-hizb al-sha'bi al-dimuqrati*) and the Party of Justice (*hizb al-'adala*) – openly made propaganda for Asad but were nevertheless forced by the authorities to cease their activities.

10. On this subject, cf. H.G. Lobmeyer, *Opposition und Widerstand in Syrien seit 1963* (Hamburg, forthcoming).

11. CP-Politbureau, (*Hiwarat* Dialogues), no. 0 (zero) (July 1993), p 4.

12. Interviews, Paris, 1991.

13. It was definitely not only the role of Islam which generated the violent protests.

14. After some successful operations by the security forces against Islamists, the regime had, as early as autumn 1980, boastfully announced the defeat of the Muslim Brotherhood.

15. Since 1982 Syria's Islamists found themselves cut off from domestic events. This became clear from the clandestine periodical *al-Nadhir* (the *Warner*) which was published until the early 1990s. In its section 'News from the Provinces' *al-Nadhir* until 1982 reported extensively on events inside Syria. After the Hama events this section was predominantly concerned with Lebanon; for events in Syria itself *al-Nadhir* almost exclusively reprinted articles from Arab (mostly Iraqi or Jordanian) newspapers.

16. In 1986 the armed opposition resumed its activities with a series of bomb attacks causing hundreds of deaths. The most spectacular incidents happened in spring of that year: on 17 April, Syria's Independence Day, a total of 150 military cadets were killed in several attacks against buses in northern Syria; in May, 140 people were killed during an attack on the railroad linking Aleppo to Lattakiya. Several hitherto unknown groups claimed responsibility. According to the Paris-based Arab journal *al-Watan*

al-'arabi 583 (16 May 1986), the person responsible for these two attacks was a Syrian from Hama whose family had been killed by security forces in February 1982.

17. On that subject see C. Kutschera, 'L'éclipse des frères musulmans syriens', *Les Cahiers de l'Orient* 7 (1987), pp 121–31; and 'When the brothers fall out', *The Middle East* (April 1988); J. Perera, 'The shifting fortunes of Syria's Muslim Brethren', *The Middle East* (May 1987). For an inside view of the 1986 split see the interviews of 'Adnan Sa'd al-Din to *al-Watan al-'arabi* 590 (3 May 1988) and 591 (10 June 1988). In early 1990 Asad again made use of the principle of *divide et impera*; at that time the Arab press reported that the Syrian regime had contacted 'personalities of the exiled Syrian opposition' (*al-sharq al-awsat*, 17 February 1990). According to the reports which had obviously been launched by the regime, 'Issam al-'Attar, in the 1960s leader of the Muslim Brotherhood, was among these personalities. 'Attar denied this categorically in a letter to *al-sharq al-awsat*; however, ultimately this letter was not published in the Saudi *al-sharq al-awsat* but in the Iraqi *al-Thawra* (3 March 1990).

18. The Muslim Brotherhood even issued declarations allegedly signed by the 'Communist Party' in order to weaken the leftist opposition.

19. In particular this applies to the pro-Jadid Ba'th Party and the PCA. Unlike the other parties, the PCA has its stronghold in the countryside; until the neutralization in the 1980s, its front organization 'Popular Committees' (*lijan sha'biyya*) was strongly supported by Palestinian refugees in Syria.

20. The Revolutionary Workers' Party is a breakaway group of the Ba'th Party; it was founded and, until his death, led by Yasin al-Hafiz. He was one of the authors of the famous Ba'th Party document 'Some Theoretical Propositions' (*ba'd al-muntalaqat al-nadhariyya*) which was presented to the 6th National Congress of the Ba'th Party in October 1963.

21. It is not unusual anywhere in the world for parties to split and for two parties with identical names to dispute over each other's legitimacy. However, in Syria there is a considerable number of parties which have not only doubled but multiplied three- and even fourfold. To deepen the confusion, most of these parties are represented in the NPF as well as in the opposition ranks. The least complicated case is that of the Muslim Brotherhood which exists in two versions both of which oppose the current regime. More disconcerting is the case of those parties which split into three. There are three Ba'th parties (one in power and two in opposition), three CPs (two in the NPF, one in opposition) and three Movements of Arab Socialists (one in the NPF and two in opposition). Finally, no fewer than four parties call themselves ASU (two represented in the NPF [cf Kienle, *Entre jama'a*, p 24], two figuring in the opposition). Similarly, one wing each of the opposition Movements of Arab Socialists and ASUs is represented in the Gathering, while their homonyms participate in the National Front for the Salvation of Syria (see the Front's manifesto in *al-Thawra*, Baghdad, 22 February 1990) and had apparently joined the former Alliance in the middle of the 1980s. For the ASU opposition, cf the interview with Muhammad al-Jarah, secretary-general of the ASU represented in the former Alliance, in *al-Watan al-'arabi* 594 (1 July 1988).

22. The Sudanese government reportedly attempted to mediate between the Syrian regime and the Muslim Brotherhood and, as a precondition, to reconcile the rival Brotherhood wings with each other (*al-Hayat*, 18 May 1992).

23. *Al-mawqif al-dimuqrati* 6 (November 1991), p 7.

24. A. Turkmani, *Da'wa ila tahrir al-'aql al-'arabi min istimrar al-isti'adad li 'l-qubul bi 'l-istibdad – muqariba hawla jadl al-khass wa al-'amm fi mas'ala al-dimuqratiyya* (Call to Free the Arab Mind from the Continuing Willingness to Admit Oppression – Essay on a Particular and General Dispute over the Problem of Democracy) (unpublished manuscript, Damascus, 1993), p 2.

25. The CP-Politbureau's *Nidal al-Sha'b* (People's Struggle), which was superseded by *al-Mawqif al-dimuqrati* (Democratic Point of View), is only one such case; since 1990 the pro-Jadid Ba'th Party has been publishing *al-Badil al-dimuqrati* (Democratic Alternative) alongside *al-Dimuqrati* (Democrat) established in 1981. The Workers' Revolutionary Party now makes known its opinion in *al-Dimuqrati al-'arabi* (Arab Democrat).

26. The title of the party's periodical, *al-Dimuqrati al-'arabi*.

27. The mobilizing effect of events in Eastern Europe on the Syrian opposition becomes visible in a document of the PC-Politbureau: Syrian Communist Party, Central Committee, *Ma'atiyat al-wad' al-duali wa mu'ashirat al-wad' al-'arabi wa 'l-muhimmat allati yatruhuha* (The Condition of the International Situation, the Indicators of the Arab Situation and the Requirements they Impose), October 1991.

28. *Hawla al-qawmiyya al-'arabiyya: mu'atayat al-madi wa tahadiyyat al-hadir* (On Arab Nationalism: the Situation in the Past and the Actual Challenges) interview with Jamal al-Atasi, *al-Mustaqbal al-'arabi* 15/5 (May 1992), pp 121–33, here p 128.

29. *Al-mawqif al-dimuqrati* 7 (December 1991), p 11.

30. *Qiyadat al-thawra al-islamiyya fi suriya* (Leadership of the Islamic Revolution in Syria), *Bayan al-thawra al-islamiyya fi suriya wa minhajuha* (Manifesto and Programme of the Islamic Revolution in Syria) 1 Muharram 1401/9 November 1980 (Damascus). *Al-jabha al-islamiyya fi suriya* (The Islamic Front in Syria), *Mithaq al-jabha al-islamiyya fi suriya* (Charter of the Islamic Front in Syria) (Damascus, 11 January 1981).

31. On this subject see: H. G. Lobmeyer, 'Islamic ideology and secular discourse: the Islamists of Syria', *Orient* (Hamburg), 32/3 (1991), pp 395–418.

32. *Qiyada jama'at al-ikhwan al-muslimin fi suriya* (Leadership of the Society of the Muslim Brotherhood), *Suriya fi dau' al-mutaghayarat al-dualiyya wa al-'arabiyya* (Syria in the Light of the International and Arabic Changes) (May 1990); reprinted in *al-bayan*, 16 (July 1990).

33. Interview, Paris, 1991.

34. S. Hawwa, *Jund Allah takhtitan* (Projecting the Army of God) (Cairo, 1988), pp 108–9.

35. J. al-Atasi, 'Al-muthaqifun al-dimuqratiyyun wa thawra al-sha'b al-thaqafiyya' (The democratic intellectuals and the intellectual people's revolution), *Dirasat nasariyya* 4 (n d), p 4.

36. Editorial of *al-bayan*, 16 (July 1990). For the regime's move towards the opposition in 1990 cf above note 16.
37. *Al-mawqif al-dimuqrati* 5 (June 1991), p 9.
38. Ibid.
39. Ibid.
40. Cf *Al-watan al-'arabi* 587 (13 May 1988) to 599 (5 August 1988).
41. Press information of the CDF, 5 April 1993. The arrested members probably belong to a wing of the party that reportedly espouses political liberalization.
42. In the present context societal opposition is defined in terms of groups whose members are, temporarily or permanently, organized on the basis of common social backgrounds, interests, or identities and whose political demands are related to their position in society. Contrary to political opposition in the narrow sense of the term, societal opposition does not strive to replace the regime in power but tries to influence its politics.
43. The first was signed by 52 journalists, writers and poets; the second was signed by six lawyers. Both communiqués are reprinted in *Al-mawqif al-dimuqrati* 1 (February 1991).

Chapter 6

1. For two sophisticated variants of these approaches see, respectively, S. Farsoun and W. Carroll, 'State capitalism and counter-revolution in the Middle East: a thesis', in B.H. Kaplan (ed), *Social Change in the Capitalist World Economy* (Beverly Hills, CA, 1978); and J. Leca, 'Social structure and political stability: comparative evidence from the Algerian, Syrian and Iraqi cases', in A. Dawisha and W. Zartman (eds), *Beyond Coercion: The Durability of the Arab State* (London, 1988), pp 164–202.
2. E. Longuenesse, 'The class nature of the State in Syria', *MERIP Reports* 9/4 (1979), pp 3–11.
3. For evidence on the Ba'th state, see my *Authoritarian Power and State Formation in Ba'thist Syria: Army, Party, and Peasants* (Boulder, CO, 1990).
4. On the economic crisis, see G. Meyer, 'Economic development in Syria since 1970', in J.A. Allan (ed), *Politics and the Economy in Syria* (London, 1980), pp 40–62; V. Perthes, 'The Syrian economy in the 1980s', *Middle East Journal* 46/1 (1992), pp 37–58.
5. P. Seale, *Asad of Syria: The Struggle for the Middle East* (London, 1988), p 457. On the bourgeoisie, see also V. Perthes, 'A look at Syria's upper class. The bourgeoisie and the Ba'th', *Middle East Report* 170/21 (May–June 1991), pp 31–7.
6. Y.M. Sadowski, 'Cadres, guns & money: the eighth regional congress of the Syrian Ba'th', *MERIP Reports* 15/6 (July–August 1985).
7. *Tishrin*, 4–5 December 1989.
8. E. Kienle, ch 7 of the present volume.
9. Asad's speech, Foreign Broadcast Information Service, *Daily Report: Middle East and North Africa*, 17 May 1990, p 27.

10. *Middle East* (September 1991), p 21.
11. S. Heydemann, 'Liberalization from above and the limits of private sector autonomy in Syria: the role of business associations', paper presented at Middle East Studies Conference (Austin, TX, 1990).
12. Hizb al-ba'th al-'arabi al-ishtiraki, *Taqarir al-mu'tamar al-qutri al-thamin wa muqarraratuhu* (Reports and Resolutions of the 8th National Congress) (Damascus, 1985), pp 35–58.
13. Syrian Arab Republic, *Statistical Abstract* (Damascus), 1976, pp 151–2, and 1991, pp 76–7.
14. F.H. Lawson, ch 9 of the present volume.

Chapter 7

1. M. Seurat, under the name of G. Michaud, 'Terrorisme d'Etat, terrorisme contre l'Etat: le cas syrien', *Esprit* (October–November 1984), pp 188–201; reprinted in M. Seurat, *L'Etat de barbarie* (Paris, 1989), pp 35–52.
2. H. Arendt, *The Origins of Totalitarianism* (New York, 1973), p 466. Freedom of individuals to chose and decide, according to Arendt, is the *condition sine qua non* of politics, and individuals enjoy such freedom only if they can move, which presupposes freedom of movement and space between them, though not a space as spacious as a suffocating and isolating desert; cf e.g. H. Arendt, *Was ist Politik? Aus dem Nachlass, herausgegeben von Ursula Ludz* (München, 1993), p 11 in conjunction with pp 28f.
3. The annual and ad hoc reports published by Amnesty International, give ample evidence of these events.
4. Cf e.g. V. Perthes, 'Syria's parliamentary elections. Remodelling Asad's political base', *Middle East Report* 174/22 (January–February 1992), pp 15–18; also Perthes in the present volume.
5. Cf e.g. *Middle East Economic Digest (MEED)*, 19 February 1993, p 30.
6. Among the vast literature on the Egyptian experience cf e.g. R.A. Hinnebusch, *Egyptian Politics under Sadat: The Post-Populist Development of an Authoritarian Modernizing State* (Cambridge, 1989); C.H. Moore, 'Money and power: the dilemma of the Egyptian *infitah*', *Middle East Journal* 40/4 (autumn 1986); R. Owen, 'Socio-economic change and political mobilization: the case of Egypt', in G. Salamé (ed), *Democracy without Democrats? The Renewal of Politics in the Muslim World* (London, 1994), pp 183–99; R. Springborg, *Mubarak's Egypt: Fragmentation of the Political Order* (Boulder, CO, 1989); J. Waterbury, *The Egypt of Nasser and Sadat: The Political Economy of Two Regimes* (Princeton, NJ, 1983). As to developments in Syria, cf R.A. Hinnebusch, *Authoritarian Power and State Formation in Ba'thist Syria: Army, Party, and Peasants* (Boulder, CO, 1990); V. Perthes, *Staat und Gesellschaft in Syrien 1970–1989* (Hamburg, 1990), pp 223ff.
7. *MEED*, 17 May 1991, p 22; for full text see e.g. Mu'assasat al-Nuri (ed), *Qanun istithmar al-amwal fi al-Jumhuriyya al-'arabiyya al-suriyya* (Damascus, 1991), trans in Damascus Chamber of Commerce (ed), *Law*

No. 10 of Encouraging Investment (Damascus, 1991).

8. Cf e.g. Waterbury, *Egypt*.

9. For details cf e.g. M. Chatelus, 'La croissance économique: mutation de structures et dynamisme des déséquilibres', in A. Raymond (ed), *La Syrie d'aujourd'hui* (Paris, 1980); R.A. Hinnebusch, 'Syria', in E. Murphy and T. Niblock (eds), *Economic and Political Liberalization in the Middle East* (London, 1993), pp 177–203; M.H. Kerr, 'Hafiz al-Asad and the changing patterns of Syrian politics', *International Journal* 28/4 (1973); E. Kienle, *Ba'th v. Ba'th: The Conflict between Syria and Iraq 1968–1989* (London, 1990), pp 43f; Perthes, *Staat*, pp 97ff; V. Perthes, 'The Syrian private industrial and commercial sectors and the state', *International Journal of Middle East Studies* 24/2 (May 1992), pp 207–30; E. Picard, 'Ouverture économique et renforcement militaire en Syrie', *Oriente Moderno* 59/7–9 (July–December 1979).

10. For these parties cf e.g. N. Muhammad, *Al-haraka al-qawmiyya al-'arabiyya fi Suriyya min khilal tarikh tanzimatiha al-siyasiyya* (Damascus, 1987); P. Seale, *The Struggle for Syria: A Study of Post-War Arab Politics 1945–1958* (London, 1965).

11. For an optimistic account of the NPF's role, cf P. Seale, *Asad of Syria. The Struggle for the Middle East* (London, 1988), pp 169ff; for an opposite view on the seat(s) of power in contemporary Syria, cf e.g. H. Batatu, 'Some observations on the social roots of Syria's ruling military group and the causes for its dominance', *Middle East Journal* 35/3 (1981), pp 331–44.

12. This is well illustrated in Y.M. Sadowski, 'Patronage and the Ba'th: corruption and control in contemporary Syria', *Arab Studies Quarterly* 9 (1987), pp 442–61; and 'Ba'thist ethics and the spirit of state capitalism: patronage and the party in contemporary Syria', in P.J. Chelkowski and R.J. Pranger (eds), *Ideology and Power in the Middle East: Studies in Honour of George Lenczowski* (Durham and London, 1988).

13. Cf e.g. Hinnebusch, 'Syria', p 188; Perthes, *Staat*, pp 91ff and ch 3 of the present volume.

14. As to the state or regime as creator of classes, see M. Seurat, 'Les populations, l'Etat et la société', in Raymond, *La Syrie,* pp 87–140.

15. For economic developments in the 1980s, cf Hinnebusch, 'Syria', pp 177–202; particularly pp 186ff; E. Kienle, 'Entre *jama'a* et classe: le pouvoir politique en Syrie contemporaine', *Revue du Monde Musulman et de la Méditerranée* 59–60 (1991–92), pp 211–40; E. Kienle, 'Syria, the Kuwait war and the new world order', in J. Ismael and T. Ismael (eds), *The Gulf War and the New World Order* (Gainsville, FL, 1993); Perthes, *Staat*, pp 103–34; Perthes, 'Syrian private', pp 207–30 and ch 3 of the present volume; S. Pölling, ch 7 of the present volume.

16. Cf H. Hopfinger, 'Kapitalistisches Agro-Business in einem sozialistischen Land? Syrien versucht neue Wege in der Landwirtschaft', *Die Erde* 121 (1990), pp 157–76.

17. For details, cf Perthes, *Staat*, pp 103ff; Hinnebusch, 'Syria', pp 177–202, particularly pp 186ff, 193; N. Sukkar, ch 2 of the present volume.

18. Cf Perthes, 'Syria's Parliamentary', and ch 3 of the present volume.
19. See J. Bahout, ch 4 of the present volume.
20. Figures as quoted by EIU, *Country Report: Syria*, no. 3, 1992, pp 15f; the exchange rate is about $1 = S£ 45.
21. EIU, *Country Report: Syria*, no. 1, 1993, pp 14f.
22. In the 1990 budget investment was put at S£ 24.49 billion. The Syrian budget is traditionally subdivided into two main sections, one covering current expenditure, the other capital investment. Figures as quoted by EIU, *Country Report: Syria*, no. 1, 1992, p 17.
23. EIU, *Country Report: Syria*, no. 2, 1992, p 14.
24 The commercial exchange rate is approximately US $1 = S£ 20.1.
25. At the time of writing this third exchange rate is at US $1 = S£ 11.225.
26. EIU, *Country Report: Syria*, no. 2, 1992, p 14.
27. GDP at market prices, estimate given in EIU, *Country Report: Syria*, no. 1, 1993, p 3.
28. EIU, *Country Report: Syria*, no. 1, 1992, p 16.
29. EIU, *Country Report: Syria*, no. 3, 1992, p 20f.
30. Kienle, *Ba'th v. Ba'th*, p 145.
31. For budgetary figures, cf EIU, *Country Report: Syria*, no. 1, 1992, pp 16f; for GDP figure, cf EIU, *Country Report: Syria*, no. 1, 1993, p 3.
32. IISS, *The Military Balance 1992–93* (London, 1992), pp 218ff; this source, however, puts Syrian defence expenditure unrealistically high at 13 per cent of GDP.
33. EIU, *Country Report: Syria*, no. 1, 1992, p 18.
34. United Nations (ed), *Demographic Yearbook 1989* (New York, 1991), p 123.
35. EIU, *Country Report: Syria*, no. 4, 1992, p 28.
36. EIU, *Country Report: Syria*, no. 4, 1992, p 28, total figure based on figures given for metal and metal products, machinery and equipment and transport equipment.
37. EIU, *Country Report: Syria*, no. 1, 1993, p 24.
38. Distinction introduced by M. Seurat, 'Etat et industrialisation dans l'Orient arabe', in CERMOC (ed), *Industrialisation et changements sociaux dans l'Orient arabe* (Beirut, 1982), pp 27–67.
39. World Bank, *World Debt Tables 1992–93* (Washington, DC, 1992), vol II, p 394.
40. EIU, *Country Report: Syria*, no. 1, 1992, p 26.
41. EIU, *Country Report: Syria*, no. 1, 1992, pp 25f in conjunction with no. 3, 1992, p 23 and no. 4, 1992, p 15.
42. *Al-Hayat*, 21 April 1993.
43. EIU, *Country Report: Syria*, no. 2, 1992, p 23.
44. EIU, *Country Report: Syria*, no. 3, 1992, p 23.
45. *Al-Hayat*, 29 December 1992; EIU, *Country Report: Syria*, no. 1, 1992, p 10.
46. EIU, *Country Report: Syria*, no. 1, 1993, p 24.
47. EIU, *Country Report: Syria*, no. 3, 1993, p 22.
48. EIU, *Country Report: Syria*, no. 4, 1992, p 17; Perthes, *Staat*, p 109.

49. *Al-Hayat*, 15 March 1993; EIU, *Country Report: Syria*, no. 4, 1992, p 6.
50. EIU, *Country Report: Syria*, no. 4, 1992, p 27.
51. EIU, *Country Report: Syria*, no 2, 1992, p 22 quoting *Syrie et Monde Arabe* put the public sector share in total export earnings at about 63 per cent for the first ten months of 1991.
52. EIU, *Country Report: Syria*, no. 1, 1992, p 7.
53 Total figures as given by EIU, *Country Report: Syria*, no. 4, 1992, p 6.
54. *al-Hayat*, 22 April 1993.
55. EIU, *Country Report: Syria*, no. 3, 1992, pp 15f; by the end of 1992 companies operating under Law no. 10 had pledged to create 56,382 jobs, cf EIU, *Country Report: Syria*, no. 1, 1993, p 15.
56. IISS (ed), *The Military Balance* (London) for 1977 onwards; also Springborg *Mubarak's Egypt*, ch 4.
57. IISS, *The Military Balance 1992–93* (London, 1992), pp 122f.
58. Cf e.g. IISS, *The Military Balance 1992–93*.
59. E.g. Owen, 'Socio-economic Change'.
60. J. Waterbury, 'The potential for political liberalization in the Middle East', in G. Salamé (ed), *Democracy without Democrats? The Renewal of Politics in the Muslim World* (London, 1994), pp 23–47.
61. E.g. Moore, 'Money and power'; Waterbury, *Egypt*.

Chapter 8

1. For the Arabic version of the Ta'if Agreement, see e.g. *Al-sharq al-awsat*, 24 October 1989.
2. J. Bahout, 'Liban: les élections législatives de l'été 1992', *Maghreb-Machrek* 139 (January–March 1993), pp 53–84.
3. For an analysis of the Ta'if Agreement, see J. Maila, *The document of national understanding: a commentary* (Oxford, May 1992); and A.R. Norton, 'Lebanon after Ta'if: is the civil war over?', *Middle East Journal* 45/3 (summer 1991), pp 457–74.
4. General 'Awn opposed the Ta'if Agreement not because he objected to domestic reforms, but because he disagreed with the role attributed to Syrian forces under that agreement. The Ta'if Agreement not only legalized Syria's occupation of Lebanon, but even praised Damascus for its commitment to the future security of its neighbouring country; thus the document repudiated General 'Awn's 'war of liberation', which aimed precisely to end Syria's military presence in Lebanon.

   Hizbullah, on the other hand, critizised the agreement because it re-emphasized political confessionalism as introduced by the National Pact of 1943 and did not favour the implementation of an Islamic regime.

   Amal objected to the agreement because it felt that the position of the speaker, although enhanced, was not commensurate with the power and size of the Shi'a community.

   The Progressive Socialist Party opposed the agreement because it did not allocate any position of formal power to the Druze. Even though the creation of a senate was on the cards – as a concession to the demands of the Druze community (the president of this new chamber was supposed to be a Druze – the circumstances that would lead to its eventual creation were so remote that it rendered this concession theoretical.

The Palestinians, finally, were against the agreement for two reasons. First of all, they opposed the inordinate Syrian influence which could severely control their movements if not crush them; and secondly they sought a clear definition of the relationship that would govern relations between the Lebanese government and Palestinian civilians.

5. The section dealing with the restoration of Lebanese sovereignty was the subject of a prior agreement between the Arab Higher Tripartite Committee and Syria. The Lebanese members of parliament were prevented from making any changes to this section of the document. Among other things, this section called on Syria to help the Lebanese army to extend its authority over all of Lebanon for a maximum of two years after which the Syrian forces would be stationed in the Biqa' or in other places if necessary. The length of their stay in the Biqa' and elsewhere will be determined by common accord.

The issue of a final Syrian military withdrawal would have to be based on the result of negotiations between Syria and the Lebanese Government of National Unity. In this respect, the Ta'if document resulted in the virtual legalization of Syria's military presence in Lebanon – a presence whose legality had been contested ever since 1982.

To the contrary, Syria was given the right to acquire strategic military positions in the Biqa' which in turn raised fears that the future stability and status of the Lebanese territory would be subordinated to the hazards of the Israeli–Syrian confrontation.

6. For a copy of the treaty, see *Lebanon Report* 2/6 (June 1991), special supplement.

7. J. Maila, 'Le traité de fraternité: une analyse', *Les Cahiers de l'Orient* 24/4 (1991), p 79.

8. For a copy of the Defence Pact see *Lebanon Report* 2/10 (October 1991).

9. Maila, 'Le traité', p 88. Maila argues that the main problem still resides in the frank and unambiguous recognition of Lebanon by Syria – a fact that requires an exchange of ambassadors. Although Lebanon and Syria have signed many treaties prior to the Treaty of Brotherhood, such an exchange of ambassadors has never taken place. The true paradox of the treaty resides in the fact that it *implies* a recognition of Lebanon precisely at a time when Lebanon's independence is merely theoretical.

10. Initially, many Lebanese businessmen feared that Syria might impose restrictions over private enterprise in Lebanon. In addition, it was felt that Syria's interest in the Lebanonese economy was limited to the protection of a free-trade area that would provide valuable financial services and vital trade links with the West. As envisaged, the economic treaty would include areas of co-operation such as the establishment of a joint customs commission, the signing of agreements on resource sharing, and granting 'most favoured nation' status to Syria.

11. The break-up of the customs union in 1950 adversely affected Lebanese

producers and parts of the services sector. In contrast, its termination had more favourable effects on Syria: see C. Gates, 'The emergence of the political economy of modern Lebanon', unpublished D.Phil thesis (Oxford, 1987).

12. M. Buheiry, *Beirut's Role in the Political Economy of the French Mandate, 1919–39* (Oxford, n d).

Chapter 9

1. C. Cordahi, 'Syria: sticking to its principles', *Middle East International (MEI)*, 19 April 1991, p 16.
2. M. Jensen, 'Asad not the stumbling block', *MEI*, 17 May 1991, p 6; G. H. Jensen, 'Syria and Lebanon: flip – and now flop?', *MEI*, 25 October 1991, p 7.
3. G. H. Jensen, 'Flip', pp 7–8; J. Muir, 'Syrians refuse the bait', *MEI*, 22 November 1991, pp 5–6.
4. L. Andoni, 'The Washington talks: deadlock or the end?', *MEI*, 6 March 1992, p 3.
5. Syrian Television Domestic Service, 28 October 1992.
6. Ibid., 3 November 1992.
7. *al-Ba'th*, 24 November 1992.
8. *Kifah al-'ummal al-ishtiraki* 17 December 1992; *Tishrin*, 16 December 1992.
9. *al-Ba'th*, 18 March 1993.
10. *al-Diyar*, 16 April 1993.
11. *al-Watan*, 27 April 1993.
12. *Tishrin*, 28 April 1993.
13. *al-Ba'th*, 4 May 1993.
14. Syrian Television Domestic Service, 14 May 1993.
15. *Tishrin*, 8 September 1992.
16. *Middle East Economic Digest (MEED)*, 8 May 1992.
17. *Syrie et Monde Arabe*, August 1992.
18. Ibid., September 1992.
19. Ibid., *MEED*, 11 September 1992.
20. *MEED*, 28 August 1992.
21. *MEED*, 11 and 25 September 1992. The terms of the May 1991 investment law are discussed in detail by Nabil Sukkar in his essay in this volume.
22. Damascus Radio Domestic Service, 2 December 1992.
23. *MEED*, 25 December 1992.
24. Interviews, Damascus, November 1992.
25. *MEED*, 20 November 1992.
26. *MEED*, 27 November and 25 December 1992.
27. *Kifah al-'Ummal al-ishtiraki*, 17 December 1992; *Syrie et Monde Arabe*, December 1992.
28. On the political role of the larger landholders during the 1980s, see F.H. Lawson, 'From Neo-Ba'th to Ba'th Nouveau', *Journal of South Asian and*

Middle Eastern Studies 14 /2 (winter 1990), pp 1–21.
29. Syrian Arab Republic, *Statistical Abstract* (Damascus, August 1987), Table 37/16.
30. *MEED*, 8 June 1990.
31. V. Perthes, 'The Syrian private industrial and commercial sectors and the state', *International Journal of Middle East Studies*, 24/2 (May 1992), p 211.
32. Ibid., pp 212–13.
33. *MEED*, 9 October 1992; *Syria Times*, 2 April 1993.
34. *Syrie et Monde Arabe*, March 1992.
35. *MEED*, 10 May and 28 June 1991.
36. *MEED*, 12 July and 2 August 1991.
37. F.H. Lawson, 'Domestic transformation and foreign steadfastness in contemporary Syria', *Middle East Journal* 48/1 (winter 1994), pp 47–64.
38. G.H. Jensen, 'Syria: keeping the lid on', *MEI*, 11 October 1991, p 11; E. Kienle, 'Entre *jama'a* et classe: le pouvoir politique en Syrie contemporaine', *Revue du Monde Musulman et de la Méditerranée* 59–60 (1991), pp 221–40.
39. *MEED*, 22 March 1991.
40. *MEED*, 20 November 1992.
41. *MEED*, 3 July, 27 November and 18 December 1992 and 8 January 1993.
42. *Syrie et Monde Arabe*, March 1993.
43. Interviews, Damascus, January 1993.
44. Syrian Television Domestic Service, 16 May 1993.
45. *Syrie et Monde Arabe*, December 1992.
46. See Lawson, 'Domestic transformation'.
47. *MEED*, 20 November and 25 December 1992.
48. F.H. Lawson, 'Libéralisation économique en Syrie et Irak', *Maghreb-Machrek*, 128 (April–June 1990), pp 27–52.
49. Lawson, 'Domestic transformation'.

Notes on Contributors

Joseph Bahout is *chercheur* at the Centre d'Etudes et de Recherches sur le Moyen-Orient Contemporain (CERMOC) in Beirut.

Raymond A. Hinnebusch is Professor of Politics at the College of St Catherine, St Paul, Minnesota.

Eberhard Kienle is Lecturer in Politics of the Middle East at the School of Oriental and African Studies, University of London.

Fred H. Lawson is Associate Professor of Government at Mills College, Oakland, California.

Hans Günter Lobmeyer is Research Officer at the Arbeitsstelle Politik des Vorderen Orient of the Freie Universität, Berlin.

Fida Nasrallah is Deputy Director of the Centre for Lebanese Studies in Oxford.

Volker Perthes is Research Officer at the Stiftung Wissenschaft und Politik (SWP) in Ebenhausen near Munich.

Sylvia Pölling works as Senior Editor for the Economist Intelligence Unit (EIU), London.

Patrick Seale is a writer on contemporary Middle Eastern issues based in London.

Nabil Sukkar previously worked as an economist for the World Bank and now heads the Syrian Consulting Bureau for Development and Investment in Damascus.

Bibliography

'Ammash, Husayn Murhij, *Tajawuz al-ma'ziq. Muntaliqat al-islah al-iqtisadi fi Suriya* (Overcoming the Dilemma. Points of Departure for Economic Reform in Syria) (Damascus, 1992)

Andoni, Lamis, 'The Washington talks: deadlock or the end?', *Middle East International*, 6 March 1992

Arab Socialist Ba'th Party (ASBP) (Hizb al-ba'th al-'arabi al-ishtiraki), Syrian Region, Regional Leadership, *Taqarir wa muqarrarat al-mu'tamar al-qutri al-sadis al-mun'aqid fi Dimashq* 5 April 1975 to 15 April 1975 (Reports and Resolutions of the Sixth Regional Conference convened in Damascus) (Damascus, 1976)

—*Taqarir al-mu'tamar al-qutri al-thamin wa muqarraratuhu* (Reports and Resolutions of the 8th National Congress) (Damascus, 1985)

—National Leadership, *Nidal hizb al-Ba'th al-'arabi al-ishtiraki* (The Struggle of the Arab Socialist Ba'th Party) (Damascus, 1978)

Arendt, Hannah, *The Origins of Totalitarianism* (new ed; New York, 1973)

—*Was ist Politik? Aus dem Nachlass, herausgegeben von Ursula Ludz* (München, 1993)

al-Atasi, Jamal, 'Al-muthaqqafun al-dimuqratiyyun wa thawra al-sha'b al-thaqafiyya' (The democratic intellectuals and the intellectual people's revolution), *Dirasat nasariyya*, 4 (n d)

Ayalon, Ami (ed), *Middle East Contemporary Survey (MECS)*, 14 (covering 1990) (Boulder, CO, 1991)

Ayubi, N.N., 'Political correlates of privatization programs in the Middle East', *Arab Studies Quarterly* 14/2–3 (spring–summer 1992), pp 39–56

Bahout, J., 'Liban: les élections législatives de l'été 1992', *Maghreb-Machrek* 139 (January–March 1993), pp 53–84

Batatu, H., 'Some observations on the social roots of Syria's ruling military group and the causes for its dominance', *Middle East Journal* 35/3 (summer 1981), pp 331–44

Buheiry, Marwan, 'Beirut's role in the political economy of the French Mandate, 1919–39', *Papers on Lebanon* 4 (Oxford, n d)

Callaghy, T., 'Lost between state and market: the politics of economic adjustment in Ghana, Zambia, and Nigeria', in J.M. Nelson (ed), *Economic*

Crisis and Policy Choice: The Politics of Adjustment in the Third World (Princeton, NJ, 1990), pp 257–319

Cantori, Louis J., 'Political participation, consultation and state-civil society relations in the Middle East' (unpublished paper, 1991)

Chatelus, Michel, 'La croissance économique: mutation de structures et dynamisme des déséquilibres', in André Raymond (ed), *La Syrie d'aujourd'hui* (Paris, 1980)

Clawson, Patrick, *Unaffordable Ambitions? Syria's Military Build-up and Economic Crisis* (Washington, DC, 1989)

Cordahi, Cherif, 'Syria: sticking to its principles', *Middle East International* (*MEI*), 19 April 1991

van Dam, N. *The Struggle for Power in Syria: Sectarianism, Regionalism, and Tribalism in Politics 1961–1978* (London, 1979)

Damascus Chamber of Commerce, *Al-taqrir al-sanawi 1990* (Annual Report) (Damascus, 1991)

—*Law No. 10 of Encouraging Investment* (Damascus, 1991)

—*Al-taqrir al-sanawi 1991* (Annual Report) (Damascus, 1992)

Drysdale, A., 'The Syrian political elite 1966–1976: a spatial and social analysis', *Middle Eastern Studies*, 17/1, pp 3–30

Economist Intelligence Unit (EIU) (ed), *Syria Country Profile, 1992–1993* (by Sylvia Pölling) (London, 1992)

—(ed), *Country Report: Syria* (London, 1991, 1992, 1993)

Farsoun, S., and W. Carroll, 'State capitalism and counter-revolution in the Middle East: a thesis', in Barbara H. Kaplan (ed), *Social Change in the Capitalist World Economy* (Beverly Hills, CA, 1978)

Filonik, A., *Su'ubat al-zira'a al-suriyya al-haditha* (Problems of the Modern Syrian Agriculture) (Damascus, 1987)

Gates, Carolyn, 'The emergence of the political economy of modern Lebanon', unpublished D.Phil thesis (Oxford: St Antony's College, 1987)

General Federation of the Workers' Syndicates (General Federation of Trade Unions; GFTU), *Al-taqrir al-'amm li'l-mu'tamar al-ibda' al-watani wa 'l-i'timad 'ala al-that* (The General Report to the Conference on National Creativity and Self-Reliance) (Damascus, November 1987)

—*A'mal wa muqarrarat wa tawsiyyat al-mu'tamar al-thamin 'ashr li'l-ittihad al-'amm li niqabat al-'ummal fi 'l-qutr al-'arabi al-suri al-mun'aqid bi Dimashq* 21–4 September 1974 (The Proceedings, Resolutions, and Recommendations of the 18th Conference of the General Federation of Trade Unions in the Syrian Arab Region convened in Damascus) (Damascus, 1974)

Haggard, S., *Pathways from the Periphery: The Politics of Growth in Newly Industrializing Countries* (Ithaca, NY, 1990)

Haggard, Stephan and Kaufman, Robert R., 'Economic adjustment and the prospects for democracy', in S. Haggard and R.R. Kaufman, (eds), *The Politics of Economic Adjustment. International Constraints, Distributive Conflicts, and the State* (Princeton, NJ, 1992)

Hanna, Abdallah, 'Fasl min tarikh al-burjwaziyya al-suriyya', in Muhammad Jadal, *Al-burjwaziyya al-'arabiyya al-mu'asira* (Damascus, 1991)

Harik, I., 'Privatization: the issue, the prospects, and the fears', in I. Harik and D.J. Sullivan (eds), *Privatization and Liberalization in the Middle East*

(Bloomington, Indianapolis, 1992)

Hassan, Ibrahim, 'La Syrie de la guerre civile', *Peuples méditerranéens*, 12 (July–September 1980), pp 91–107

'Hawla al-qawmiyya al-'arabiyya: mu'atayat al-madi wa tahadiyyat al-hadir' (On Arab nationalism: the situation in the past and the actual challenges), Interview with Jamal al-Atasi, *Al-mustaqbal al-'arabi* 15/5 (May 1992), pp 121–33

Hawwa, Sa'id, *Jund Allah takhtitan* (Projecting the Army of God) (Cairo, 1988)

Heydemann, Steven, 'Liberalization from above and the limits of private sector autonomy in Syria: the role of business associations', paper presented at Middle East Studies Conference (Austin, TX, 1990)

—'The political logic of economic rationality: selective stabilization in Syria', in Henri J. Barkey (ed), *The Politics of Economic Reform in the Middle East* (New York, 1992)

—'Taxation without representation: authoritarianism and economic liberalization in Syria', in Ellis Goldberg, Resat Kasaba and Joel Migdal (eds), *Rules and Rights in the Middle East: Society, Law and Democracy* (Washington, DC, 1993)

Hinnebusch, R.A., *Egyptian Politics under Sadat: The Post-Populist Development of an Authoritarian Modernizing State* (Cambridge, 1989)

—*Authoritarian Power and State Formation in Ba'thist Syria: Army, Party, and Peasants* (Boulder, CO, 1990)

—'Syria', in E. Murphy and T. Niblock (eds), *Economic and Political Liberalization in the Middle East* (London, 1993), pp 177–203

Hirschman, A.O., 'The turn to authoritarianism in Latin America and the search for its economic determinants', in D. Collier (ed), *The New Authoritarianism in Latin America* (Princeton, NJ, 1979), pp 61–92

Hopfinger, H., 'Kapitalistisches Agro-Business in einem sozialistischen Land? Syrien versucht neue Wege in der Landwirtschaft', *Die Erde*, 121 (1990), pp 157–76

—'Capitalist agro-business in a socialist country? Syria's new shareholding corporations as an example', *British Society for Middle Eastern Studies Bulletin* 17/2 (1990), pp 162–70

International Institute for Strategic Studies (IISS) (ed), *The Military Balance* (London, annually)

International Monetary Fund (IMF), International Financial Statistics Yearbook (Washington, DC, 1992, 1993)

Islamic Front in Syria, al-Jabha al-islamiyya fi suriya, *Mithaq al-jabha al-islamiyya fi suriya* (Charter of the Islamic Front in Syria) (Damascus, n d)

al-Jabiri, Muhammad 'Abid, 'Ishkaliyat al-dimuqratiyya wa 'l-mujtama' al-madani fi 'l-watan al-'arabi' (The problematique of democracy and civil society in the Arab fatherland), *Al-mustaqbal al-'arabi* 15/167 (January 1993), pp 4–15

Jadal, Muhammad, *Al-burjwaziyya al-'arabiyya al-mu'asira* (Damascus, 1991)

Jensen, G.H., 'Syria: keeping the lid on', *Middle East International (MEI)*, 11 October 1991

—'Syria and Lebanon: flip – and now flop?', *MEI*, 25 October 1991

Jensen, Michael, 'Asad not the stumbling block', *Middle East International*, 17

May 1991

Kanovsky, Eliyahu, 'What's behind Syria's current economic problems?', in *Middle East Contemporary Survey 1983–84* (Tel Aviv, 1986)

Kerr, M.H., 'Hafiz al-Asad and the changing patterns of Syrian politics', *International Journal* 28/4 (1973), pp 689–706

al-Khafaji, Issam, *Al-dawla wa 'l-tatawwur al-ra'smali fi 'l-Iraq* (Cairo, 1983)

Kienle, E., *Ethnizität und Machtkonkurrenz in inter-arabischen Beziehungen: Der syrisch-irakische Konflikt unter den Ba'th-Regimen* (Berlin, 1985)

— *Ba'th v. Ba'th: The Conflict between Syria and Iraq 1968–1989* (London, 1990)

—'Entre *jama'a* et classe: le pouvoir politique en Syrie contemporaine', *Revue du Monde Musulman et de la Méditerranée* 59–60 (1991–92), pp 211–40

—*Entre Jama'a et Classe: Le Pouvoir Politique en Syrie* (Berlin, 1992)

—'Syria, the Kuwait war and the new world order', in J. Ismael and T. Ismael (eds), *The Gulf War and the New World Order* (Gainsville, FL, 1993), pp 383–98

Krämer, Gudrun, 'Liberalization and democracy in the Arab world', *Middle East Report* 174/ 22 (January–February 1992), pp 22–5, 35

Kutschera, Chris, 'L'éclipse des frères musulmans syriens', *Les Cahiers de l'Orient* 7 (1987), pp 121–31

—'When the brothers fall out', *Middle East* (April 1988)

Lawson, Fred H., 'Political-economic trends in Ba'thist Syria: a reinterpretation', *Orient* 29 (1988), pp 579–94

— 'Libéralisation économique en Syrie et Irak', *Maghreb-Machrek* 128 (April–June 1990), pp 27–52

— 'From Neo-Ba'th to Ba'th Nouveau', *Journal of South Asian and Middle Eastern Studies* 14/2 (winter 1990), pp 1–21

—'Domestic transformation and foreign steadfastness in contemporary Syria', *Middle East Journal* 48/1 (winter 1994), pp 47–64

Leca, Jean, 'Social structure and political stability: comparative evidence from the Algerian, Syrian, and Iraqi cases', in Adeed Dawisha and William Zartman (eds), *Beyond Coercion: The Durability of the Arab State* (London, 1988); reprinted in G. Luciani (ed), *The Arab State* (London, 1990)

Lobmeyer, Hans Günter, 'Islamic ideology and secular discourse: the Islamists of Syria', *Orient* (Hamburg), 32/3 (1991), pp 395–418

Longuenesse, Elizabeth, 'The class nature of the State in Syria', *MERIP Reports* 9/4 (1979), pp 3–11

—'Etat et syndicalisme en Syrie: discours et pratiques', *Sou'al* 8 (February 1988), pp 97–130

Mahmud, Sadiq, *Hiwar hawla Suriyya* (Cairo, 1992)

Maila, Joseph, 'Le traité de fraternité: une analyse', *Les Cahiers de l'Orient* 24/4 (1991)

— 'The document of national understanding: a commentary', *Prospects for Lebanon* 4 (Oxford, May 1992)

Meyer, Günter, 'Economic development in Syria since 1970', in J.A. Allan (ed), *Politics and the Economy in Syria* (London, 1980), pp 40–62

Moore, C.H., 'Money and power: the dilemma of the Egyptian *infitah*', *Middle East Journal* 40/4 (autumn 1986), pp 634–50

Mu'assasat al-Nuri (ed), *Qanun istithmar al-amwal fi al-Jumhuriyya al-'arabiyya al-suriyya* (Damascus, 1991); trans in Damascus Chamber of Commerce (ed), *Law No. 10 of Encouraging Investment* (Damascus, 1991)

Muhammad, N., *Al-haraka al-qawmiyya al-'arabiyya fi Suriyya min khilal tarikh tanzimatiha al-siyasiyya* (Damascus, 1987)

Muir, Jim, 'Syrians refuse the bait', *Middle East International*, 22 November 1991

Norton, A.R., 'Lebanon after Ta'if: is the civil war over?', *Middle East Journal* 45/3 (summer 1991), pp 457–74

O'Donnell, G., *Modernization and Bureaucratic Authoritarianism: Studies in South American Politics* (Berkeley, CA, 1973)

Owen, R., 'Socio-economic change and political mobilization: the case of Egypt', in G. Salamé (ed), *Democracy without Democrats? The Renewal of Politics in the Muslim World* (London, 1994)

Perera, Judith, 'The shifting fortunes of Syria's Muslim Brethren', *Middle East* (May 1987)

Perthes, Volker, *Staat und Gesellschaft in Syrien 1970–1989* (Hamburg, 1990)

—'Einige kritische Bemerkungen zum Minderheitenparadigma in der Syrienforschung', *Orient* 31/4 (1990), pp 571–82

—'A look at Syria's upper class. The bourgeoisie and the Ba'th', *Middle East Report* 170/21 (May–June 1991), pp 31–7

—'Syria's parliamentary elections. Remodelling Asad's political base', *Middle East Report* 174/22 (January–February 1992), pp 15–18, 35

—'The Syrian economy in the 1980s', *Middle East Journal* 46/1 (winter 1992), pp 37–58

—'The Syrian private industrial and commercial sectors and the state', *International Journal of Middle East Studies* 24/2 (May 1992), pp 207–30

—'The private sector, economic liberalization, and the prospects of democratization: the case of Syria and some other Arab countries', in Ghassan Salamé (ed), *Democracy without Democrats? The Renewal of Politics in the Muslim World* (London, 1994)

Picard, Elizabeth, 'Syria returns to democracy: the 1973 legislative elections', in Guy Hemet et al. (eds), *Elections Without Choice* (London, 1978)

—'L'emprise du général Assad sur l'Etat syrien se renforce', *Maghreb-Machrek* 80 (1978), pp 13–14

—'Ouverture économique et renforcement militaire en Syrie', *Oriente Moderno* 59/7–12 (July–December 1979), pp 663–76

—'La Syrie de 1946 à 1979', in André Raymond (ed), *La Syrie d'aujourd'hui* (Paris, 1980)

—'Y a-t-il un problème communautaire en Syrie?', *Maghreb-Machrek* 87 (janvier–mars 1980), pp 7–21

—'Espace de Référence et Espace d'Intervention du Mouvement Rectificatif au Pouvoir en Syrie 1970–1982', Thèse de III° Cycle (Paris, 1985)

Pool, David,'The links between economic and political liberalization', in T. Niblock and E. Murphy (eds), *Economic and Political Liberalization in the Middle East* (London, 1993)

Qasem, Riad, 'Syria: rapid growth in foreign trade activity', *Arab Economist* 11 (April 1979), pp 23–7

Qiyadat al-thawra al-islamiyya fi suriya, *Bayan al-thawra al-islamiyya fi suriya wa minhajuha* (Manifesto and Programme of the Islamic Revolution in Syria) (Damascus, 1 Muharram 1401/9 November 1980)

Report of the Eighth Party Congress and its Resolutions (Damascus, 1985)

Richards, Adam and Waterbury, John, *A Political Economy of the Middle East. State, Class, and Economic Development* (Boulder, CO, 1990)

Sadowski, Yahya M., 'Cadres, guns & money: the eighth regional congress of the Syrian Ba'th', *MERIP Reports* 15/6 (July–August 1985)

—'Patronage and the Ba'th: corruption and control in contemporary Syria', *Arab Studies Quarterly* 9 (1987), pp 442–61

—'Ba'thist ethics and the spirit of state capitalism: patronage and the party in contemporary Syria', in P.J. Chelkowski and R.J. Pranger (eds), *Ideology and Power in the Middle East: Studies in Honour of George Lenczowski* (Durham and London, 1988)

—(ed), *Democracy without Democrats? The Renewal of Politics in the Muslim World* (London, 1994)

Salih, Amani 'Abd al-Rahman, 'Al-ta'addudiyya al-siyasiyya fi al-watan al-'arabi: dirasa li'l-namuzaj al-misri wa'l-maghribi' (Political pluralism in the Arab fatherland: a study of the Egyptian/Moroccan pattern), *Al-fikr al-istratiji al-'arabi* 10 (October 1991), pp 85–120

Seale, Patrick, *The Struggle for Syria: A Study of Post-War Arab Politics 1945–1958* (London, 1965)

—*Asad of Syria. The Struggle for the Middle East* (London, 1988)

—'Asad: between institutions and autocracy', in Richard T. Antoun and Donald Quataert (eds), *Syria. Society, Culture, and Polity* (Albany, NY, 1991)

Seurat, Michel, 'Les populations, l'état et la société', in André Raymond (ed), *La Syrie d'aujourd'hui* (Paris, 1980)

—'Etat et industrialisation dans l'Orient arabe', in CERMOC (ed), *Industrialisation et changements sociaux dans l'Orient arabe* (Beirut, 1982), pp 27–67

—(under the name of G. Michaud) 'Terrorisme d'Etat, terrorisme contre l'Etat: le cas syrien', *Esprit* (October–November 1984), pp 188–201; reprinted in Seurat, Michel, *L'Etat de barbarie* (Paris, 1989), pp 35–52

—*L'Etat de barbarie* (Paris, 1989)

Springborg, R., *Mubarak's Egypt: Fragmentation of the Political Order* (Boulder, CO, 1989)

Sukkar, Nabil et al., *Nahwa iqtisad ishtiraki mutatawwar fi'l-qutr al-'arabi al-suri: muqtarahat li-i'adat al-tawazun li'l-iqtisad wa iqamat idara iqtisadiyya la-markaziyya* (1987)

Syrian Arab Republic (SAR), Ministry of Planning, *Tahlil al-wad' al-rahin fi qita' al-sina'at al-tahwiliyya li al-sana'wat 1979–1983* (Analysis of the Position of the Manufacturing Sector for the Years 1979–1983) (Damascus, December 1984)

Syrian Arab Republic (SAR) (annually) *Statistical Abstract* (Damascus: Central Bureau of Statistics, 1976, 1981, 1987, 1988, 1991, 1992)

—Al-Jumhuriyya al-'arabiyya al-suriyya, Wizarat al-iqtisad wa 'l-tijara al-kharijiyya, *Al-qanun raqm 10 li tashji' al-istithmar min 4/5/1991 wa 'l-ta'limat al-tanfiziyya min 28/5/1991* (Damascus, 1991)

—Al-Jumhuriyya al-'arabiyya al-suriyya, Ri'asat majlis al-wuzara', *Al-qirar raqm 7 m.w. bi ta'limat al-tanfiziyya li'l-qanun raqm 10 'l-'am 1991* (Damascus, 1991)

Syrian Communist Party (SCP), *Al-mu'tamar al-khamis li'l-hizb al-shuyu'i al-suri, ayyar 1980* (The 5th Conference of the Syrian Communist Party, May 1980) (Damascus, n d)

—Central Committee, *Ma'atiyat al-wad' al-duali wa mu'ashirat al-wad' al-'arabi wa 'l-muhimmat allati yatruhuha* (The Condition of the International Situation, the Indicators of the Arab Situation and the Requirements of the Impose) (October 1991)

Turkmani, Abd Allah, *Da'wa ila tahrir al-'aql al-'arabi min istimrar al-isti'adad li 'l-qubul bi 'l-istibdad – muqariba hawla jadl al-khass wa al-'amm fi 'l-mas'ala al-dimuqratiyya* (Call to Free the Arab Mind from the Continuing Willingness to Admit Oppression – Essay on a Particular and General Dispute over the Problem of Democracy) unpublished manuscript (Damascus, 1993)

United Nations (ed), *Demographic Yearbook* (New York, 1991)

Waterbury, J., *The Egypt of Nasser and Sadat: The Political Economy of Two Regimes* (Princeton, NJ, 1983)

—'The potential for political liberalization in the Middle East', in G. Salamé (ed), *Democracy without Democrats? The Renewal of Politics in the Muslim World* (London, 1994)

World Bank, *World Development Report* (Washington, DC, 1988)

—World Debt Tables 1992–93 (Washington, DC, 1992)

Index